Military Service Tribunals and Boards in the Great War

While a plethora of studies have discussed why so many men decided to volunteer for the army during the Great War, the experiences of those who were called up under conscription have received relatively little scrutiny. Even when the implementation of the respective Military Service Acts has been investigated, scholars have usually focused on only the distinct minority of those eligible who expressed conscientious objections. It is rare to see equal significance placed on the fact that substantial numbers of men appealed, or were appealed for, on the grounds that their domestic, business, or occupational circumstances meant they should not be expected to serve. David Littlewood analyses the processes undergone by these men, and the workings of the bodies charged with assessing their cases, through a sustained transnational comparison of the British and New Zealand contexts.

David Littlewood is Lecturer in the School of Humanities at Massey University, New Zealand.

Routledge Studies in First World War History

Series Editor: John Bourne, The University of Birmingham, UK

The First World War is a subject of perennial interest to historians and is often regarded as a watershed event, marking the end of the nineteenth century and the beginning of the 'modern' industrial world. The sheer scale of the conflict and massive loss of life means that it is constantly being assessed and reassessed to examine its lasting military, political, sociological, industrial, cultural and economic impact. Reflecting the latest international scholarly research, the Routledge Studies in First World War History series provides a unique platform for the publication of monographs on all aspects of the Great War. While the main thrust of the series is on the military aspects of the conflict, other related areas (including cultural, visual, literary, political and social) are also addressed. Books published are aimed primarily at a post-graduate academic audience, furthering exciting recent interpretations of the war, while still being accessible enough to appeal to a wider audience of educated lay readers.

For a full list of titles in this series, please visit https://www.routledge.com/history/series/WWI

Also in this series:

Aerial Propaganda and the Wartime Occupation of France, 1914–18
Bernard Wilkin

The Great War and the British Empire
Culture and Society
Edited by Michael Walsh and Andrekos Varnava

The Royal Flying Corps, the Western Front and the Control of the Air, 1914–1918
James Pugh

Military Service Tribunals and Boards in the Great War
Determining the Fate of Britain's and New Zealand's Conscripts
David Littlewood

Military Service Tribunals and Boards in the Great War
Determining the Fate of Britain's and New Zealand's Conscripts

David Littlewood

LONDON AND NEW YORK

First published 2018
by Routledge
2 Park Square, Milton Park, Abingdon, Oxon OX14 4RN

and by Routledge
711 Third Avenue, New York, NY 10017

Routledge is an imprint of the Taylor & Francis Group, an informa business

© 2018 David Littlewood

The right of David Littlewood to be identified as author of this work
has been asserted by him in accordance with sections 77 and 78 of the
Copyright, Designs and Patents Act 1988.

All rights reserved. No part of this book may be reprinted or reproduced or
utilised in any form or by any electronic, mechanical, or other means, now
known or hereafter invented, including photocopying and recording, or in
any information storage or retrieval system, without permission in writing
from the publishers.

Trademark notice: Product or corporate names may be trademarks or
registered trademarks, and are used only for identification and explanation
without intent to infringe.

British Library Cataloguing in Publication Data
A catalogue record for this book is available from the British Library

Library of Congress Cataloging in Publication Data
Names: Littlewood, David, author.
Title: Military service tribunals and boards in the Great War: determining
the fate of Britain's and New Zealand's conscripts / David Littlewood.
Description: Abingdon, Oxon [UK]; New York: Routledge, 2017. |
Series: Routledge studies in first World War history | Includes
bibliographical references and index.
Identifiers: LCCN 2017027283| ISBN 9781138206601 (hardback: alk. paper) |
ISBN 9781315464497 (ebook)
Subjects: LCSH: Courts-martial and courts of inquiry–Great Britain–
History–20th century. | Courts-martial and courts of inquiry–New Zealand–
History–20th century. | Military courts–Great Britain–History–20th
century. | Military courts–New Zealand–History–20th century. | Draft–Law
and legislation–Great Britain–History–20th century. | Draft–Law and
legislation–New Zealand–History–20th century. | Conscientious objection–
History–20th century. | World War, 1914–1918.
Classification: LCC K4754 .L58 2017 | DDC 343.41/0122–dc23
LC record available at https://lccn.loc.gov/2017027283

ISBN: 978-1-138-20660-1 (hbk)
ISBN: 978-1-315-46449-7 (ebk)

Typeset in Times New Roman
by Deanta Global Publishing Services, Chennai, India

This book is dedicated to the individuals who engaged with the British and New Zealand exemption systems. While some of their sentiments may appear strange or even distasteful to a modern audience, they are surely best viewed as quintessentially human responses to a time of profound uncertainty. I only hope all those involved would agree with at least part of what I have to say.

Contents

	List of figures	viii
	Series editors preface	ix
	Acknowledgements	xi
	Abbreviations	xii
	Introduction	1
1	Setting the boundaries	10
2	Judges and juries	33
3	Willing and able to go?	53
4	Autonomy or compliance?	79
5	Army first?	107
6	Those troublesome few	129
7	Work or fight?	148
	Conclusions	161
	Bibliography	168
	Index	179

Figures

3.1	Appellants as a proportion of the eligible population	57
3.2	Representation of occupational classes among the New Zealand appellants	60
6.1	The boards' verdicts on appeals lodged by conscientious objectors	140
7.1	Positive 'concrete verdicts' as a proportion of all verdicts delivered	149
7.2	Types of 'concrete verdict' delivered by the division's tribunals	150
7.3	Positive 'concrete verdicts' and dismissals with time as a proportion of all verdicts delivered	151
7.4	Sample 'concrete verdicts' delivered by the boards	156
7.5	Sample 'concrete verdicts' compared to all 'concrete verdicts' delivered by the boards	157

Series editors preface

The British Empire entered what would become known as the Great War on the assumption that it would be a war fought on terms of limited British military liability, in which the British contribution to the defeat of Germany would be naval and economic. This comfortable assumption rapidly unravelled. By the late spring of 1915, Britain had raised a mass army by voluntary means at the cost of considerable economic dislocation. The *ad hoc* expeditionary forces raised by Australia, Canada and New Zealand had already learned the true human costs of modern war on the battlefields of Flanders and Gallipoli. The establishment of a British Ministry of Munitions, in the wake of the 'shell scandal', presaged the move to a 'war economy'. 'Manpower', a word coined in 1915, became central to the political, economic and military agenda. And at the heart of the 'manpower question' was the spectre of conscription. In Britain it was eventually realised that it was not only impossible but also unfair to conduct a modern, industrialised war without the ability to compel some men to serve and to prevent others from doing so. Within a year, conscription was fully established and without the political and social upheaval that many had feared. New Zealand followed in August 1916, again with comparatively little political or public disquiet. But in Australia conscription was rejected after two bitter and divisive referendums, in October 1916 and November–December 1917. The Canadian Prime Minister Robert Borden forced conscription through Parliament in August 1917, but at the cost of considerable opposition, some of it violent.

Britain's liberal values and voluntarist tradition were recognised by the possibility of conscripted men applying for exemptions from military service. These values were shared in New Zealand. Both countries established systems to assess objections. The British system was based on 'service tribunals' and the New Zealand system on 'service boards'. The grounds for exemption were not the same in both countries and the British system was much less centralised than that of New Zealand. Tribunals and boards have not had a good press, and have often been portrayed as engines of military oppression, treating objectors with contempt and prioritising the need for soldiers above all else. This view stems in part from the focus on applications for exemption from military service on grounds of 'conscience'. As David Littlewood shows in this most welcome, innovative and perceptive study, 'conscientious objectors', both on grounds of religion, and

x *Series editors preface*

even more so on grounds of politics, were harshly treated in both countries – and widely derided by the general public. This has led to neglect, until recent times, of the economic nature of most claims for exemption in both countries, claims often made not only by individuals but also by their employers. Dr Littlewood shows convincingly that the tribunals and boards, and especially the tribunals, operated far more leniently than has often been thought as they attempted to balance the needs of the armed forces, the economy and – not least – the locality.

Writing comparative history is never easy, but Dr Littlewood has carried it off triumphantly. His study not only throws new light on the operation of conscription in both countries, but also on the 'policies, attitudes and prejudices' of British and New Zealand society at war, together with important issues of 'imperial loyalty' and 'Britishness' in the wider 'British world'.

John Bourne
University of Wolverhampton, UK

Acknowledgements

This study derives from a 2015 PhD thesis at Massey University, and so owes a tremendous debt to my supervisors: Associate Professor James Watson and Dr John Griffiths. My other colleagues in the School of Humanities have always given great encouragement, none more so than Associate Professor Kerry Taylor, who continues to demonstrate tremendous faith in my abilities. Thank you also to Professor Glyn Harper, Dr Geoff Watson, Professor Sir Hew Strachan, Professor Katie Pickles and Dr Jock Philips for their assistance at various stages along the way.

I have experienced dedicated assistance at all of the repositories listed in the bibliography. However, a special mention must go to the staff at the Huddersfield Local Studies Library and the Kirklees branch of the West Yorkshire Archive Service, who managed to locate several previously undiscovered treasures on my behalf. It has been a great pleasure to work alongside the team at Routledge, particularly Rob Langham and Michael Bourne. Thank you for taking this work on and for all your efforts in bringing it to completion.

My greatest debt is to my wife, Kat, whose love and support always make me feel incredibly lucky. Family members have been behind me throughout and I particularly want to thank my Dad for his tireless efforts obtaining sources for me in the UK.

David Littlewood

Abbreviations

AG	*Ashburton Guardian*
AJHR	*Appendix to the Journals of the House of Representatives*
ANZ	Archives New Zealand
AP	Sir James Allen papers
AS	*Auckland Star*
AsqP	Herbert Henry Asquith papers
ATL	Alexander Turnbull Library
BC	*Barnsley Chronicle*
BI	*Barnsley Independent*
BL	British Library
BLTF	Birstall Local Tribunal files
BN	*Batley News*
BodL	Bodleian Library
BSP	British Socialist Party
CSG	*Cleckheaton & Spenborough Guardian*
CVG	*Colne Valley Guardian*
DDN	*Dewsbury District News*
DEN	*Dannevirke Evening News*
DR	*Dewsbury Reporter*
ECAT	East Central Division Appeal Tribunal
EP	*Evening Post*
FS	*Feilding Star*
GRA	*Grey River Argus*
GT	*Goole Times*
HBT	*Hawke's Bay Tribune*
H.C.	House of Commons
HE	*Holmfirth Express*
HEx	*Huddersfield Examiner*
HHP	Harris Hoyle papers
HNS	*Hawera & Normanby Star*
HORP	Herbert Otto Roth papers
H.R.	House of Representatives
ILP	Independent Labour Party

Abbreviations xiii

KA	West Yorkshire Archive Service, Kirklees
L.C.	Legislative Council
LGB	Local Government Board
MARO	Munitions area recruitment officer
ME	*Marlborough Express*
MES	*Manawatu Evening Standard*
MW	*Maoriland Worker*
NA	National Archives
NEB	National Efficiency Board
NZG	*New Zealand Gazette*
NZH	*New Zealand Herald*
ODT	*Otago Daily Times*
OO	*Ossett Observer*
P	*Press*
PBH	*Poverty Bay Herald*
PCE	*Pontefract & Castleford Express*
ROT	*Rodney and Otamatea Times, Waitemata and Kaipara Gazette*
ST	*Southland Times*
TH	*Taranaki Herald*
VTC	Volunteer Training Corps
W	*Worker*
WC	*Wanganui Chronicle*
WDT	*Wairarapa Daily Times*
WE	*Wakefield Express*
WSHC	Wiltshire and Swindon History Centre
WT	*Waikato Times*

Introduction

On 7 October 1916, Albert Walker, a blanket raiser living in the Yorkshire town of Dewsbury, explained why he should be exempted from conscription into the British Army. He was the sole support of his father, who had been seriously injured in a textile mill accident, and a sister who looked after the family home. Three of his brothers were away serving at the front, and two others had recently been called up by the military authorities. In view of this precarious domestic situation, and the sacrifices already made by his family, Walker was granted a certificate of conditional exemption.[1] Seven months later, Charles Sneddon made a similar plea at Hawera in the Taranaki region of New Zealand. In addition to owning an 897-acre farm, he was working his father's property twelve miles away, which carried four hundred breeding ewes and forty head of cattle. The proceeds from these two holdings provided for his mother and father, who were aged eighty and seventy-one, respectively. On the strength of this testimony, Sneddon was awarded *sine die* (indefinite) relief from joining the army.[2] Although they both had to renew their claims in the years that followed, Walker and Sneddon were always successful in obtaining further exemption and thereby spent the remainder of the Great War at home.[3]

These accounts exemplify a critical part of the wartime experience in Britain and New Zealand, but one that has not been fully analysed by historians. While a plethora of studies have discussed why so many men chose to volunteer for the army during 1914 and 1915, the outlooks of those who were subsequently called up under conscription have received relatively little scrutiny.[4] Even when the implementation of the respective Military Service Acts has been examined, scholars have overwhelmingly focused on the minority of individuals who expressed outright resistance towards being compelled to fight. It is rare to see equal significance placed on the fact that, like Albert Walker and Charles Sneddon, substantial numbers of prospective conscripts appealed, or were appealed for, on the grounds their domestic, business or occupational circumstances meant they should not be expected to serve. In Britain, specially constituted military service tribunals determined many of these cases, whereas military service boards were established to hear every claim lodged by eligible New Zealanders.

Most studies of the tribunals have given disproportionate attention to the hearings of conscientious objectors. During the inter-war period, several commentators

2 Introduction

established the orthodoxy that these occasions were marked by intolerance, vitriol and an unjustified refusal to grant the absolute exemption, as opposed to relief from combatant service, which was necessary to satisfy the beliefs of many objectors.[5] This interpretation has been contested by a few appraisals that advance more balanced conclusions. While admitting the tribunals' members could be unnecessarily abusive, these historians suggest that many of them did the best they could to implement the ambiguously worded and poorly regulated 'conscience clause'.[6] Nonetheless, most works on the British exemption system still highlight the tribunals' allegedly harsh treatment of conscription's moral and political opponents.[7]

Some attempts have been made to evaluate the tribunals' operations more broadly. In doing so, the relevant scholars have frequently challenged the 'traditional' portrayal of cogs in an impersonal and bureaucratic conscription machine. James McDermott maintains that the receipt of highly ambiguous guidance meant the tribunals operating in Northamptonshire had to develop their own policies. With the freedom to allocate degrees of importance between the army and the community, some were prepared to modify, or even ignore, official directions if they perceived them as a threat to local interests.[8] According to Adrian Gregory, the tribunals were part of an 'extremely complex, devolved, and flexible' recruitment system and operated in a very public setting.[9] Being local, often elected, dignitaries, their members tended to steer a middle course between the demand to root out 'shirkers' and the need to protect the economy and their own political prospects by not acting too harshly.[10] Similarly, Robin Barlow, Keith Grieves, Ivor Slocombe and Philip Spinks each acknowledge that individual tribunals were receptive to the military's needs, but contend that they often prioritised an efficient allocation of manpower that would not threaten their district's productivity.[11]

The historiography regarding the boards is even more limited in nature. Some studies of the New Zealand home front ignore the exemption system entirely. More common is a focus on only those men who cited religious or political objections to performing military service.[12] It has generally been admitted that the boards possessed little discretion in these cases. However, P. S. O'Connor asserts that they arbitrarily determined exemption should only be granted to groups that possessed written articles against bearing arms, while Paul Baker maintains some deserving individuals were denied a recommendation for non-combatant service.[13] Much stronger criticism has fastened around the boards' conduct during hearings. Gwen Parsons claims their members were more interested in challenging an appellant's beliefs than with assessing his claim to exemption, Ian McGibbon finds that 'humanitarian arguments against involvement in war cut no ice', and Graham Hucker characterises the boards' overall attitude as one of 'disdain'.[14]

Only a handful of recent studies have adopted a wider perspective. James Belich and John Martin assert that the boards readily embraced the concept of essential industries, while Keith Scott suggests most appellants in the Otago region were treated with 'considerable leniency'.[15] Yet such positive appraisals are rare. Sonia Inder, Lisa James and Kerry Stratton all contend that most agricultural and pastoral claimants had their cases dismissed, while Baker maintains the appeal bodies were always more likely to refuse exemption than to grant it.[16] For Parsons, the fact the boards dealing with Dunedin and Ashburton men were 'cautious and even sceptical about the appellant's claims' meant few appeals were allowed outright.[17] Hucker does concede that the board operating in Taranaki judged each case on its merits, but also finds that most verdicts showed a 'degree of inconsistency, even indecision'.[18]

Despite these partial expansions in scope, substantial issues continue to afflict both the British and New Zealand historiographies. Those scholars who have looked beyond conscientious objectors have carried out either impressionistic analyses of an entire country, or detailed examinations of just one appeal body or locality. The former approach necessarily lacks depth, while the latter raises important questions over sample size and representativeness. Both methods also run the risk of allowing particular cases to assume disproportionate significance, and of making rare or unusual occurrences appear commonplace. A further problem is that studies of the two exemption systems have remained almost totally confined within a national framework. Not a single mention is made of the boards in any work that considers the tribunals. From the New Zealand perspective, the only effort to relate events to those in the imperial centre is Baker's comment that the early British experience of conscription provided a 'mainly negative' example.[19]

This book addresses these issues by conducting a sustained transnational comparison of the tribunals' and boards' operations. Three areas are examined throughout. First, the degree of influence that the respective governments and militaries exerted over their exemption systems. Second, the proportion of eligible men who appealed, or were appealed for, and the grounds that were cited in support of these claims. Finally, the attitudes adopted by the tribunals' and boards' members and how likely they were to grant exemption to different social and occupational groups.

Such an approach offers a myriad of benefits. The number of cases brought before the tribunals ran into the millions, while tens of thousands of eligible New Zealanders were also the subjects of exemption claims.[20] Having so many individuals under their jurisdiction meant the appeal bodies played a crucial part in the highly charged debates surrounding manpower allocation during the second half of the Great War. Furthermore, every verdict the tribunals and boards delivered was a seminal moment for the man concerned. If success meant seeing out the war in relative safety, refusal would at best strain family and business arrangements, and at worst lead to death or serious injury at the front. Arthur Slack described the occasion of his hearing as a 'vitally important day in my life', while the anguish of witnessing their son being denied an exemption certificate proved too much for one couple in the West Riding of Yorkshire, who committed suicide just a few hours later.[21]

The methods by which the appeal bodies reached their decisions are equally revealing. An oft-stated complaint about Great War sources is that they are limited in extent and heavily weighted towards the middle and upper classes.[22] This is emphatically not the case for the tribunals' and boards' sittings, which brought together individuals from every walk of life and were extensively reported in

4   *Introduction*

the press. The appellants before one tribunal were described as a 'motley group of young and old, clean and dirty, rich and poor', while the observer of a board sitting noted how 'the blacksmith straight from his forge, the labourer from the waterside, the bush-man from the backblocks, rubs shoulders with the musician, slaughterman, flying-school pupil, and ship's cook'.[23] Crucially, the traditional burden of proof was reversed, with the appellants having to establish the merits of their claim under questioning by supplying evidence of the surrounding circumstances. As a result, the testimony not only facilitates comparisons between the attitudes of British and New Zealand men towards performing military service, but also between the contested understandings of citizenship, identity and masculine duty that played a vital role in determining who would be exempted.

There is strong precedent for adopting a transnational perspective. The late 1990s witnessed the emergence of what is commonly termed 'British World' scholarship, an approach that rejects the utility of purely national histories in favour of drawing comparisons between different parts of the former British Empire. It also challenges the notion that a rigid core/periphery relationship existed between Britain and the dominions, and instead advocates the symbiotic interpretation of 'Britishness' as a category for analysis.[24] As Katie Pickles has noted, the fact 'Britishness' was promoted most extensively during times of conflict makes the study of war and society an obvious point of interest.[25] Several historians working in Britain have readily embraced these concepts, particularly when analysing networks of people and shared cultural institutions.[26] 'British World' methodologies took longer to gain a foothold in New Zealand, partly due to the long-standing emphasis on tracing that country's supposedly distinctive nationalism. Recently, however, there has been a growing recognition of the need to re-examine the implications of New Zealand's imperial past.[27] Indeed, Giselle Byrnes advances the *New Oxford History of New Zealand* as a response to Peter Gibbons's entreaty to 'dissolve or decentre "New Zealand" as a subject'.[28] When doing so, she explicitly promotes transnationalism on the basis that it identifies 'connections and linkages that are comparable with each other and occur more or less simultaneously'.[29]

The East Central Division of the West Riding of Yorkshire provides a focus for the British element of this book. Under the Military Service Act of January 1916, appeal tribunals were established in each county to hear claims lodged against the verdicts of the district-level local tribunals. However, due to the abnormally large size of its population, the West Riding was divided into four separate jurisdictions. One of these was the East Central Division, which centred on the county boroughs of Barnsley, Dewsbury, Huddersfield and Wakefield, and on the boroughs of Batley, Morley, Ossett and Pontefract. The attractions of this area as a point of comparison for New Zealand are substantial. Their populations were roughly the same, with 810,454 people residing in the division in 1911 compared to 1,070,910 in New Zealand, while a similar number of people lived in their largest settlements: Huddersfield (107,821) and Auckland (102,676).[30] Moreover, the division broadly contained a mix of urban and rural and industry and agriculture, which also characterised New Zealand's society and economy. As a result, the

Introduction 5

relationship is between two cross-sections, rather than being skewed towards any particular group.

Another significant factor concerns the availability of sources. In 1921, the Ministry of Health decreed that the tribunals' records were not 'of sufficient public value to justify their preservation' and should be destroyed, with the exception of those pertaining to the Lothian and Peebles Appeal Tribunal, the Middlesex Appeal Tribunal and the London-based Central Tribunal.[31] Thankfully, this order was ignored in several cases, and the records of the East Central Division's local tribunals enjoy an uncommonly high survival rate. The Kirklees branch of the West Yorkshire Archive Service holds the minute books of both the Huddersfield Local Tribunal and the Spenborough Local Tribunal, alongside the Batley Local Tribunal's register of cases. Further documents pertain to the Marsden and Birstall appeal bodies. The former are located in the papers of Harris Hoyle, the tribunal's trade unionist member, and include statistics on verdicts, correspondence between Hoyle and his colleagues, and annotated sitting agendas. For Birstall, the extant files contain the clerk's rough minutes, letters to and from the tribunal members, and annotated agendas for each hearing.

These documents provide a wealth of information, but they only cover part of the division and do not divulge the appellants' motivations or the rationale behind many of the tribunals' verdicts. Newspapers play a critical role in mitigating these absences. Each of the division's principal towns has at least one accessible publication for the conscription period, and their combined coverage also takes in most of the less populous districts that hosted tribunal sittings. The local press took a great interest in the workings of the exemption system, reporting on the appointment of the tribunals' members and on reactions to their decisions. Each publication also carried extensive accounts of appeal hearings, which usually provide the only record of what occurred in terms of the questions asked, the statements made, and the attitudes of the tribunals' members.

Although the East Central Division provides an important focus, the British element of this book extends well beyond its borders. To examine whether the situation in the division reflected wider patterns, a range of primary and secondary sources have been used to draw comparisons with other parts of the country. Historians have specifically analysed the tribunals operating in Audenshaw, Calne, Leek, Stratford-upon-Avon, Carmarthenshire and Northamptonshire, while there are also memoirs and/or archival documents relating to Bristol, Birmingham, Leeds, Preston and Middlesex. Accessing the records held at the British Library, Imperial War Museum and National Archives has also permitted conclusions to be drawn on official manpower policies and the tribunals' responses to them, in addition to the overall rate of appealing within Britain.

The selection of New Zealand allows for a detailed comparison. During the early years of the twentieth century, moves towards an empire-wide system of defence gathered increasing momentum. The matter was debated at the 1907 and 1911 imperial conferences, an imperial general staff was established, and several of the dominions implemented compulsory military training for their youths and young males. However, only New Zealand, which regarded itself as the most

6   *Introduction*

'British' and most 'loyal' of the dominions, extended this latter initiative to any great degree once hostilities began. Like its British counterpart, the New Zealand Government obtained sufficient popular consent to introduce a fulsome measure of conscription during 1916.[32] New Zealand also looked to the British experience for lessons in relation to compulsory military service, and included roughly similar grounds of appeal within its Military Service Act.

The situation in the other dominions was very different. No form of conscription was ever mooted for South Africa over fears that it would incite open rebellion among the already resentful Afrikaners and among the majority black population.[33] In Australia, the Labor Government of Prime Minister William Hughes took several steps towards introducing a compulsion bill, only to be thwarted by the results of two popular referendums.[34] Although conscription was implemented in Canada and Newfoundland, this only took place during August 1917 and May 1918, respectively, and through the passage of legislation that provided a whole swathe of loopholes for exemption.[35] In short, a comparison between Britain and New Zealand embodies most of the experience of conscription within the empire.

Information regarding the New Zealand boards has been obtained from Defence Department files, which outline the methods used to appoint the appeal bodies' members and the genesis of any official instructions issued to them. Additional contents comprise statements of the cabinet's policies on exemptions, government and Defence Department correspondence with the boards, general returns on verdicts, and the board chairmen's valedictory reports. These records are more revealing than the tribunal minute books and registers in terms of the appeal bodies' attitudes and how they were administered. However, they provide much less detail on individual claims.

Newspapers are the primary means of supplementing these files. The total coverage of the consulted publications takes in nearly every town at which the boards heard cases. Like their British counterparts, New Zealand newspapers were avid followers of the exemption process and described hearings at length. These reports are of considerable importance, as only they detail particular appeals in terms of the grounds raised and the testimony supplied. Moreover, an absence of board minute books means newspapers are the sole source for determining the verdict delivered in each claim.

This study begins by examining the key decisions taken before the tribunals' and boards' operations commenced. Chapter 1 analyses their initial discretion to determine cases and the extent to which this was circumscribed by the respective governments and militaries. Chapter 2 then considers the appointments made to the various positions within the exemption systems, while Chapter 3 looks at the proportion of men who were the subjects of appeals, and how frequently the various grounds were cited. In Chapter 4, the focus is on the degree of autonomy that the appeal bodies were willing to exercise once sittings were underway. The board and tribunal members themselves are central to Chapter 5, which examines the attitudes they adopted during hearings. A more specific scope is adopted in Chapter 6: how the appeal bodies treated the claims of conscientious objectors.

Introduction 7

Finally, Chapter 7 analyses the overall verdicts delivered by the tribunals and boards to determine the relative likelihood of them granting exemption.

Analysing these points of comparison reveals several striking differences. Large numbers of tribunals were established with diverse and locally chosen memberships, whereas the personnel for the handful of boards were appointed according to a prescribed formula. Moreover, the tribunals received a plethora of ambiguous directions, which, when combined with a tendency to prioritise the needs of their communities, led to significant inconsistencies of procedure and decision. In contrast, the New Zealand government exerted strong centralised control over its exemption system, an approach that coincided with the boards' desire to achieve uniformity.

There were few similarities between the two countries, but those that did occur were highly significant. While historians have tended to focus on conscientious objectors, a clear majority of the British and New Zealand appellants expressed an earnest desire to join the army, were it not for their existing domestic or occupational commitments. Furthermore, and in direct contradiction to the common understanding, both the tribunals and the boards were more likely to award some period of relief than to simply confirm a man's conscription.

Notes

1 *Batley News* (*BN*), 14 Oct. 1916, 7.
2 *Hawera & Normanby Star* (*HNS*), 19 May 1917, 2 and 15 Jun. 1917, 5; *Wanganui Chronicle* (*WC*), 21 May 1917, 4.
3 *HNS*, 16 Oct. 1917, 5 and 7 Jun. 1918, 5.
4 John Morton Osborne, *The Voluntary Recruiting Movement in Britain, 1914–1916* (New York: Garland, 1982), 73–105; Catriona Pennell, *A Kingdom United: Popular Responses to the Outbreak of the First World War in Britain and Ireland* (Oxford: Oxford University Press, 2012), 143–62; David Silbey, *The British Working Class and Enthusiasm for War, 1914–1916* (London: Frank Cass, 2005), 49–124; J. M. Winter, *The Great War and the British People* (Cambridge: Harvard University Press, 1986), 29–37; Glyn Harper, *Johnny Enzed: The New Zealand Soldier in the First World War, 1914–1918* (Auckland: Exisle, 2016), 18–27; Jock Phillips, *A Man's Country?: The Image of the Pakeha Male – A History*, rev. ed. (Auckland: Penguin, 1996), 158–63; Matthew Wright, *Shattered Glory: The New Zealand Experience at Gallipoli and the Western Front* (Rosedale: Penguin, 2010), 45–48.
5 W. J. Chamberlain, *Fighting for Peace: The Story of the War Resistance Movement* (London: No More War Movement, 1928), 47–53; John W. Graham, *Conscription and Conscience: A History, 1916–1919* (London: George Allen and Unwin, 1922), 65–89; Philip (Viscount) Snowden, *An Autobiography*, vol. 1, *1864–1919* (London: Ivor Nicholson and Watson, 1934), 403–10; Adrian Stephen, "The Tribunals," in *We Did Not Fight: 1914–1918 Experiences of War Resisters*, ed. Julian Bell (London: Cobden-Sanderson, 1935), 381–82.
6 Rachel Barker, *Conscience, Government and War: Conscientious Objection in Great Britain, 1939–45* (London: Routledge and Kegan Paul, 1982), 29–43; Martin Ceadel, *Semi-Detached Idealists: The British Peace Movement and International Relations, 1854–1945* (Oxford: Oxford University Press, 2000), 220–22; Thomas C. Kennedy, *The Hound of Conscience: A History of the No-Conscription Fellowship, 1914–1919* (Fayetteville: University of Arkansas Press, 1981), 89–105; John Rae, *Conscience*

8   *Introduction*

and Politics: The British Government and the Conscientious Objector to Military Service, 1916–1919* (London: Oxford University Press, 1970), 33–67, 94–133; Keith Robbins, *The Abolition of War: The Peace Movement in Britain, 1914–1919* (Cardiff: University of Wales Press, 1976), 79–84.

7   Sascha Auerbach, "Negotiating Nationalism: Jewish Conscription and Russian Repatriation in London's East End, 1916–1918," *Journal of British Studies* 46, no. 3 (2007): 600–604; Lois S. Bibbings, *Telling Tales About Men: Conceptions of Conscientious Objectors to Military Service during the First World War* (Manchester: Manchester University Press, 2009), 29–31; David Boulton, *Objection Overruled* (London: MacGibbon and Kee, 1967), 123–39; Will Ellsworth-Jones, *We Will Not Fight: The Untold Story of the First World War's Conscientious Objectors* (London: Aurum, 2007), 62–78; Caroline Moorhead, *Troublesome People: Enemies of War, 1916–1986* (London: Hamish Hamilton, 1987), 31–34; A. J. Peacock, *York in the Great War: 1914 to 1918* (York: York Settlement Trust, 1993), 376, 517–18; Cyril Pearce, *Comrades in Conscience: The Story of an English Community's Opposition to the Great War*, rev. ed. (London: Francis Boutle, 2014), 134–63.

8   James McDermott, *British Military Service Tribunals, 1916–1918: "A Very Much Abused Body of Men"* (Manchester: Manchester University Press, 2011), 5–8.

9   Adrian Gregory, "Military Service Tribunals: Civil Society in Action, 1916–1918," in *Civil Society in British History: Ideas, Identities, Institutions*, ed. Jose Harris (Oxford: Oxford University Press, 2003), 178.

10   Ibid., 186.

11   Robin Barlow, "Military Tribunals in Carmarthenshire, 1916–1917," in *The Great War: Localities and Regional Identities*, ed. Nick Mansfield and Craig Horner (Newcastle: Cambridge Scholars, 2014), 18–19; Keith Grieves, "Mobilising Manpower: Audenshaw Tribunal in the First World War," *Manchester Region History Review* 3, no. 2 (1989): 24–27; Ivor Slocombe, "Recruitment into the Armed Forces during the First World War: The Work of the Military Tribunals in Wiltshire, 1915–1918," *Local Historian* 30, no. 2 (2000): 108; Philip Spinks, "'The War Courts': The Stratford-upon-Avon Borough Tribunal, 1916–1918," *Local Historian* 32, no. 4 (2000): 212.

12   Stevan Eldred-Grigg, *The Great Wrong War: New Zealand Society in WWI* (Auckland: Random House, 2010), 232–35; Damien Fenton, *New Zealand and the First World War, 1914–1919* (Auckland: Penguin, 2013), 34–35; Michael King, *The Penguin History of New Zealand* (Auckland: Penguin, 2003), 301–302; Christopher Pugsley, *On the Fringe of Hell: New Zealanders and Military Discipline in the First World War* (Auckland: Hodder and Stoughton, 1991), 225–35; Matthew Wright, *Reed Illustrated History of New Zealand* (Auckland: Reed, 2004), 266.

13   P. S. O'Connor, "The Awkward Ones – Dealing with Conscience, 1916–1918," *New Zealand Journal of History* 8, no. 2 (1974): 132–33; Paul Baker, *King and Country Call: New Zealanders, Conscription and the Great War* (Auckland: Auckland University Press, 1988), 173–75.

14   Gwen A. Parsons, "'The Many Derelicts of the War'?: Repatriation and Great War Veterans in Dunedin and Ashburton, 1918 to 1928" (PhD thesis, University of Otago, 2008), 36; Ian McGibbon, "The Price of Empire, 1897–1918," in *Frontier of Dreams: The Story of New Zealand*, ed. Bronwyn Dalley and Gavin McLean (Auckland: Hachette Livre NZ, 2005), 239; Graham Hucker, "The Rural Home Front: A New Zealand Region and the Great War, 1914–1926" (PhD thesis, Massey University, 2006), 169.

15   James Belich, *Paradise Reforged: The Story of the New Zealanders from the 1880s to the Year 2000* (Auckland: Penguin, 2001), 101; John E. Martin, "Blueprint for the Future? 'National Efficiency' and the First World War," in *New Zealand's Great War: New Zealand, the Allies and the First World War*, ed. John Crawford and Ian McGibbon (Auckland: Exisle, 2007), 523; Keith Douglas Scott, *Before ANZAC,*

Beyond Armistice: The Central Otago Soldiers of World War One and the Home They Left Behind (Auckland: Activity Press, 2009), 215.

16 Sonia Inder, "Middlemarch, 1914–1918" (Research essay, University of Otago, 1992), 36; Lisa James, "Doing Their Duty: The Impact of Conscription on Farming Families in New Zealand during the Great War" (Research essay, Victoria University of Wellington, 2006), 30–38; Kerry Stratton, "'Doing Their Bit': The Impact of the First World War on the Inhabitants of Tuapeka County" (Research essay, University of Otago, 1992), 102; Baker, *King and Country Call*, 117–23.

17 Parsons, "Many Derelicts," 48.

18 Hucker, "Rural Home Front," 172–78.

19 Baker, *King and Country Call*, 86.

20 David Littlewood, "'Willing and Eager to go in Their Turn'?: Appeals for Exemption from Military Service in New Zealand and Great Britain, 1916–18," *War in History* 21, no. 3 (2014): 338–54.

21 Diary Entry, 17 Jan. 1916, Arthur Slack Papers, Documents 18453, Imperial War Museum, London (IWM); *Huddersfield Examiner* (*HEx*), 1 Dec. 1916, 4.

22 David Monger, *Patriotism and Propaganda in First World War Britain: The National War Aims Committee and Civilian Morale* (Liverpool: Liverpool University Press, 2012), 12; Pennell, *A Kingdom United*, 9.

23 Ellsworth-Jones, *We Will Not Fight*, 67–68; *New Zealand Herald* (*NZH*), 29 Sep. 1917, 1 (supplement).

24 Phillip Buckner and R. Douglas Francis, "Introduction," in *Canada and the British World: Culture, Migration, and Identity*, ed. Phillip Buckner and R. Douglas Francis (Vancouver: University of British Columbia Press, 2006), 1–9.

25 Katie Pickles, "The Obvious and the Awkward: Postcolonialism and the British World," *New Zealand Journal of History* 45, no. 1 (2011): 85–87.

26 Brad Beaven, *Visions of Empire: Patriotism, Popular Culture and the City, 1870–1939* (Manchester: Manchester University Press, 2012); Kathleen Wilson, ed., *A New Imperial History: Culture, Identity and Modernity in Britain and the Empire, 1660–1840* (Cambridge: Cambridge University Press, 2004); Angela Woollacott, *Gender and Empire* (Basingstoke: Palgrave Macmillan, 2006).

27 Felicity Barnes, *New Zealand's London: A Colony and Its Metropolis* (Auckland: Auckland University Press, 2012); James Belich, *Replenishing the Earth: The Settler Revolution and the Rise of the Anglo-World, 1783–1939* (Oxford: Oxford University Press, 2009); Charlotte Macdonald, *Strong, Beautiful and Modern: National Fitness in Britain, New Zealand, Australia and Canada, 1935–1960* (Wellington: Bridget Williams Books, 2011).

28 Giselle Byrnes, "Introduction: Reframing New Zealand History," in *The New Oxford History of New Zealand*, ed. Giselle Byrnes (Melbourne: Oxford University Press, 2009), 2; Peter Gibbons, "The Far Side of the Search for Identity: Reconsidering New Zealand History," *New Zealand Journal of History* 37, no. 1 (2003): 39.

29 Byrnes, "Introduction," 14.

30 *1911 Census of Great Britain*; *1911 Census of New Zealand*.

31 Circular, Ministry of Health R. 293, 27 Mar. 1922, MH 47/5, UK National Archives, Kew (NA).

32 Mark David Sheftall, *Altered Memories of the Great War: Divergent Narratives of Britain, Australia, New Zealand and Canada* (London: I. B. Tauris, 2009), 91.

33 Timothy C. Winegard, *Indigenous Peoples of the British Dominions and the First World War* (Cambridge: Cambridge University Press, 2012), 165–66.

34 E. M. Andrews, *The ANZAC Illusion: Anglo-Australian Relations during World War I* (Cambridge: Cambridge University Press, 1993), 121–24.

35 J. L. Granatstein and J. M. Hitsman, *Broken Promises: A History of Conscription in Canada* (Toronto: Oxford University Press, 1977), 84–85; Winegard, *Indigenous Peoples*, 162–65.

1 Setting the boundaries

The formal conscription of large numbers of men for overseas military service was unprecedented in the history of both Britain and New Zealand. Taking such a radical step created the very real prospect of dissent, or even outright resistance, so the respective governments had to find ways of making their legislative and regulatory enactments appear as necessary and as equitable as possible. One promising means of achieving these objectives was to grant all eligible men the right to appeal for exemption. This would allow individuals who were engaged in essential wartime occupations to be retained on the home front, while also reassuring the public that only those men who might reasonably be expected to serve would be compelled to do so.[1] Yet if the overall concept of exemptions possessed obvious attractions, determining exactly how much discretion the tribunals and boards should have to judge individual cases proved to be anything but straightforward. Indeed, the final decision would ultimately hinge on a plethora of political, economic, social and cultural deliberations.

There was some upturn of militarism in British society prior to the Great War, challenging long-established attitudes. During the nineteenth century, the continental move towards conscription had been rejected in favour of retaining a small professional army recruited through volunteering. Suspicions dating back to the rule of Oliver Cromwell and the major generals in the seventeenth century, the fact it was largely recruited from minority groups, and the apparent security provided by the Royal Navy, meant the army was 'ignored and often abhorred by wider society'.[2] However, these attitudes underwent some revision due to a humiliating series of defeats in the 1899–1902 Boer War, which, by amplifying fears that the 'British race' was declining physically, encouraged a turn towards eugenics and 'efficiency'.[3] One manifestation of this shift was the popularity of youth organisations such as the Boys' Brigades and Boy Scouts, each of which stressed the benefits of sport, religion and military discipline.[4] The post-Boer War period also saw the emergence of the National Service League. Established to push for the introduction of compulsory military training, this body boasted Lord Roberts, Britain's most revered soldier, as its president. With the additional stimulants of 'invasion' literature and a belief that German naval and imperial ambitions threatened Britain's vital interests, 40 percent of young males belonged to a youth organisation by 1914, while the

Setting the boundaries 11

National Service League claimed to have nearly one hundred thousand members in 1912.[5]

Nevertheless, pre-war militarism lacked both depth and popular appeal. The primary aim of the scouts was to train good citizens for the empire, not to indoctrinate militarism, and the martial outlook of the Boys' Brigades was mitigated by a greater emphasis on social control. Furthermore, membership of a movement did not necessarily equate to identifying with or absorbing all its teachings.[6] Of greater significance is that most adolescent men were not part of a youth organisation at the outbreak of war; the working class in particular tended to remain aloof.[7] Likewise, the National Service League remained an association of the higher echelons of society and 'never became a true mass movement'.[8] A dearth of political support for the league's objectives meant that no attempt to introduce a measure of compulsion passed its second reading in Parliament. Those army reforms that were undertaken further illustrate a lack of militarist sentiment. The Secretary of State for War was forced to operate within a tightly constrained budget, while the new Army Reserve simply consisted of old auxiliary units melded into a Territorial Force, which was consistently unable to meet even its modest manpower targets. Furthermore, the 120,000-man complement of the new British Expeditionary Force marked an overall decrease in the army's frontline strength.[9]

This background made it inevitable that the wartime drift towards conscription would be slow and haphazard. The issue was completely swept aside during the early months, as a flood of volunteers overwhelmed Britain's enlistment machinery. Recruitment was co-ordinated at a national level by the Parliamentary Recruiting Committee, an essentially apolitical body comprising government ministers, MPs and party officials.[10] However, in a foretaste of subsequent manpower initiatives, the committee first delegated the implementation of its proposals to local organisations, and then acquiesced to the formation of locally raised 'pals battalions'.[11] Adhering to its ideological traditions, the Liberal Government, headed by Prime Minister Herbert Asquith, adopted a policy of 'business as usual'. This entailed a minimum of state interference in the economy and the lives of the populace, under which volunteering was allowed to proceed without restrictions.

By late 1914, it had become clear that such a *laissez-faire* approach was contributing to an unsustainable loss of skilled personnel from war industries.[12] The first attempt to mitigate this issue involved 'badging' essential workers to protect them from the attentions of recruiting officers. Between December 1914 and July 1915, the Admiralty supplied around four hundred thousand war service badges to companies involved in the production of munitions. Although it was considerably more reluctant to impede the flow of men to the front, from March 1915 the War Office issued over eighty thousand badges to individuals making small arms and ammunition. Yet the role of both these departments was limited to providing badges to the relevant firms; it was individual employers who controlled their distribution.[13]

Two million men had enlisted by the middle of 1915, but several factors then pushed conscription to the top of the political agenda. The most pressing was a decline in volunteering. In September 1914, the number of enlistments had

12   Setting the boundaries

averaged 116,000 per week; by June 1915 it averaged only 100,000 per month.[14] This was particularly worrying given that the Secretary of State for War, Lord Kitchener, had promised the French that Britain would double its army's strength to seventy divisions.[15] While volunteering was coming under considerable strain, support for conscription within the government was growing. In May 1915, several Conservatives joined the cabinet as part of the new Coalition, bringing their pro-conscription sentiments with them. Then the 'shells scandal', which saw a lack of artillery rounds blamed for the heavy casualties suffered at the Battle of Neuve-Chapelle, led to the establishment of a Ministry of Munitions with extensive directional powers over the country's industries. That body also replaced the Admiralty and War Office as the sole badging authority, although the allocation of these awards remained the preserve of individual employers.[16]

Asquith recognised that conscription was becoming increasingly necessary, but resolved to wait until its viability had been assessed. His first move was to authorise a census of the population aged fifteen to sixty-five, which was undertaken on 15 August 1915. Continuing the earlier reliance on local bodies, the National Register was organised and the responses tabulated by local registration authorities: the urban and rural district councils and borough councils, in conjunction with local recruiting officers and labour exchanges.[17] The results showed 5,158,211 eligible men, of whom 1,519,432 were 'starred' as being employed in essential occupations. Using a 25 percent ratio for medical rejection, the available manpower pool was estimated at 2.7 million.[18]

A War Policy Committee was then formed to consider future recruitment. Testimony before this body revealed a cabinet divided between supporters of conscription, mostly Conservative, and opponents, mostly Liberal. Despite four of its six members being pro-conscription, the committee's official report merely outlined the available options going forward.[19] Of greater significance were two minority reports. The first, by Austen Chamberlain, Winston Churchill, Lord Selborne and Lord Curzon, asserted that Britain would not obtain sufficient men through volunteering.[20] In contrast, the Labour Party's representative on the committee, Arthur Henderson, cautioned that moving to compulsory service without first proving its necessity would split the cabinet and alienate the working classes.[21] Asquith was therefore left 'in a fix'.[22] Calls for conscription were becoming incessant, but to introduce it prematurely might bring down the government and fracture the 'national unity' that he was so desperate to preserve.

In the belief conscription would only gain general assent if the alternative was proven to have failed, Asquith resolved to give volunteering one last chance. Under what became known as the Derby Scheme, publicly announced on 19 October 1915, the local registration authorities, local parliamentary recruiting committees, and local recruiting officers organised a canvass of all males of military age to try and persuade them to enlist directly, or to attest their willingness to serve when required. The attestees were then placed into age groups, numbered one to twenty-three for the unmarried and twenty-four to forty-six for the married, to be summoned in order by royal proclamation. Badged and 'starred' men were asked to attest, but promised that their occupation would render them immune from call-up.[23]

The Derby Scheme's appeals process embodied the existing trends of localism and decentralisation. At its head was the President of the Local Government Board (LGB), Walter Long, who was tasked with overseeing the establishment of a tribunal in each of the more than two thousand local registration districts, and with their subsequent administration. A firm believer in the sound judgment of local bodies, Long adopted, or even expanded, on the provisions of the scheme that granted them an important role.[24] He delegated responsibility for appointing the tribunals' members to the local registration authorities, merely recommending that each body consist of up to five individuals who were capable of exercising 'impartial and balanced judgment'.[25] Attested men could apply to a tribunal for postponement of their call-up on hardship grounds; employers could plead for the retention of their staff by citing necessity in the workplace. When determining these claims, Long instructed the tribunals to both 'facilitate recruiting' and protect the 'vital industrial and financial interests of the country'.[26] Such wording left considerable scope for interpretation, difficult to harmonise among so many bodies, as well as indicating willingness for the tribunals to exercise discretion. However, the scheme's architects did not have complete faith that local men would always make the 'correct' decisions. As the first of several checks on their powers, any reservist or employer who felt their case had been incorrectly rejected could appeal to a government-appointed Central Tribunal sitting in London.[27]

The local tribunals enjoyed only slightly less freedom in cases brought by men who felt they should have been immune from call-up. Special colliery courts were appointed to deal with claims relating to men employed underground or at the surface of coal mines.[28] Left to determine all other appeals for protection, the tribunals were asked to heed the original 'starring' criteria, alongside the lists of reserved occupations drawn up to supplement them. If a man could prove his calling came within the scope of these documents, the tribunals were obliged to treat him as being safeguarded from recruitment.[29] Yet while the lists of 'starred' and reserved occupations might have brought an element of centralised control into the exemption system, the fractured state of Britain's manpower allocation meant they in fact did the opposite. The Ministry of Munitions, the Admiralty, the Home Office and the Board of Agriculture each contributed to the main lists. Additional occupations were then assessed by an inter-departmental Reserved Occupations Committee sitting at the Board of Trade, which formulated its own schema after hearing from over four thousand firms and employees.[30] There were also allegations that the original 'starring' had been badly carried out and accusations that some men had deliberately misrepresented the nature of their work.[31] This meant the tribunals had to go beyond merely establishing whether a man's occupation appeared on the lists; they had to determine why he had not been 'starred' in the first place and whether he was actually employed as stated.

The appeals process was partly subject to the influence of the War Office, which attached a military representative and advisory committee to each tribunal. The former individuals were appointed directly by the military hierarchy, while the latter were groups of up to five men chosen by the local parliamentary

14   *Setting the boundaries*

recruiting committees for their knowledge of an area's economic circumstances.[32] This team was charged with screening every application for postponement or immunity. If they assented to a claim, it could be granted without the need for a formal tribunal hearing. Where an application was deemed contestable, a brief would be prepared for the military representative, who would then attend the appeal sitting to question the appellant and advocate for a refusal. In any case where he subsequently believed the tribunal had afforded relief incorrectly, the military representative could apply to the Central Tribunal for a review. The military representative was also permitted to challenge the immunity from call-up of any man employed outside of munitions work.[33] Clearly these were powerful prerogatives. They signalled a belief that local bodies might prove excessively lenient and must be constrained from doing so lest they threaten the supply of men to the army.

Yet there were substantial limitations on the War Office's influence. First, its military representatives had no right to refuse claims or to take part in making decisions at appeal hearings. Second, the tribunals could always reject the views that the military representatives put forward. Finally, although the War Office instructed the military representatives and advisory committees on what attitudes to adopt, their willingness to follow its directives was far from guaranteed. As individuals connected to the local economy, the advisory committees were hardly likely to counsel for wholesale losses of men to the front. Furthermore, a desire to minimise public concern over the army's role in the exemption system led to the selection of military representatives who were also familiar to the community in which they would serve.[34] This proved to be an unfortunate decision from the military's perspective, with the War Office lamenting as early as February 1916 that 'in certain cases the military representative has allowed his sympathy for individual hard cases or the special business needs of the locality to outweigh his responsibility in obtaining men for the Army'.[35]

The outcome of the Derby Scheme marked the beginning of the end for volunteering. On 2 November 1915, Asquith informed the House of Commons that the measure would only be deemed a success if it brought in 'everybody of military age and capacity who is left after you have completely supplied the other national necessities'.[36] Failure to do so would lead to conscription, a commitment reinforced by what became known as 'Asquith's pledge', which stipulated that any married men who attested would be off-limits until every single man had been 'dealt with'.[37] The final results of the scheme were along way short of achieving these goals. Only 840,000 single men of military age attested out of 2.2 million. Removing the 'starred' and the unfit reduced this figure to an estimated 318,533 who were readily 'available'. From 2.8 million married men, the numbers of attestees was 1.3 million, of whom 403,921 were 'available'.[38] In many respects the fate of volunteering had already been sealed, as the Allied conference at Chantilly had seen Britain commit to a sustained offensive against the German lines in the coming year. With the failure of the Derby Scheme and the need to secure every available man for the front, Asquith agreed to place a Military Service Bill before Parliament in January 1916.

Setting the boundaries   15

Military values exercised a much greater influence in pre-war New Zealand, where something of a dual identity was prevalent by the last decade of the nineteenth century. Strong attachment to Britain co-existed with a nascent nationalism that asserted New Zealanders were in many ways superior to 'Old Britons', a perception that usually revolved around the attributes of physical fitness and personal daring.[39] If the Boer War kindled militarism in sections of British society, this national self-image meant it reinforced an existing martial trend in New Zealand. Support was overwhelming: six and a half thousand individuals served overseas, the Volunteer Force swelled to over seventeen thousand members, and substantial sums of public money were donated to pay for supplies and equipment.[40] The aftermath of the war illustrated the government's appraisal of its role in the military affairs of the empire. There was certainly a desire to offer more assistance to Britain against the rise of German power. Yet a simultaneous, and perhaps greater, concern was New Zealand's position as an isolated imperial outpost. Geographically remote and with a small population and long coastline, the dominion had already been gripped by fear of a Russian invasion in the late nineteenth century. Attention had since shifted to the possibility of attack by Japan, particularly after its comprehensive victory in the Russo–Japanese War of 1904–1905. Official rhetoric therefore promoted a shared commitment to imperial defence. New Zealand must demonstrate its willingness and ability to assist Britain, so that Britain would feel compelled to come to New Zealand's aid if required.[41]

These beliefs stimulated a desire for increased military preparedness. At a time when reforms of the British Army were impeded by budgetary constraints, New Zealand doubled its defence expenditure between 1909 and 1913, while an offer to buy Britain a frontline battleship received overwhelming public support.[42] The clearest illustration of New Zealand's greater militarism was the introduction of compulsory military training. Established to push for this measure in 1906, the National Defence League could soon boast over seven thousand members.[43] Much of this expansion resulted from the perceived overseas threats, but was also facilitated by New Zealand's 'tradition of "big government"'.[44] Successive administrations had responded to working class unrest by introducing welfare measures that went considerably further than those of most other countries. This, in turn, fostered a growing belief that 'the state had the right to demand certain duties of its citizens'.[45] It took two years of war for Britain to introduction conscription, whereas New Zealand's 1909 Defence Act for the compulsory military training of twelve- to twenty-one-year-olds was opposed by only a handful of MPs. There were protests, particularly in Christchurch, from pacifists and trade unionists, and thousands were prosecuted for failing to parade.[46] Yet other groups rallied to the system's support and the overwhelming majority of youths and young men did report for training as ordered.[47]

Despite this greater martial tendency, New Zealand witnessed few calls for conscription during the early stages of the Great War. Indeed, the issue was scarcely raised due to a rush of volunteers, numbering fourteen thousand in the first week alone. Rather than sending all these men overseas, the Defence Department dispatched the 8,499-strong Main Body and arranged for its strength

16 *Setting the boundaries*

to be maintained through bimonthly reinforcement drafts. This approach meant there was no immediate role for many of the men who had come forward, leading the Defence Department to conclude that it did not need to play an active part in recruitment.[48] By January 1915 the situation had altered somewhat, as a realisation the conflict could be long and difficult meant public attitudes began to shift towards regarding volunteering as a duty. It was at this point that official steps were finally taken to encourage enlistment. However, the Minister of Defence, James Allen, proved extremely resistant to local initiatives, arguing it was 'far better that recruiting should be in hands of the Defence Department'.[49]

Several events in the middle of 1915 hardened attitudes towards volunteering. News of the heavy casualties at Gallipoli arrived at the end of April and was quickly followed by the sinking of the British ocean liner *Lusitania* by a German U-Boat. The former occasioned national pride; the latter led to determination to defeat an unscrupulous enemy. Between them they sparked another flood of volunteers and demands for New Zealand to increase its military commitment. The Coalition Government had already raised the strength of the Main Body in April, and in August it did so again, necessitating larger reinforcement quotas.[50] This period also saw the first fears New Zealand might struggle to meet its obligations, an impression strengthened when Allen erroneously remarked that sufficient recruits were not coming forward. A belief that all young men should go to the front now became widespread. Sports teams were targeted, employers pressured their single staff to enlist and white feathers were distributed to those perceived to be 'shirkers'.[51] Nevertheless, calls for conscription remained limited, given an absence of actual shortages and a reluctance to act before Britain.

Demands for compulsory service began in earnest when there was a real danger of New Zealand failing to meet its commitments. Allen had finally countenanced local measures to encourage volunteering in April 1915. However, these produced ever-decreasing returns and the first crisis came when the October reinforcement quota was only just filled in time. Much of the blame for this episode was directed at the Defence Department, with the continued time-lapse between enlistment and mobilisation cited as a disincentive to potential volunteers. Critics argued the solution lay in immediate mobilisation through local camps. Yet Allen constantly rejected such proposals, citing cost and efficiency.[52] The difficulties of obtaining a regular and orderly flow of recruits led many in the government to recognise the benefits of conscription, but they worried about the working-class dissent that might result from introducing it prematurely.[53]

The government therefore determined it must do everything possible to make volunteering work, and arranged for a National Register of males aged between seventeen and sixty. Like its British equivalent, this measure was justified on the grounds of efficient manpower allocation.[54] Yet there were two important differences. The New Zealand register circumvented local authorities by asking respondents to post their forms directly to the Government Statistician, and required individuals to state their degree of willingness to enlist. When the results were released on 7 December 1915, they showed that of 187,593 males of military age, 58.5 percent were prepared to volunteer for overseas service, 23.2 percent would serve in a civil capacity and 18.3 percent would volunteer for neither.[55] Anger at the latter group was exacerbated by a recruiting shortage over Christmas, widely attributed to the fact eligible men would not enlist while so many 'shirkers' remained at large.

The government now found itself in the same 'fix' that had so worried Asquith. Conscription appeared to be necessary, but potential resistance meant it could only be introduced after the alternative was shown to have failed. The commencement of a new Recruiting Scheme in February 1916 was explicitly justified by the fact Britain had only abandoned volunteering after a 'most exhaustive and systematic personal canvass' proved unsuccessful.[56] Each district, county and borough was to establish a committee made up of local authority members and other representative persons, which would then appoint canvassers to interview eligible men to try and persuade them to enlist.[57] Despite these basic similarities with the Derby Scheme, there were some notable differences. While local bodies would carry out the New Zealand measure, its direction would be in the hands of a Recruiting Board consisting of: the Prime Minister, William Massey; the Deputy Prime Minister, Sir Joseph Ward; and Allen, thereby giving it a more centralised character.[58] Men who agreed to enlist were not allocated to groups to be called in order, but could choose when they wished to mobilise. This removed the need for claiming postponement and meant there would be no formal appeal hearings or appeal bodies. The only comparable mechanism pertained to men engaged in essential industries, for whom employers could apply directly to the Minister of Munitions and Supply, Arthur Myers, for an exemption badge. After investigating the circumstances, Myers would make a recommendation to Allen, who would then decide whether the claim should be upheld.[59]

If the methodology of the Recruiting Scheme differed from its British forebear, the result was largely the same. Most local bodies promised their co-operation. However, many expressed a preference for conscription rather than another attempt to stimulate volunteering, and there was a distinct reluctance to pressure men into enlisting. Such attitudes frequently led to a dilatory approach, with other bodies complaining of an inability to find sufficient canvassers.[60] Those on the receiving end of the scheme also failed to meet expectations. Some asserted they would only enlist when they 'saw "the other fellow" compelled to do his share', whereas others simply failed to report as they had promised.[61] After every reinforcement draft from February to April mobilised with a greater shortage than the last, it was clear that the final test of volunteering had never got off the ground.[62] On 27 March 1916, Massey announced that the government would introduce a Military Service Bill to Parliament in May.

The drafting of Britain's conscription legislation was a predominantly civilian affair. In September 1915, the Lord Privy Seal, Lord Curzon, and the Conservative MP and publicist Leo Amery had put together a 'Sketch of Possible Scheme of Compulsory Military Service'.[63] It was this blueprint that the Cabinet Committee, established on 15 December, used as a starting point for preparing the Military Service Bill. Under Long's chairmanship, the committee comprised: Curzon; the Conservative Attorney General, Frederick Smith; the Liberal Lord President of

18 *Setting the boundaries*

the Council, Lord Crewe; and Sir John Simon, the Liberal Home Secretary and only member of the cabinet who opposed conscription on principle. Although it did consult with the departmental staff of the War Office, no member of the committee had a direct connection to the military.[64] Once a draft had been produced it was referred to the full cabinet for approval. Certainly, the subsequent discussions involved Kitchener, with other prominent members of the War Office also being asked for their input. However, Kitchener did not insist on any substantive changes, while the objections made by the Adjutant General and Director of Personnel Services to the wide scope of the 'conscience clause' were all rebuffed.[65]

In contrast, political concerns exerted a substantial influence on the proposed legislation, and ensured that localism and decentralisation would remain at the forefront. Asquith had attempted to mitigate potential resistance by asserting that conscription would be solely a means of redeeming his 'pledge' that no attested married men would be taken before all the available singles.[66] Yet the pretence that the Bill was a necessary extension of the Derby Scheme could only be maintained if their provisions were kept similar. The final draft, introduced by Asquith to the Commons on 5 January 1916, displayed several manifestations of this approach. First, it only applied to unattested men who had been unmarried on 2 November 1915, the date of the 'pledge', and who were aged between eighteen and forty-one on 15 August 1915, those who had been canvassed.[67] Second, it preserved the right of a man or his employer to appeal, with the Cabinet Committee noting that the permissible grounds 'correspond, as far as possible, to those in which exemption can be obtained under the Derby Scheme'.[68] A claim might be lodged

> on the ground that it is expedient in the national interests that he or they should, instead of being employed in military service, be engaged in other work; or on the ground that the man ... has any person dependent on him who, if the man was called up for army service, would be without suitable means of subsistence.[69]

Third, the responsibility for interpreting these provisions would remain with the same local tribunals established under the scheme. Indeed, one of Asquith's main arguments when trying to assuage the possible reluctance of MPs to countenance conscription was that appeals would be determined by bodies operating 'in every locality, as close as may be to a man's doors'.[70] The membership of these tribunals could now be expanded up to twenty-five, but the local registration authorities would continue to make any appointments.

Many of the new elements in the tribunals' brief would provide them with greater discretion. Under the Derby Scheme they had only been able to postpone the call-up of men who appealed on hardship or occupational grounds, whereas the Bill allowed for the granting of certificates of exemption from military service. Such relief could be stipulated as temporary, as dependent on certain conditions being met, or as absolute, with the tribunals having the power to review or renew a certificate on their own initiative or on the application of its holder. Moreover, deviations from the principle of mirroring the previously available

Setting the boundaries 19

grounds promised to give the tribunals two extra categories of cases to determine. First, they would be permitted to grant exemption on the basis of 'ill-health or infirmity'.[71] Second, during the final cabinet discussions, the Bill was amended to allow men to appeal on the grounds of a 'conscientious objection to the undertaking of combatant service', with an associated provision for exemption 'from combatant duties only'.[72] This change was carried out just two days after Simon's resignation from the government, a move that had prompted fears the former Home Secretary might mobilise Liberal opposition to the Bill. Given this timing, it seems the 'conscience clause' was a rushed effort to nullify potential dissent.[73]

If other features of the Bill appeared to signal a departure from localism and decentralisation, they in fact served to reinforce those trends. The first was the result of lobbying by the Ministry of Munitions, whose officials argued that local tribunals would lack the wider perspective necessary to judge which men were vital for maintaining production. At its insistence, a sub-section was inserted that would permit government departments to direct that any war service badges previously issued to men engaged on essential work should now be treated as certificates of exemption from conscription.[74] The second was the ability of each government department to grant exemption to 'men, or classes or bodies of men' directly in its employment, and to certify that 'men, or classes or bodies of men' whose work came within its 'sphere' were engaged in work of 'national importance' and should be entitled to relief.[75] These two measures would place substantial numbers of men outside the tribunals' jurisdiction and limit their discretion in other cases. However, given that they revolved around keeping men in their employment, they would largely apply to individuals who had been immune from call-up anyway under the Derby Scheme. Furthermore, the issuing of individual certificates would remain in the hands of employers rather than a central authority, while involving every government department in the exemption system would make it even more difficult to impose central controls.

A third significant proposal was the introduction of appeal tribunals. It would be to these bodies that dissatisfied appellants and employers would have the right to refer their claims, whereas a case would only proceed to the Central Tribunal if an appeal tribunal gave its permission. Unlike the local tribunals, the appeal tribunals would be appointed by the government and at a county level rather than for each registration district.[76] However, the primary consequence of their establishment was that instead of going before a central body in London, the clear majority of claims would be dealt with in their county of origin by people from that area.

The degree of War Office influence was to remain limited. Long outlined that the advisory committees (which were not mentioned in the Bill) would continue in their role as 'grand juries' by clearing 'the lists of cases where the facts are so evident that it would not be worth while' for the tribunals to investigate.[77] In doing so, they would again be partnered by military representatives, who would appear at exemption hearings to contest doubtful claims. The Bill also provided for the unrestricted right of the military representatives to request that exemption certificates be reviewed and to refer cases to the appeal tribunals.[78] Even the LGB regarded this latter mechanism more as a safeguard for the army against

20 *Setting the boundaries*

'any laxity on the part of the local tribunal' than as a means of protecting the appellants.[79] However, exercising either of these prerogatives would only bring the case before the same or a higher tribunal; the military representatives were to have no control over the final verdict. The Bill and the debates surrounding it certainly gave no prospect of the War Office obtaining directional powers over the appeal bodies. The LGB would be responsible for addressing any difficulty 'in relation to the operation of this Act with respect to local tribunals'.[80] Furthermore, the majority of questions and amendments concerning the tribunals were dealt with by Long, who gave an explicit assurance that they would be 'civilian in character and not military'.[81] Finally, it was specified that once the Bill had been passed, Long would draw up and issue regulations regarding the constitution and procedures of the appeal bodies.

While New Zealand's conscription legislation shared the imprint of political expediency, the military had a much greater role in its drafting. The cabinet was given ample opportunity to discuss the Military Service Bill and to make alterations. Nevertheless, Allen had a particularly prominent role in its development. He wrote that this work had kept him 'fully occupied'; Myers identified him as the principal architect; and it was he, not Myers or the Prime Minister, who outlined the proposed legislation to the House of Representatives on 30 May 1916.[82] The Bill's central features were designed to obtain the broadest possible public consent. Not only was there a fear of working-class unrest, but the government was also a coalition and the House was divided almost equally between Reform and Liberal members. Several MPs had already called for the application of strong compulsion, whereas others remained doubtful whether such a perceived assault on individual liberties was warranted at that juncture, or even at all.[83] The Bill struck a balance between these positions. Each recruiting district would try and meet its monthly reinforcement quota through volunteering, but failure to do so would result in the balloting of conscripts to make up the shortage. A First Division of the unmarried, widowers without children and those married after 1 May 1915 would be exhausted initially, followed by the predominantly married men of the Second Division. Where no sons had enlisted from a family with at least two eligible men, all the sons would be available for immediate conscription regardless of their status.[84]

Several of the Bill's features appeared to signify an intention to 'de-politicize' the boards and afford them considerable discretion.[85] There would be no granting of exemptions by government departments and no legislative privileging of certain occupational classes, as 'it has been proved from experience in Britain that the exempting by classes was a mistake'.[86] Instead, Allen stressed that every reservist, or his employer, would have to lodge an appeal and that the boards would be responsible for determining each case on its merits. Claims could be made 'on the grounds that it is contrary to public interest, or because there are domestic circumstances or other reasons why his calling up will be the cause of undue hardship to himself or to others'.[87] The key terms of these provisions were not defined and would require the boards to determine how they should be interpreted and applied. In each case, the relevant board could dismiss the appeal, adjourn it for rehearing at a set date, adjourn it *sine die* (indefinitely) or allow it.[88] These decisions would always be final, as the proposed legislation did not allow for any higher bodies to which claims might be referred.

However, further sections and statements demonstrate that New Zealand's exemption system would be highly centralised. There was no provision for relief based on medical unfitness or, initially, on the grounds of conscientious objections. The three members of each board would be appointed by the government rather than by the local authorities, and would only hold their positions at the executive's 'pleasure'.[89] Allen also divulged that the current thinking envisaged only one board in each of the four military districts: Auckland, Wellington, Canterbury and Otago. Although he went on to state that 'we may have to establish a Board in each military group', even this would only mean twenty-one appeal bodies, far fewer proportionately than in Britain.[90] Rather than being based in a local district, the boards would need to travel around the country and hold sittings in many different places.

The combined effects of these policies would be threefold. First, the board members would be less influenced by local concerns than the personnel of the tribunals. Their position would not be dependent on the goodwill of local authorities, and perhaps the local population, and they might be without a personal connection to their place of sitting. Second, the boards would sometimes lack the familiarity with local conditions that the tribunals possessed. A final impact concerned central direction. Like their British counterparts, the boards would be free, in the absence of any regulations, to decide their own approach.[91] However, the government's right to choose the appeal bodies' personnel would allow it to select individuals who could be relied upon to adopt the 'correct' attitude and who would be amenable to applying instructions. It would be far easier to produce directions for a handful of boards than for over two thousand tribunals, with Allen making repeated reference to the importance of uniformity.[92] The New Zealand government would also be better able to monitor the activities of its appeal bodies, both to determine if regulations were required and to ensure they were implemented in the desired manner.

Despite firm assurances to the contrary, it was clear the military would play a significant role in New Zealand's exemption system. When introducing the Bill, Allen stated that he knew 'of no reason why military men should be on the Appeal Boards' and the proposed legislation made no mention of military representatives or advisory committees.[93] Allen even explicitly guaranteed the boards would 'not be under military control', but would be the responsibility of Myers and his Ministry of Munitions and Supply.[94] Yet the parliamentary process itself contradicted this assertion. Not only did Allen introduce the Bill and explain its sections regarding exemptions, he also responded to questions or comments during the debates; made statements regarding the proposed number, constitution and procedure of the boards; steered the Bill through the committee stage; and proposed every government amendment.[95] One MP even stated that he hoped to influence 'the Minister of Defence, when he makes regulations for the exemption Board', a comment that passed without contradiction.[96] In contrast, no questions were put

22 *Setting the boundaries*

to Myers and his speech on the Bill failed to make a single mention of the boards. This must have made it abundantly clear that the direction of the appeal bodies would be the preserve of the Minister of Defence. Yet no opposition was raised to this eventuality, indicating that New Zealand MPs were more willing to countenance military oversight than their British counterparts.

The amendments made to the British Bill extended the limits of the tribunals' discretion. To ameliorate fears that conditional exemptions might produce a form of 'industrial compulsion', the grounds for occupational appeals were expanded to

> that it is expedient in the national interests that he should, instead of being employed in military service, be engaged in other work in which he is habitually engaged or in which he wishes to be engaged or, if he is being educated or trained for any work, that he should continue to be so educated or trained.[97]

In addition, a sub-section was inserted that would allow a man who left the employment on which his exemption depended two months to find similar work and apply for a renewal. This 'grace' period would also apply in any case where a certificate expired or was withdrawn.[98] Another concern for the government was that conscription might cause high-profile disputes with conscientious objectors who refused to work under military direction. It therefore accepted an amendment that would permit the tribunals to make an objector's certificate conditional on him 'being engaged in some work which, in the opinion of the local tribunal, is of national importance'.[99]

The greatest increase in the tribunals' discretion resulted from a widening of the permissible grounds for hardship cases. Several amendments were tabled that would have compelled the appeal bodies to grant exemption in certain circumstances, particularly to the only son of a widowed mother.[100] Long agreed that the fact the initial provision only applied to men with dependents meant it was too restrictive, but firmly opposed any wording that specified exactly when exemption should be granted. He instead moved the insertion of a replacement sub-section: 'that serious hardship would ensue if a man were called up for Army service owing to his special financial, business or domestic obligations'.[101] Clearly, this version was far broader and more open to interpretation. Indeed, some MPs argued that it was too wide and would lead to vast numbers of exemptions.[102] In response, Long had the word 'special' replaced by 'exceptional' and made it so appeals brought under the provision could not receive an absolute exemption.[103] Despite these caveats, the tribunals' discretion in hardship cases had been considerably enhanced.

Long also ensured that the local registration authorities retained considerable freedom in making appointments to the local tribunals. Several MPs supported an amendment stipulating that half the members of each body must be drawn from trade unions, while Labour MP Philip Snowden moved that a fifth of all members should be women.[104] From the other end of the political spectrum came agitation that no individual who was a 'pronounced opponent' of conscription should be allowed to serve.[105] Long's answer was that no definite prescription regarding the tribunals' constitution should be formulated, as the varied occupational and political circumstances across the country made general rules impractical. Furthermore, if anti-conscriptionists were to be prevented from sitting, then 'common justice' required that supporters of universal compulsion should also be barred.[106] He instead promised that guidelines would be issued to the local authorities advocating for labour representation and the appointment of suitable women if they were available.

Unlike these divisive aspects of the appeals process, the role of the military proved uncontroversial. The only lengthy speech on the matter was made by Long, who maintained that the military representatives and advisory committees were a crucial part of the recruiting system and acted as a balance to the interests of 'the people and any machinery they may create for themselves'.[107] A lack of comment on this assertion makes it impossible to know exactly how it was received. Nevertheless, the fact many of conscription's staunchest opponents remained silent again illustrates that the level of military influence was perceived to be limited.

The completion of the committee stage marked the end of changes to the proposed British exemption system. It was hardly mentioned in the third reading debate, which the Bill passed by 383 votes to 36.[108] The Military Service Act received the Royal Assent on 27 January and took effect on 10 February 1916.

The New Zealand Bill received only limited amendments, thereby retaining its decidedly centralised character. A major point of contention was the level of independence that the boards should possess. On one side were those MPs, predominately Liberal, who, reflecting their party's traditional hostility towards 'class' interests, welcomed Allen's insistence that the appeal bodies would be allowed complete freedom to determine claims.[109] They argued that providing for automatic exemptions or issuing directions would make the system inequitable by privileging certain groups.[110] On the other side were MPs who regarded the government's apparent willingness to grant the boards freedom of action as a cause of great concern. The majority were Reform members who, while generally accepting that the legislation should not exempt occupational classes, believed this placed an onus on the government to issue detailed instructions regarding which men should be considered essential.[111] Although MPs discussed this matter at length, the Bill's double-sided implications, seeming to give the boards latitude while also allowing the government to exercise central control, was enough to satisfy both sides. Only one pertinent amendment was moved from outside the executive: that the sole surviving son of a family in which at least one had been killed should automatically have his appeal granted. Whereas Long had ensured there would be no concrete prescriptions in the British hardship clause, this change was approved without a division.[112]

A further potential reduction in the boards' independence was proposed in the Legislative Council, New Zealand's appointed upper chamber: to allow the government to establish a Final Appeal Board if required. Allen prompted the House to accept this amendment on the basis that 'it was for the sake of uniformity, and to provide a means of giving general directions'.[113] Like the Central Tribunal, the Final

24 *Setting the boundaries*

Appeal Board would have the power to review and overturn verdicts. However, while Long had stated that the Central Tribunal would only issue guidance, the Final Appeal Board would be able to rule on any question of interpretation, administration or procedure, with the boards being obliged to carry out its instructions.[114]

The New Zealand Bill did eventually receive its own 'conscience clause', but one with highly restrictive wording. Allen believed that obtaining the widest public backing for conscription required a concession to objectors.[115] He therefore introduced an amendment to permit appeals from a man who 'objects in good faith to military service on the ground that such service is contrary to his religious belief'.[116] A number of MPs had already insisted that it would be 'monstrous' if the views of Christian pacifists were not provided for, with a few basing their arguments on the precedent of the British Act.[117] However, most were thinking only of the Quakers and emphasised that any section must be formulated to prevent 'shirkers' from benefitting.[118] Such misgivings prompted these MPs to join with the opponents of religious exemption in defeating Allen's proposal.

The government then introduced a modified amendment in the Council. On the condition of performing non-military work in New Zealand, this would exempt men who, since the outbreak of war, had been members of a religious body, the tenets and doctrines of which declared military service to be 'contrary to divine revelation'.[119] Some councillors lamented that this wording was far more prohibitive. It would disqualify individually held objections, as well as men who belonged to denominations that were not opposed to military service.[120] That exemption would definitely be confined to a handful of 'small bodies' convinced a majority of councillors to vote in favour, but even this proved too liberal for the elected House.[121] A compromise had to be reached stating the alternative service would be non-combatant rather than non-military, could include the Army Service Corps or Medical Corps, and could be 'in or beyond New Zealand'.[122] One of the leading proponents of religious exemption complained these new stipulations 'left very little provision at all', while other members labelled the modified amendment pointless, as the denominations it was intended to benefit would refuse to accept non-combatant service.[123] This perceived irrelevance persuaded many opponents of an allowance for religious objectors to vote for the amendment, as it finally passed by forty-four votes to seventeen.

Two major elements of centralisation received little comment and no amendments. The first was the selection of the boards' personnel. During the debates, all manner of permutations for the ideal constitution were suggested.[124] Yet only a handful of MPs postulated who should be responsible for making the appointments. The fact most remained silent implies a tacit acceptance of the right of the government, rather than local authorities, to determine the boards' membership. A second uncontroversial area was the number of appeal bodies. Most MPs simply spoke of 'the boards' in a manner that suggests they were prepared to accept however many the government felt necessary.[125] Some even initially referred unquestioningly to a single 'board'.[126] Despite scattered calls for an appeal body to be established in each military group or in each 'major centre', nowhere was it argued that every locality should have its own board.[127]

Setting the boundaries 25

There were strong hints that the military's role in appeals was likely to be strengthened. When MPs debated the legislation, not one of them called for an army presence on the boards. Rather, a large group of them applauded Allen's insistence that no officers would be selected, claiming this would raise public confidence in the impartiality of the exemption system.[128] Yet Allen had come to regret the definitiveness of his earlier pronouncement. He proceeded to contradict it flatly at the end of the second reading debate, by stating the Defence Department would 'raise no objection' to military membership and that 'we have no desire to put a man who has worn Khaki on the Boards if the House does not so wish, but my advice is to leave the matter to the judgment of the Government'.[129] By this point the House had, in no uncertain terms, stated its objections to having military men on the appeal bodies. It was also disingenuous to ask MPs to leave the matter to 'the government', when it was plain Allen himself would be administering the boards. Finally, while somewhat distancing himself from the appointment of former soldiers, Allen did not rule out the use of existing officers or men commissioned specifically for the role. Allen clearly envisaged a military presence at appeal hearings. However, his remarks to this effect occasioned no dissent or proposed amendments from MPs.

The New Zealand Bill passed its third reading by forty-four votes to four.[130] Due to the prolonged wrangle between the House and the Council over conscientious objectors, it did not finally pass into law as the Military Service Act until 1 August 1916.

The regulations and instructions issued to Britain's tribunals enshrined the principles of localism and decentralisation. Drawn up and issued by Long, formal regulations were dispatched on 3 February 1916, accompanied by LGB Circular R. 36, Long's elaboration on their content. The tribunals' would have the right to determine what evidence should be admissible, which witnesses should be called, and to conduct any case in private if they deemed it necessary.[131] There was little direction over the verdicts they should reach, with Long stressing that 'the Local Government Board cannot advise Local Tribunals or particular persons on individual cases'.[132] He instead confined himself to articulating general principles, namely that every man who came within the Act 'and who is available for military service should undertake military service'.[133] Long was slightly more specific in regard to conscientious objectors, asserting that

> while care must be taken that the man who shirks his duty to his country does not find unworthy shelter behind this provision, every consideration should be given to the man whose objection genuinely rests on religious or moral convictions.[134]

However, nothing in this plea would circumscribe a tribunal's ability to determine cases in the manner it desired.

There was even latitude over the claims of men who asserted their occupation was included on the list of certified occupations: those callings that the government departments identified as being of 'national importance'. This document was

26 *Setting the boundaries*

similar in scope to the lists of 'starred' and reserved occupations it superseded.[135] While the tribunals were obliged to exempt any man who demonstrated that he was employed in an occupation marked 'MM' (for munitions), the tasks of establishing whether he was employed as stated, and whether his calling was covered by the list, would still need to be carried out. Even if engagement in a certified occupation was proven, the appeal bodies could refuse exemption if they agreed with the military representatives that it was unnecessary for a man to remain in civilian employment.[136]

The instructions also extended the tribunals' discretion in regard to individuals who had attested under the Derby Scheme. To forestall accusations that these men were being punished for expressing their willingness to serve, the government endeavoured to place them on the same footing as the conscripts. This included allowing the tribunals to grant them exemption, rather than just postponement, and providing that the appeal tribunals would deal with any disputed decisions. In addition, the lists of 'starred' and reserved occupations became obsolete, with those attested men who were so entitled being protected by the same list of certified occupations that applied to unattested men.[137]

In contrast, directions issued to the boards greatly increased the centralisation of New Zealand's exemption system. While Allen had suggested to MPs that an appeal body might be required in each of the twenty-one military groups, the Recruiting Board instead opted to establish only one for each of the four military districts.[138] The official justification revolved around the need to secure consistency of procedures and verdicts. Indeed, the newly appointed board chairmen were immediately summoned to Wellington to 'consider the Act, and the proposed regulations, and to deal with questions of uniformity of judgment and other points necessary for smooth working'.[139]

The government also restricted the boards' discretion over occupational appeals. On 10 October 1916, a regulation was gazetted stipulating that, when considering public interest cases, 'the Board shall, unless it sees good reason to the contrary, accept as sufficient [evidence] a certificate by the Minister of Defence'.[140] So strong was this wording that the Solicitor General, John Salmond, claimed it created 'a serious risk of undermining public confidence in the impartiality, integrity, and fairness of the administration of the Military Service Act'.[141] A discussion of the matter then took place in cabinet, where it was decided to canvass the opinion of the Attorney General, Alexander Herdman.[142] He maintained that Salmond had gone beyond his remit by considering the political implications of the certificates rather than their legality. The government had 'ample authority' to issue the documents, as the Act required the boards to comply with any regulations that were made. Nevertheless, the Attorney General did concur with Salmond that using the certificates could create political problems. Given the choice of directing the boards through regulations or through conferences with their members, Herdman favoured the latter, as 'Regulation 9 to my mind savours of a mandate from the Government and of interference with the judicial functions of the Boards.'[143] Despite these misgivings, Allen decided that being able to protect essential individuals made issuing the certificates worth the risk. Salmond

Setting the boundaries 27

was certainly correct to argue that they amounted to a 'practical compulsion' of the boards, by applying considerable pressure to accept appeals and creating an impression that the appellant deserved exemption before any testimony had been heard.[144] Allen was later to state that he had 'no reason to believe that the Boards would not accept the certificate in every case'.[145]

The government then proceeded to issue further instructions. To prevent economic dislocation, a list of industries considered essential was set out to include: coal mining, farming, shearing, freezing works, shipping and leather and boot factories. Allen also explained that the boards would be expected to adopt a hierarchy for public interest cases: men employed in the stated industries should be considered for exemption, those outside them should not.[146] This list and the need to adhere to it was further emphasised to the board chairmen at a conference called with the intention of achieving 'a uniform policy'.[147] Four days later, a letter was sent to the appeal bodies that again outlined which industries the government considered essential.[148] Its desire to avoid potentially militant opposition to conscription also prompted the government to make special allowances for members of the 'strategic unions'.[149] The boards were directed to exempt all seamen with at least twelve months' experience, all *bona fide* slaughtermen and, with particular emphasis, all coal miners.[150]

Another crucial step was the attachment of a military representative to each board. The role of these individuals partly resembled that of their British counterparts, as they were charged with screening appeals to determine whether they had any merit, and with preparing a case against those considered doubtful. During hearings, they had the 'right to be heard in opposition thereto, to produce evidence and to cross-examine witnesses', but were not permitted to take part in reaching verdicts.[151] However, in other respects the position of New Zealand's military representatives was very different. They would not have the assistance of a local advisory committee, while the lack of higher appeal bodies meant they would be unable to challenge the boards' initial verdicts. Of even greater importance is that New Zealand's military representatives were deliberately assigned to boards that would operate away from their places of residence. Again, the stated rationale was to promote impartiality.[152] Yet it meant the military representatives would lack the local knowledge possessed by their British counterparts, would be less susceptible to community sentiment, and would be more receptive to official instructions.

The relative positions of the military representatives encapsulate the significant variances between the two exemption systems. In Britain, localism and decentralisation were the dominant themes of recruitment policy from the beginning. These principles were then further enshrined in the Military Service Act, which established tribunals wielding wide discretionary powers in every local registration district. The administration of these bodies was entrusted to Long, who proved an active proponent of their freedom to judge appeals. Certainly, the government's faith in the tribunals was not absolute, but its system of checks and balances on their independence only increased the local and fragmented nature of the appeals process. As for the War Office, it was in no position to control the tribunals directly, and the fact its own appointees were local men

28 *Setting the boundaries*

meant even their willingness to follow instructions was uncertain. The situation in New Zealand was the complete opposite. Only a handful of boards were set up, meaning they would be much less local and much more responsive to central direction. Moreover, the government quickly demonstrated a willingness to circumscribe the appeal bodies' powers by issuing extensive instructions regarding men employed in essential industries. Greater military influence was ensured by the fact that Allen, as Minister of Defence, would act as the primary overseer of the boards.

Introducing conscription and developing an exemption system had proven to be a long and complex undertaking in both countries. Yet all the respective administrators had done to this point was establish a framework. They now confronted the equally fraught task of putting some flesh on the bones.

Notes

1 George Q. Flynn, *Conscription and Democracy: The Draft in France, Great Britain, and the United States* (Westport: Greenwood Press, 2002), 5; Jonathan Mein, Anne Wares and Sue Mann, eds., *St Albans: Life on the Home Front, 1914–1918* (Hatfield: University of Hertfordshire Press, 2016), 44.
2 Gerard J. DeGroot, *Blighty: British Society in the Era of the Great War* (London: Longman, 1996), 15.
3 Alan G. V. Simmonds, *Britain and World War One* (Abingdon: Routledge, 2012), 9–11; Winter, *Great War*, 8–21.
4 Ian F. W. Beckett, "The Nation in Arms," in *A Nation in Arms: A Social Study of the British Army in the First World War*, ed. Ian F. W. Beckett and Keith Simpson (Manchester: Manchester University Press, 1985), 4–5.
5 Hew Strachan, *The First World War*, vol. 1, *To Arms* (Oxford: Oxford University Press, 2001), 145; Anne Summers, "Militarism in Britain before the Great War," *History Workshop Journal* 2, no. 1 (1976): 113.
6 Ian F. W. Beckett, *The Amateur Military Tradition, 1558–1945* (Manchester: Manchester University Press, 1991), 199.
7 Niall Ferguson, *The Pity of War* (London: Penguin, 1998), 15.
8 R. J. Q. Adams and Philip P. Poirier, *The Conscription Controversy in Great Britain, 1900–18* (Columbus: Ohio State University Press, 1987), 20.
9 Beckett, "Nation in Arms," 6–7.
10 Roy Douglas, "Voluntary Enlistment in the First World War and the Work of the Parliamentary Recruiting Committee," *Journal of Modern History* 42, no. 4 (1970): 564–85.
11 Osborne, *Voluntary Recruiting*, 60–67.
12 David Lloyd George, *War Memoirs of David Lloyd George*, rev. ed. (London: Odhams Press, 1938), 1:172.
13 Humbert Wolfe, *Labour Supply and Regulation* (Oxford: Humphrey Milford, 1923), 24–27.
14 *Statistics of the Military Effort of the British Empire during the Great War, 1914–1920* (London: HMSO, 1922), 364.
15 Adams and Poirier, *Conscription Controversy*, 103.
16 Wolfe, *Labour Supply*, 29.
17 Peter Simpkins, *Kitchener's Army: The Raising of the New Armies, 1914–16* (Manchester: Manchester University Press, 1988), 148.
18 Adams and Poirier, *Conscription Controversy*, 98.
19 Report, War Policy Committee, 6 Sep. 1915, CAB 37/134/9, NA.

Setting the boundaries 29

20 Supplementary Memorandum, War Policy Committee, 7 Sep. 1915, CAB 37/134/7, NA.
21 Supplementary Report, War Policy Committee, 7 Sep. 1915, CAB 37/134/5, NA.
22 Adams and Poirier, *Conscription Controversy*, 116.
23 Report on Recruiting by the Earl of Derby, K.G., Director General of Recruiting, 1916, Cd. 8149, at 3.
24 Walter Long, *Memories* (London: Hutchinson, 1923), 228–29.
25 Circular, LGB R. 1, 26 Oct. 1915, MH 47/142, NA.
26 Circular, LGB R. 2, 19 Nov. 1915, MH 47/142, NA.
27 Circular, LGB R. 1, 26 Oct. 1915, MH 47/142, NA.
28 Circular, LGB R. 35, 3 Dec. 1915, MH 10/80, NA.
29 Circular, LGB R. 4, 19 Nov. 1915, MH 47/142, NA.
30 Runciman, 77 Parl. Deb., H.C. (5th ser.) (1916), 332; Memorandum, "Reserved Occupations," 20 Mar. 1916, CAB 37/144/47, NA.
31 Derby to Asquith, 25 Nov. 1915, Asquith Papers (AsqP), MSS Asquith 82, Bodleian Library, Oxford (BodL).
32 Ministry of National Service, "The Recruiting Code," 1 Jan. 1918, p. 63, NATS 1/95, NA; Memorandum, "Advisory Committees to Assist the Military Authorities," 24 Nov. 1915, MH 47/142, NA.
33 Circular, LGB R. 3, 19 Nov. 1915, MH 47/142, NA.
34 *HEx*, 19 Nov. 1915, 2.
35 Director General of Recruiting, "Group and Class Systems: Notes on Administration," February 1916, p. 5, MH 47/142, NA.
36 Asquith, 75 Parl. Deb., H.C. (5th ser.) (1916), 520.
37 Ibid.
38 Memorandum, Lord Derby on the Results of the Derby Scheme, 20 Dec. 1915, AsqP, MSS Asquith 82, BodL.
39 Belich, *Paradise Reforged*, 78.
40 Peter Cooke and John Crawford, *The Territorials: The History of the Territorial and Volunteer Forces of New Zealand* (Auckland: Random House, 2011), 113–15.
41 Paul Moon, *New Zealand in the Twentieth Century: The Nation, the People* (Auckland: HarperCollins, 2011), 37–38; Steven Loveridge, *Calls to Arms: New Zealand Society and Commitment to the Great War* (Wellington: Victoria University Press, 2014), 33–34.
42 *New Zealand Official Yearbook, 1914* (Wellington: Government Printer, 1914), 270; Wright, *Shattered Glory*, 38.
43 Eldred-Grigg, *Great Wrong War*, 15–16.
44 Baker, *King and Country Call*, 11.
45 Ibid., 12.
46 David Grant, *Field Punishment No. 1: Archibald Baxter, Mark Briggs & New Zealand's Anti-Militarist Tradition* (Wellington: Steele Roberts, 2008), 23–26; R. L. Weitzel, "Pacifists and Anti-Militarists in New Zealand, 1909–1914," *New Zealand Journal of History* 7, no. 2 (1973): 129–47.
47 Cooke and Crawford, *Territorials*, 170.
48 John Crawford, "'I Get Blamed for Everything': Enduring the Burdens of Office, James Allen as Minister of Defence in 1915," in *Endurance and the First World War: Experiences and Legacies in New Zealand and Australia*, ed. David Monger, Sarah Murray and Katie Pickles (Newcastle: Cambridge Scholars, 2014), 20.
49 *Evening Star*, 27 Nov. 1914, 3.
50 *Evening Post* (*EP*), 19 Apr. 1915, 6; Allen to Birdwood, 12 Aug. 1915, Allen Papers (AP), ALLEN 1 9, Archives New Zealand, Wellington (ANZ).
51 *NZH*, 27 May 1915, 8; *EP*, 28 May 1915, 3.
52 *Feilding Star* (*FS*), 29 Nov. 1915, 2; *WC*, 18 Dec. 1915, 4.
53 Allen to Godley, 4 Jan. 1916, AP, ALLEN 1 1 M 1/15/2, ANZ.

30   Setting the boundaries

54 Allen, 174 NZ Parl. Deb., H.R. (1916), 805.
55 "National Register," *Appendix to the Journals of the House of Representatives (AJHR)*, 1916, H-35.
56 Circular, Constitution of Recruiting Board, 14 Feb. 1916, AD 82 8 84, ANZ.
57 Circular, Recruiting Board to Local Bodies, Feb. 1916, AD 1 713 9/169/2, ANZ.
58 Circular, Recruiting Board to Town Boards, Feb. 1916, AD 1 713 9/162/2, ANZ.
59 Myers to Allen, 8 Jun. 1916 and Allen to Myers, 9 Jun. 1916, AD 1 10/483, ANZ.
60 Commander Wellington Military District to Headquarters NZ Military Forces, 20 Apr. 1916 and Commander Group 6 to Wellington Military District Headquarters, 3 May 1916, AD 1 713 9/169/2, ANZ.
61 *EP*, 15 Feb. 1916, 3; Commander Group 7a to Wellington Military District Headquarters, 1 May 1916, AD 1 713 9/169/2, ANZ.
62 Gibbon to Gray, 7 Mar. 1916 and 3 Apr. 1916, AD 1 713 9/169/2, ANZ.
63 Asquith to the King, 12 Oct. 1915, AsqP, MSS Asquith 8, BodL.
64 Long, *Memories*, 224; Rae, *Conscience and Politics*, 23.
65 Major-General Sir Wyndham Childs, *Episodes and Reflections: Being Some Records from the Life of Major-General Sir Wyndham Childs* (London: Cassell, 1930), 148.
66 Asquith, 75 Parl. Deb., H.C. (5th ser.) (1916), 520.
67 "Military Service (No. 2) Bill," 6 Jan. 1916, WO 32/9348, NA.
68 "Military Service Bill," Draft 297-7, 30 Dec. 1915, CAB 37/139/67, NA.
69 "Military Service (No. 2) Bill," 6 Jan. 1916, WO 32/9348, NA.
70 Asquith, 77 Parl. Deb., H.C. (5th ser.) (1916), 961.
71 "Military Service (No. 2) Bill," 6 Jan. 1916, WO 32/9348, NA.
72 "Military Service Bill," Draft 297-9, 4 Jan. 1916, AsqP, MSS Asquith 82, BodL.
73 Martin Ceadel, *Pacifism in Britain, 1914–1945: The Defining of a Faith* (Oxford: Clarendon Press, 1980), 38–39.
74 Rt. Hon. Christopher Addison, *Four and a Half Years: A Personal Diary from June 1914 to January 1919* (London: Hutchinson, 1934), 1:161.
75 "Military Service (No. 2) Bill," 6 Jan. 1916, WO 32/9348, NA.
76 Ibid.
77 Long, 78 Parl. Deb., H.C. (5th ser.) (1916), 738–39.
78 "Military Service (No. 2) Bill," 6 Jan. 1916, WO 32/9348, NA.
79 Forty-Sixth Annual Report of the Local Government Board, 1917, Cd. 8697, at 21.
80 Long, 78 Parl. Deb., H.C. (5th ser.) (1916), 1010.
81 Ibid., 745.
82 Allen to Godley, 11 Jul. 1916, AP, ALLEN 1 2 M1/15/3, ANZ; Myers, 175 NZ Parl. Deb., H.R. (1916), 773.
83 Wilford, 175 NZ Parl. Deb., H.R. (1916), 60; Veitch, 81; Statham, 140; Wilkinson, 184.
84 Allen, 175 NZ Parl. Deb., H.R. (1916), 484–91.
85 Baker, *King and Country Call*, 117; Parsons, "Many Derelicts," 44.
86 Allen, 175 NZ Parl. Deb., H.R. (1916), 486.
87 Ibid., 487.
88 New Zealand Military Service Act, 1916, 7 Geo. 5, no. 8, secs. 25–30.
89 Ibid., sec. 19(3).
90 Allen, 175 NZ Parl. Deb., H.R. (1916), 646.
91 New Zealand Military Service Act, 1916, 7 Geo. 5, no. 8, sec. 21.
92 Allen, 177 NZ Parl. Deb., H.R. (1916), 186; *EP*, 27 Sep. 1916, 6.
93 Allen, 175 NZ Parl. Deb., H.R. (1916), 490.
94 Ibid.
95 175 NZ Parl. Deb., H.R. (1916), 511, 590, 646, 782–84.
96 Pearce, 175 NZ Parl. Deb., H.R. (1916), 534.
97 78 Parl. Deb., H.C. (5th ser.) (1916), 970.
98 Long, 78 Parl. Deb., H.C. (5th ser.) (1916), 574–75.
99 Ibid., 556.

Setting the boundaries   31

100 MacCallum Scott, 78 Parl. Deb., H.C. (5th ser.) (1916), 344.
101 Long, 78 Parl. Deb., H.C. (5th ser.) (1916), 350.
102 Mond, 78 Parl. Deb., H.C. (5th ser.) (1916), 352; Annan-Bryce, 357.
103 Long, 78 Parl. Deb., H.C. (5th ser.) (1916), 558, 974; Military Service Act, 1916, 5 & 6 Geo. 5, c. 104, sec. 2(1)(b).
104 Walsh, 78 Parl. Deb., H.C. (5th ser.) (1916), 749; Snowden, 750.
105 Long, 78 Parl. Deb., H.C. (5th ser.) (1916), 741.
106 Ibid.
107 Ibid., 738.
108 78 Parl. Deb., H.C. (5th ser.) (1916), 1037–42.
109 David Hamer, *The New Zealand Liberals: The Years of Power, 1891–1912* (Auckland: Auckland University Press, 1988), 41–43.
110 Anstey, 175 NZ Parl. Deb., H.R. (1916), 571; Dickie, 594; Forbes, 607; Talbot, 622.
111 A. K. Newman, 175 NZ Parl. Deb., H.R. (1916), 498–99; Wilkinson, 507–08; Pearce, 534; Young, 640.
112 175 NZ Parl. Deb., H.R. (1916), 694.
113 Allen, 176 NZ Parl. Deb., H.R. (1916), 519 and 177 NZ Parl. Deb., H.R. (1916), 186.
114 New Zealand Military Service Act, 1916, 7 Geo. 5, no. 8, sec. 31.
115 O'Connor, "Awkward Ones," 118–19.
116 175 NZ Parl. Deb., H.R. (1916), 694.
117 T. A. H. Field, 175 NZ Parl. Deb., H.R. (1916), 563; those members who cited the British precedent were McCombs, 175 NZ Parl. Deb., H.R. (1916), 550; Webb, 566; and Witty, 760.
118 Hudson, 175 NZ Parl. Deb., H.R. (1916), 546; Walker, 553; Wright, 556.
119 177 NZ Parl. Deb., H.R. (1916), 238.
120 Paul, 176 NZ Parl. Deb., L.C. (1916), 353.
121 Barr, 176 NZ Parl. Deb., L.C. (1916), 347–49; Carson, 363.
122 176 NZ Parl. Deb., H.R. (1916), 519 and 177 NZ Parl. Deb., H.R. (1916), 331.
123 Isitt, 177 NZ Parl. Deb., H.R. (1916), 335; Hornsby, 337; Herries, 337–38; Sykes, 340.
124 Craigie, 175 NZ Parl. Deb., H.R. (1916), 533; Wright, 557; Anstey, 571; Dickie, 594.
125 Ell, 175 NZ Parl. Deb., H.R. (1916), 775.
126 Witty, 175 NZ Parl. Deb., H.R. (1916), 492; Wilkinson, 507–08.
127 T. W. Rhodes, 175 NZ Parl. Deb., H.R. (1916), 590; Okey, 601; Newman, 559.
128 Witty, 175 NZ Parl. Deb., H.R. (1916), 492–93.
129 Allen, 175 NZ Parl. Deb., H.R. (1916), 646.
130 175 NZ Parl. Deb., H.R. (1916), 786.
131 "The Military Service (Regulations) Order, 1916," 3 Feb. 1916, MH 47/142, NA.
132 Circular, LGB R. 36, 3 Feb. 1916, MH 47/142, NA.
133 Ibid.
134 Ibid.
135 Circular, LGB R. 40, MH 47/142, NA; N. B. Dearle, *An Economic Chronicle of the Great War for Great Britain & Ireland, 1914–1919* (London: Humphrey Milford, 1929), 60.
136 "The Military Service (Regulations) Order, 1916," 3 Feb. 1916 and Circular, LGB R. 36, 3 Feb. 1916, MH 47/142, NA; Central Tribunal, *Report of the Central Tribunal Appointed Under the Military Service Act, 1916* (London: HMSO, 1919), 10.
137 Circular, LGB R. 36, 3 Feb. 1916, MH 47/142, NA.
138 Hogan to Allen, 25 Aug. 1916, AD 1 769 22/117, ANZ; Allen to Massey, 1 Sep. 1916, AP, ALLEN 1 9, ANZ.
139 Allen to Massey, 1 Sep. 1916, AP, ALLEN 1 9, ANZ.
140 *New Zealand Gazette (NZG)*, 1916, 3208.
141 Salmond to Gray, 1 Dec. 1916, AD 82 7 30/1, ANZ.
142 Ibid.
143 Herdman to Allen, 8 Dec. 1916, AD 1 736 10/477, ANZ.

32   *Setting the boundaries*

144 Salmond to Gray, 1 Dec. 1916, AD 82 7 30/1, ANZ.
145 Allen to Coffey, 21 Mar. 1917, AD 82 4 5/1, ANZ.
146 *NZH*, 24 Nov. 1916, 8.
147 Allen to Reardon, 9 Dec. 1916, AD 82 8 74, ANZ.
148 Allen to Massey, 19 Dec. 1916, AP, ALLEN 1 9, ANZ.
149 Belich, *Paradise Reforged*, 101.
150 *EP*, 14 Feb. 1917, 8; Allen to Niall, 16 Jan. 1918, AD 82 8 74, ANZ; Allen to Webb, 2 Sep. 1916 AD 82 7 28/1, ANZ.
151 *NZG*, 1916, 3207.
152 Report, "Recruiting 1916–1918," 31 Mar. 1919, AD 1 712 9/169/2, ANZ.

2 Judges and juries

One of the most remarkable features of Britain's and New Zealand's conscription enactments was that they did not specify what types of people should be appointed to evaluate appeals. The few stipulations that were made were all highly ambiguous in their wording, and exceedingly narrow in their scope. Yet Britain's tribunal members, military representatives and advisory committee personnel, and New Zealand's board members and military representatives, would be the crucial 'human' elements in the day-to-day operation of their respective exemption systems. Thus, how the various appointments were carried out, and what traits and qualifications the chosen individuals possessed, would inevitably exert a profound influence on what took place once appeal hearings began.

The appointment of Britain's local tribunal members commenced with the formation of the Derby Scheme bodies in November 1915. When making their selections, the local registration authorities in the East Central Division proceeded much as they would have for any other committee. Nominees were moved and seconded, a vote was taken if necessary, and the successful candidates were then asked to confirm their acceptance of the position. The minutes and newspaper reports of some of these processes supply little detail on what took place beyond listing the chosen individuals. Yet such a lack of comment indicates that matters were carried through relatively smoothly in these instances. There are certainly minutes that record the personnel of tribunals being resolved upon unanimously.[1]

Nonetheless, the decision to entrust the appointments to local councils, and to afford them considerable discretion, meant several issues arose. Some were the result of tensions over previous recruiting initiatives. Following the nomination of Frank Wood as a member of the Ardsley Tribunal, it was suggested that, as a large employer, he might frequently find himself in the delicate position of hearing appeals from his own staff. Although Councillor Bury insisted Wood could be relied upon to put the country's interests first, Councillor Naylor remarked that 'there are more young men working on [his] firm to-day than any other firm in Yorkshire', and further charged that 'some of them have been anxious to enlist'.[2] Despite these misgivings, Wood was subsequently voted onto the Ardsley Tribunal. The controversy at Linthwaite proved more intractable. After several meetings had failed to agree on a fifth member for the local tribunal, Councillor Freer was finally chosen. However, his acceptance prompted two

34 *Judges and juries*

of the other nominees, Councillors Cock and Haigh, to withdraw their offers of service.[3] The *Colne Valley Guardian* attributed this impasse to the existence of two factions within the local authority, 'as widely distinct and genuinely hostile to each other as Kilkenny cats'.[4] Freer's appointment would have given the east and south wards, which had allegedly 'not lifted a finger or said one word to encourage recruiting', a total of three members, while the west ward, whose personnel had always fulfilled their patriotic duty, would have been left with only two. Cock and Haigh had therefore 'declined to act as dummies' and resigned.[5] Through an intemperate exchange of letters, and the refusal of additional west ward men to serve, this dispute rumbled on for several more weeks. Matters finally came to a head after the nomination of Councillor Livesey threatened to leave the west ward completely unrepresented. When Cock moved to protest, the council chairman asserted that the situation stemmed from his own 'foolishness' for having resigned in the first place, and Livesey's appointment was duly carried.[6]

Local concerns over the appropriateness of the Derby Scheme also led to conflict. This often revolved around a belief that conscription would be a more equitable recruiting measure. At Birstall, Councillors Holton and Flynn used their nominations to the tribunal as an opportunity to eulogise the scheme's methodology, and to praise the way it would safeguard the British ethos of volunteerism. This oratory was strongly opposed by Councillor Willans, who argued that conscription was the only equitable way to decide who should join the army. Upon his stance being criticised, Willans stated that he wanted nothing more to do with the whole process, and promptly resigned his seat on the council as well.[7] A similar dispute occurred at Ardsley, where Councillor Brook objected to being proposed as a labour representative on the tribunal. He contended that the scheme 'had nothing to do with recruiting' and raised the prospect of men escaping their military obligations through favouritism. With the support of several other councillors, Brook exclaimed that 'I am not going to be party to that kind of conscription. If they want the men I say fetch them in the proper straightforward way and have done with it.'[8] The Derby Scheme also came under fire from the opposite perspective. When Councillor Steele, manager of Barrow Colliery, was nominated for the Worsborough Tribunal, he denied the ability of any outside body to ascertain who could be spared from his workplace. Steele asserted he 'should not want to be on' the tribunal, as he must continue to approach recruitment from his colliery's perspective, rather than from a national perspective.[9]

A more widespread complication was whether the tribunals should include representatives of labour. Although Long's instructions emphasised the need for members who would exercise 'impartial and balanced judgment', they made no specific call for the working classes to be represented.[10] Some councils did not require explicit prompting and selected one, or even two, labour men for their appeal bodies. The Ossett Tribunal featured both the president of the Ossett and Horbury Trades and Labour Council, William France, and trade union official Councillor Ernest Sowden.[11] Yet this accommodating approach was notably lacking elsewhere. After a prolonged meeting of the Huddersfield Council, the district trades and labour council was informed that not only had its original nominee,

Councillor Topping, been rejected, but that a secondary proposal of Alderman Wheatley had been defeated on the casting vote of the mayor. Outraged by this rebuff and scornful of the mayor's claim that his action was 'not a class matter', the trades council promptly moved a resolution of 'emphatic protest'.[12] A similar feeling of injustice prevailed at the Pontefract Trades and Labour Council, which resolved to communicate with the Director of Recruiting over the absence of labour representation on the local borough tribunal. Indignation was expressed here over the fact the corporation was supposed to be a coalition body, with delegates maintaining that the appointments demonstrated a continued existence of 'party feeling'.[13] Acrimony from this issue could even spill into neighbouring districts. When addressing a recruiting meeting, the Mayor of Batley took the opportunity to complain that the Dewsbury Council had failed to appoint any labour representatives onto its tribunal. However, the chairman of the Dewsbury body replied that two working-class men had in fact been nominated, but had both declined to accept the position.[14]

In February 1916, the local authorities were tasked with establishing tribunals that would hear appeals under the Military Service Act, as well as taking over responsibility for cases lodged by attested men. The regulations accompanying the Act merely stipulated that there should be 'adequate representation of labour' on each appeal body.[15] While Long also supplied several recommendations, he kept these deliberately vague so that local conditions would be the primary determinants. The councils were advised to retain those individuals who had gained valuable experience under the Derby Scheme, with the primary criterion for new personnel being an ability to judge cases 'impartially' and with an eye to the 'national interests'. Labour representatives should possess the 'confidence' of the working classes, and the local authorities should 'not hesitate to appoint suitable women on the Tribunals, if they think it desirable to do so'.[16] Even more ambiguous was Long's guidance on what proportion of a tribunal should be made up of local government members. He wrote that it was 'left to the discretion' of the councils whether they went beyond their own ranks, but simultaneously asserted that 'a proportion of every Tribunal should be selected from outside the local authority'.[17]

The division's councils proved overwhelmingly receptive to the idea that current members should form the nucleus of the reconstituted bodies. Indeed, for the fifty-four military service tribunals where the relevant information is obtainable, 260 of their 361 initial members had previously sat on the Derby Scheme bodies. The newcomers were almost entirely additional members. Nonetheless, a handful of individuals used the re-organisation as an opportunity to resign. Some, such as the chairman of the Kirkburton Tribunal, did so because they intended to appeal against their own conscription and did not think it appropriate to judge the claims of others.[18] A more frequent reason was the expanded tribunal workload, which would cause membership to become increasingly onerous and thereby impinge on personal business commitments.[19] There are no recorded instances of members being removed from their position when the tribunals were remodelled.

Beyond this uncontroversial step was a substantial degree of divergence. One issue was how many individuals should be appointed to each tribunal. While

36 *Judges and juries*

anywhere between five and twenty-five members was now permitted, the implicit expectation in Long's guidance was that the number should reflect the size of a district's population, to achieve the fullest representation of its interests without becoming too cumbersome.[20] Yet this was infrequent in practice. The councils for Wakefield Borough (population 51,511 in 1911), Barnsley Borough (50,614) and Batley (36,389), despite being the third, fourth and fifth most populous districts in the division, retained the five existing members without any additions.[21] The most common approach was to expand the tribunal to six or seven members, as occurred in the two most populous districts, Huddersfield (107,821) and Dewsbury (53,351).[22] Nevertheless, certain local authorities went considerably further. At Horbury (7,509), Lepton (3,123) and Dodworth (3,284), ten members were chosen.[23] The two largest bodies outstripped even this figure, with eleven members being assigned to both the Knottingley Tribunal (6,680) and the Mirfield Tribunal (11,712).[24]

Further disparities occurred over what proportion of a tribunal's personnel should be made up of local government members. Most authorities settled on a majority of councillors supplemented by a minority of outsiders. Nonetheless, the chosen ratio differed considerably. At Knottingley nine councillors were accompanied by two outsiders, while at Castleford there were three councillors to two outsiders.[25] A handful of tribunals even contained a preponderance of individuals from beyond local government, by five to four at Darfield and six to one at Golcar.[26] In contrast, many other councils appointed only members of their own authority. At Methley, Councillor Bullimore suggested that the personnel of the existing tribunal should be increased to seven and that the public 'would have more confidence' in the appeal body if it contained someone not connected to the council. However, this motion came to nothing after Councillor Websdale argued that the public ought to have faith in their elected representatives.[27]

There was also a lack of uniformity over the entreaties of other local bodies for representation. Many groups had already been successful in this regard when the Derby Scheme tribunals were formed, but additional requests came from those who felt their claims had been unjustly ignored. In the division, the most common source was the local butchers' associations, which argued that the maintenance of efficient food distribution depended on having an expert on each tribunal who could stem the loss of men from their industry.[28] Yet the associations' large volume of petitions did not equate to successful results. The Ossett Council pointed out there were only fourteen butchers in the town, meaning their claims to representation were weaker than those of other groups, such as the thirty-seven licensed victuallers.[29] Similar reasoning was advanced at Holmfirth, where it was maintained that the butchering trade was far from the only one experiencing shortages.[30] Applications from other groups were also rejected. The Pontefract Borough Council split between those who supported the request of the local war agricultural committee for a farmer and market gardener to be added to the tribunal, and those who felt the existing membership was sufficiently representative. After discussion had failed to resolve the issue, a vote decided in favour of the status quo.[31] A similar move might have succeeded at Featherstone but for extenuating circumstances. Here Councillor Poppleton objected to a recommendation by the general purposes committee that only a farmer need be added to the tribunal. Arguing that Councillor Maxwell did not stand for the whole of the shopkeepers, Poppleton asserted that they required additional representation. When the force of this argument was recognised, Poppleton himself was nominated. However, he refused to serve, as it would mean adjudicating on the case of his own son.[32]

The question of whether to appoint women proved less controversial, but still did not produce a unanimous response. Very few women sat on Britain's tribunals, with minutes and newspaper reports indicating that the idea was not even discussed in most cases. Nonetheless, there were a handful of exceptions. There are no recorded instances in the division, although one did occur at Leeds and St Albans, of a proposal for female membership being moved and rejected.[33] All three councils where the matter was broached subsequently appointed a woman. This decision was reached amicably enough at New Mill and Ardsley East and West, where the reading of Long's guidance swiftly led to its acceptance, but was more contentious at Holmfirth.[34] In that district, the decision to increase the existing tribunal from five to seven members was followed by an animated discussion over whether the additions should be two labour representatives, or one labour representative and one woman. The matter was eventually put to the vote, with the five supporters of two labour men being defeated by the nine who favoured the counter-proposal.[35]

There was more debate over the stipulation that each tribunal must include 'adequate representation' of labour. Most of the division's councils attempted to fulfil this requirement by including a bare minimum of working class representatives. A common approach was that adopted at Huddersfield, where the tribunal was chosen in proportion to the composition of the council itself, with two Liberals, two Conservatives and one trade unionist member.[36] However, this sort of concession proved unpalatable for the majority at the Dodworth Council, where Councillor Levitt described a proposed membership that would not reflect labour's position on the authority as a 'Tory move for political purposes'. He and his labour colleagues then endeavoured to have the whole council appointed as the tribunal, but were defeated on a vote and had to settle for two labour members out of ten.[37] A more accommodating attitude was adopted elsewhere, although none of the division's councils matched those at Leeds, which allowed the three major political parties equal representation; or York, which had three trade unionists and two Liberal pacifists among its ten tribunal members.[38] Nonetheless, two labour representatives were appointed among the five members at Batley and among the seven at Ossett.[39] On the other hand, several councils contravened the regulation by refusing to select any working-class men. This was carried out in a particularly blithe manner at Cudworth, where an inquiry as to whether re-appointing the existing members would provide labour representation met with the rejoinder that 'they are all workers, sir, although none of them can do a day's work'.[40]

Even when the councils did manage to agree on the proportion of labour representatives, there were differences in how they went about selecting them. The New Mill body asked the local branch of the Independent Labour Party (ILP) to

38 Judges and juries

choose its own delegate and even afforded an extension of several weeks when it initially proved unable to do so.[41] In contrast, there was a sharp exchange at Huddersfield when the council's choice, Alderman Wheatley, refused to take a position on the tribunal in light of the trades and labour council's decision to nominate Joseph Pickles.[42] To avoid acrimony, the mayor and others argued that Pickles should be accepted, but other councillors who objected to being 'dictated to' opposed them. Only after a heated discussion was Pickles's appointment finally carried.[43]

The selection of New Zealand's board members shared some initial similarities with this British process. From the first reading of the Military Service Bill to the point where the boards were finally established, MPs and cabinet ministers were deluged with over one hundred and fifty nominations.[44] The sources of these proposals were extremely diverse. Most were put forward by organisations such as councils, trades and labour councils, branches of the Farmers' Union, or local recruiting committees, but there were also personal applications from barristers, mayors, retired gentlemen, and the editor of the *New Zealand Herald*.[45] When advancing a nominee's credentials, the emphasis was usually placed on his prominent standing in community affairs. The Waitomo County Council's proposal of Thomas Pine was based on his 'splendid' efforts to advance voluntary recruiting, while the Mayor of Onehunga asserted that his popularity within the district would guarantee widespread approval of his selection.[46]

However, a highly centralised process quickly overtook these devolved beginnings. On 10 September 1916, the Recruiting Board convened to discuss the formation of the four initial appeal bodies. Given that he was the senior figure in the absence overseas of Massey and Ward, and that the temporary replacements had no direct connection with recruiting, it is safe to assume Allen took the lead.[47] Two crucial decisions were made at this meeting, the first being that a selection criterion would be used to screen the nominees. Of course, the regulations and Long's guidance acted as a form of criteria in Britain, but the difference was that the local councils could pick and choose which directions to follow, whereas the Recruiting Board naturally applied all its own policies. Elements of the Recruiting Board's schema were similar to that urged by Long, namely that members should be outside the eligible military age, and should not have any sons who had failed to enlist when they might reasonably have been expected to do so.[48] On the other hand, Allen believed that placing men hostile to conscription on the appeal bodies would 'wreck the whole system'.[49] The most significant disparity was the Recruiting Board's decision to avoid the appointment of elected members, as their impartiality might be undermined by a desire to secure local favour and political support.[50]

The Recruiting Board's second decision was even further removed from the British approach: that each board should have a uniform structure. Their three members would consist of a stipendiary magistrate as chairman, accompanied by one member who lived in a rural area and one member who was from a city or was connected with city life. Allen claimed that 'no man has been selected because he represents any particular section of the community'. Yet the adoption of a balanced membership formula, and his subsequent statement that it was designed 'to represent as far as possible the feeling of the people in the district', strongly contradicts this assertion.[51] What the Recruiting Board appeared to do was to utilise the constitution of the arbitration court, established by the Industrial Conciliation and Arbitration Act, 1894, as a template. That body was designed to equitably represent the parties in an industrial dispute: one member was chosen by workers and one by employers, with a judge as an impartial president. Before the introduction of conscription, there had been fierce argument in New Zealand between the rural and urban communities over their respective contributions to the war effort.[52] The Recruiting Board seems to have recognised that the awarding of exemptions could exacerbate this conflict and configured the boards to try and ensure they could not be seen as biased. However, while a principle of representative members was adopted, it was representation on a much higher level than in Britain. New Zealand's military districts were far from the same, just as Britain's local registration districts were far from the same. Yet the method of appointing the tribunals allowed these differences to have an impact, whereas the criteria for the boards' membership took no account of local circumstances.

The appointment of personnel to the boards was also carried out in a centralised manner. Selection of the stipendiary magistrate chairmen was entrusted to the Minister of Justice. For the lay members, a significant development came when a deputation of trade union leaders and Labour parliamentarians met Allen to press for the inclusion of a working-class representative on each board. Allen's reply was somewhat accommodating in that he asked the main trades and labour council for each military district to nominate suitable candidates. However, he demonstrated an unwillingness to surrender control of the appointments by stressing that the trades councils would only be making suggestions and that anti-conscriptionists would be vetoed automatically.[53] This ambiguous position proved intolerable for a majority on the Auckland and Canterbury labour representation committees, both of which asserted that conditional representation was scarcely worth having, and resolved not to submit any nominations.[54] In response, Allen decided that rather than try to find working-class men for the Auckland and Canterbury boards by another means, the matter would simply be dropped and businessmen appointed instead. Even when prospective labour representatives were put forward in Wellington and Otago, the selected individuals were those who had been recommended by the Minister of Labour, rather than those suggested by the trades councils.[55] The appointment of the other members was relatively unproblematic. A provisional list was drawn up by the Recruiting Board, which was then sent to the Government Statistician and military group commanders for reports on whether each candidate satisfied the age and no-eligible-sons criteria.[56] This task being completed, the Recruiting Board made its final selections and then secured the formal approval of the cabinet.

It is possible to identify four characteristics of the typical British tribunal member. First, he was a male, given that women made up only a very small proportion of the total appointees. Second, contradicting an older portrayal of the individuals who sat on the appeal bodies, he was a civilian, with just one member across the

40 *Judges and juries*

whole division being recorded as holding a military commission.[57] Third, he took an active role in community affairs. This trait is particularly apparent in the prominence of local government personnel. Of 353 tribunal members in the division, 252 were either local aldermen or councillors, or represented their district on the West Riding County Council. The chairmen of the tribunals were nearly always aldermen or councillors, and in many cases the mayor occupied that crucial position. Furthermore, it was rare for a tribunal not to include at least one justice of the peace, with 58 of the 353 division members being so designated. Members also tended to hold prominent positions in local organisations and political clubs. A particularly strong credential was involvement in the war effort through patriotic and charitable bodies, or through membership of the local recruiting committee. Emblematic of such public servants were Cooper Firth, who was at the forefront of every Marsden initiative for 'the welfare of the men in the forces, their relatives and dependents at home, and the success of the allied cause'; and Alfred Flynn, who sat on the Birstall Council's Sanitary Sub-Committee, Old Age Pensions Committee and Distress Committee, and on the Oakwell Joint Hospital Board.[58]

The prominence of local government representatives is also reflected in the final typical trait of being middle class. Tradesmen and manufacturers were in the ascendancy on most appeal bodies and many were influential figures in one of their district's largest or most reputable businesses. Arthur Lockwood of the Linthwaite Tribunal had joined his father's company, Charles Lockwood and Sons, textile mill owners, at the age of sixteen, and had then become a partner at twenty-one and a director at thirty-five.[59] Similarly, John Furniss was the long-serving manager of the Slaithwaite Gas Works; and William Kingswell was a partner in W. H. Kingswell & Sons, furriers, silk mercers and carpet warehousemen of Wakefield.[60] Although professional men featured rather less often, there was usually one solicitor, registrar or accountant on each appeal body. Indeed, the Barnsley Borough Tribunal contained William Raley, solicitor and partner at Raley & Sons; and Edmund Rideal, solicitor and partner at E. J. F. Rideal and Son.[61]

However, there were numerous appointees who did not possess these typical attributes. The division's members included three women: Miss Hannah Baines at Ardsley East and West; Mrs E. Walker, a Quaker and president of the local Nursing Association, at Holmfirth; and Mrs C. Tinker at New Mill.[62] Although many personnel were aldermen or councillors, nearly a third of them were outside of local government, while justices of the peace were a decided minority. Taking an active role in local affairs was also not strictly necessary, given that John Crowther was appointed to the Marsden Tribunal despite being notorious for his previous insistence on anonymity.[63] Moreover, the dominance of middle-class individuals was far from absolute, given that there were the stipulated working-class representatives on most appeal bodies. It is also apparent that some members had joined the middle class from more humble beginnings. Now Mayor of Barnsley and the owner of a printing business, Alderman Henry Holden had started his working life as a pit boy.[64] Likewise, Owen Balmforth was the son of a Chartist and had risen from being an office and errand boy to his position as paid secretary of the Huddersfield Education Committee.[65] Finally, while such categories do not necessarily equate to class and might have altered in the intervening years, there were a sizeable number of members who described themselves in the *1911 Census* as being a 'worker', rather than an 'employer'.

The products that the tribunal members were making, or the tasks they were engaged in, varied considerably. This resulted from the fact that the composition of local councils tended to reflect a district's major industries. In 1916, the West Riding of Yorkshire was one of the world's leading centres of woollen textile production, making it inevitable that textiles would provide the primary source of members. Indeed, textiles accounted for the division's closest thing to a 'single industry' tribunal, with the personnel of the Marsden body comprising four woollen mill proprietors; the owner of a firm of flock, worsted and woollen warehousemen; a textile workers' trade union secretary; and an engineer's pattern maker.[66] In areas where textiles were not the primary industry, other sectors predominated. Coal mining had a particularly strong presence in the districts surrounding Wakefield and Barnsley. At Castleford, the membership reflected the importance of glass bottle manufacturing to the local economy, while Goole's status as a port accounts for the appointment of a stevedore, a ship repairer and a timber merchant among its urban tribunal personnel.[67] In the small number of rural districts, most of the members were involved with working the land and selling its produce. Beyond this overall prevalence of major industries were members drawn from a plethora of other walks of life. These individuals were chosen because they represented an influential sector in the local economy, because they were respected in local affairs, or simply because there was no one else who would take on the role. Whatever the reasoning, the division's tribunal personnel included: veterinary surgeons, doctors, rent collectors, council employees, innkeepers, bankers, architects, upholsters, merchants, insurance agents, blacksmiths, salesmen and many others. Eight councils even appointed a local clergyman to their appeal body, one of whom, the Congregationalist Reverend William Barker, was elected chairman of the Dodworth Tribunal.[68]

Substantial disparities also existed between the tribunals' labour representatives. While most other members were councillors or aldermen, the split among these individuals between those inside and outside local authorities was far more even. Most were trade union officials and usually represented men employed in the largest sector of the local economy. John Gartside, secretary of the Weavers' Association, was a member of the Saddleworth Tribunal; Harris Hoyle, secretary of the Colne Valley District of the General Union of Textile Workers, was appointed at Marsden; and William Proctor of the local miners' union took a position on the Royston appeal body.[69] Many also sat on their district's trades and labour council, and Andrew Stott at Heckmondwike, secretary of the Boot and Shoe Operatives Union, was far from the only council president to be appointed.[70]

In terms of their attitudes, the labour representatives usually sat on the local recruiting committee, or at least were not pronounced anti-conscriptionists. One of the few division tribunals to start out with two trade unionist members was that for Ossett, but William France supported the 'general desire to beat the Germans'

42 *Judges and juries*

and Ernest Sowden insisted that Britain's central war aim should be to 'break and put an end to German culture for all time'.[71] However, there were some notable exceptions. The most prominent was Ben Turner, chairman of the Batley Tribunal, Mayor of Batley, secretary of the Heavy Woollen District Branch of the General Union of Textile Workers and a member of the Labour Party National Executive. Despite arguing that recruits must be obtained in order to win the war, Turner was a committed pacifist and stated in January 1916 that 'I am as strongly opposed to conscription as I ever was'.[72] Similarly, Joseph Pickles had been a pre-war member of the Huddersfield Committee Against Compulsory Military Service and, when nominated for the tribunal by the local trades and labour council, was instructed that he would be failing in his duty if he did not press for the exemption of any man who was reluctant to serve.[73]

The membership of the East Central Division Appeal Tribunal (ECAT) also demonstrated both typical and atypical features. While responsibility for establishing these higher bodies had been formally awarded to the government, Long decided that the task would best be carried out by the various county council chairmen, acting in conjunction with other 'representative persons'. These committees were asked to follow much the same guidance as for the local tribunals, although Long described it as 'expedient' for at least one appointee to have legal training, and specifically recommended chamber of commerce members for consideration. Otherwise the county authorities were free to select whomsoever they pleased.[74] The ECAT's compliment of eight members was intended to represent the division's main centres and to cover most of its geographical extent. Long's advice was followed with the selection of two chamber of commerce members, and emphatically endorsed in that all eight appointees were justices of the peace. Two labour men were also included, the first of whom was Ben Turner, who had to resign his chairmanship of the Batley Tribunal to take up this higher position. He was joined by one of the nominees put forward by the Huddersfield and District Trades and Labour Council, Ben Littlewood, secretary of the Huddersfield Branch of the General Union of Textile Workers, a member of the ILP, and, like Turner, an outspoken opponent of conscription.[75]

The ECAT's occupational profile only partly mirrored that of the local tribunals. There was one professional man in the form of Edward Lancaster, a Barnsley auctioneer and land agent.[76] The typical dominance of the textile industry also held sway, with five current or retired manufacturers constituting the remaining members. They comprised: the chairman, Thomas Norton, a former partner in Norton Brothers fancy cloth milling firm, who was now chairman of the Barnsley (Staincross) Petty Sessions and a deputy lieutenant of the county; Edward Bruce, president of the Huddersfield Chamber of Commerce and a director of Crowther, Bruce and Co. Ltd., woollen manufacturers; Joe Haley of Dewsbury, a partner in Messrs. Hepworth and Haley, blanket and rug manufacturers; Frederick Mallalieu, cloth mill owner of Delph; and Edmund Stonehouse, Mayor of Wakefield and the owner of M. P. Stonehouse Ltd., woollen cloth spinners.[77] Where the ECAT differed from many of the local tribunals was in the lack of any tradesmen, farmers or representatives of the division's other major industries.

Judges and juries 43

In contrast to these myriad instances of diversity, there was only one major difference between the memberships of the New Zealand boards. These bodies all followed the occupational formula laid down by the Recruiting Board, beginning with the appointment of a stipendiary magistrate as chairman. The choice for the Auckland Board fell on Frederick Burgess, who was magistrate for the Thames district in 1916.[78] His counterpart on the Wellington body was Daniel Cooper, a former deputy registrar of the Supreme Court.[79] James Evans, a magistrate at Nelson, was appointed to preside in Canterbury, while Howell Widdowson, the principal magistrate at Dunedin, chaired the Otago Board.[80] The Recruiting Board's formula was also met by the appointment of a city man to each board, but the difficulties over obtaining nominees for labour representatives made this the single point of disparity. The urban personnel on the Auckland and Canterbury boards were both businessmen, George Elliott, a company director of Auckland, and James Milton, a retired run-holder of Christchurch.[81] These were very different backgrounds to those of the Wellington and Otago boards' urban members. As secretary to a number of trade unions, including the Wellington Waterside Workers' Federation, David McLaren had previously represented Labour as Mayor of Wellington and as MP for Wellington East, while Edward Kellett was president of the Otago Carpenters' Union.[82]

There was no such divergence when it came to the final appointment to each body, that of a country resident. Filling this role on the Auckland Board was John McCaw, a government valuer who had recently begun farming on his own account at Matamata.[83] William Perry, a leading figure in the Farmers' Union and a sheep farmer at Masterton, represented the Wellington Military District's rural areas.[84] The Canterbury Board included Edgar Studholme of Waimate, a son of one of the earliest sheep farming families in New Zealand.[85] Lastly, Otago's country member was Alfred Dillon Bell, one of his district's largest sheep farmers, a member of the Farmers' Union and the brother of Francis Henry Dillon Bell, the leader of New Zealand's Legislative Council.[86]

The board members were similar in several other ways. Due to the Recruiting Boards' careful vetting process, they were all above the military age, and none had sons who had failed to join the colours. Furthermore, the desire to avoid elected personnel was very nearly achieved, with only McCaw breaching this stipulation by being a member of the Matamata County Council.[87] The final common attribute was a strong belief in the war effort. Some of the members' 'official rhetoric' emphasised the defence of Britain and the empire, supporting Keith Sinclair's contention that such prominent persons adhered to the concept of 'imperial federation, to imperialism'.[88] However, they just as frequently espoused the need to preserve the liberty and prosperity of New Zealand from a brutal and authoritarian enemy.[89] The majority had sent at least one son to the front and several had lost family members killed in action.[90] Moreover, Milton was the officer in charge of the Christchurch Citizens' Defence Corps, while the government had personally supplied McCaw with a car and a sergeant major in 1914 and 1916 so that he could 'go round the District and try to recruit as many [men] as possible'.[91] Even the two labour representatives were far from the anti-conscriptionists that

44   *Judges and juries*

Allen so feared. Although McLaren had started out as a militant trade unionist who opposed the introduction of compulsory military training in 1909, he had since broken away from radicalism and spent the early years of the war touring the country urging workers to enlist.[92] Kellett was also an active recruiter, had sent two volunteer sons to the front, and, upon his election as vice-president of the Dunedin Labour Representation Committee in November 1916, promptly resigned the next day, stating that such a position was incompatible with his pro-conscription sentiments.[93]

The initial appointments to the division's tribunals provoked a considerable amount of local criticism, some of which was brushed aside. These unsuccessful protestations concerned a perceived lack of 'adequate' labour representation. Councillor Jackson raised this complaint at Mirfield, arguing that a current tribunal member, Councillor Platt, could not be regarded as speaking for the working class. Yet this claim was swiftly undermined by reference to Platt's forty-eight years of trade union service, and it was further pointed out that Mr. Jenkins also represented labour on the appeal body.[94] A similar rebuff occurred at Huddersfield, when the district trades and labour council, angered by the course the tribunal's early operations were taking, sent a deputation to the local authority to press for the appointment of two additional labour men. On receiving this petition, the Huddersfield Council resolved that it had great confidence in the tribunal and saw 'no necessity for adding to its number'.[95] The issue of working-class representation proved even more contentious at Saddleworth. Here the resignation of one member prompted the trades and labour council to argue that they no longer had a representative, and to nominate Albert Hewkin as a replacement. When this proposal was seconded at the local authority, several other councillors objected on the basis that John Gartside, secretary of the Weavers' Association, was already acting as a voice for labour. Hewkin's supporters countered that Gartside's union was not a member of the trades council, that the engineering unions should be represented, and that two labour men on a tribunal of five was not unreasonable, given that most appeals derived from the working classes. Unconvinced by these arguments, Hewkin's opponents attempted to block his appointment by moving John Edwards instead. On the matter being put to the vote, Edwards was added to the tribunal ahead of Hewkin by seven votes to three.[96]

Other remonstrations managed to bring about significant changes. The Spen Valley Trades and Labour Council, displeased that only one labour man had been appointed to both the Spenborough and the Heckmondwike tribunals, wrote to the respective authorities asking for those numbers to be doubled. Although this request was declined at Heckmondwike, a majority on the Spenborough Council voted to appoint Councillor Firth as an additional labour representative.[97] Similar success was achieved at Dewsbury, where the Heavy Woollen District Trades and Labour Council petitioned the local authority over the fact its tribunal contained no spokesmen of the working classes. In response, the Dewsbury Council obligingly appointed two of the trades council's nominees, Councillor Halstead and Benjamin Turner.[98] A considerably more protracted affair was that concerning the Goole Urban Tribunal. This began when the sole labour representative was forced to resign from the Derby Scheme appeal body and no replacement was appointed on the tribunal's subsequent reconstitution. The resulting protest from the trades and labour council initially proved fruitless, as the local authority narrowly rejected a motion to appoint two working-class men.[99] Yet the matter did not close there. A complaint over the lack of labour representation was raised in Parliament, to which Long replied that he would personally investigate the matter.[100] A month later, the Goole Council asked its finance committee to reconsider the appointment of working-class representatives. When that body recommended the preservation of the status quo, it provoked a stormy session of the full council, which decided to refer the question back to the finance committee. Eventually, over two months after the issue was first broached, John Cone of the Sailors' and Firemen's Union and Percy Colbridge of the Engineers' Society were both added to the Goole Urban Tribunal.[101]

Such personnel changes did not occur in New Zealand, where Allen proved unresponsive to local disquiet. The most serious challenge to the initial appointments came from the Auckland City Recruiting Committee. In late August 1916, the Commandant to the Military Forces within New Zealand, Major General Alfred Robin, met with that body on his own initiative and asked them to submit nominations for the Auckland Board. Keen to oblige, the committee suggested three prominent candidates, including the Mayor of Auckland. Having been approached by such a high-ranking military figure, the committee clearly believed these recommendations would carry considerable weight. Unsurprisingly, therefore, its members were outraged when all their nominees were subsequently overlooked, with Allen being informed that such a snub could 'only be taken as a practical indication that [the committee's] services [were] no longer required'.[102] A discomforted Minister of Defence quickly travelled to Auckland for a consultation. After a rather heated discussion, the committee, although privately re-affirming its dissatisfaction, was persuaded to maintain public silence and to recommence its recruiting activities.[103] Other local organisations lodged their own protests. The Southland War Funds Committee complained that no representative from their region had been placed on the Otago Board and expressed its 'fears that agricultural and pastoral interests will therefore suffer, the conditions in this province requiring special local knowledge'.[104] Bodies representing the West Coast of the South Island and the Nelson region advanced much the same argument, but none of these remonstrations could persuade Allen to make any changes.[105]

Beyond this locally based criticism, opposition to the initial appointments came from organised labour. There were objections from various quarters about the lack of a working-class representative on the Auckland and Canterbury boards, with resentment being expressed over the relative prominence of farmers. Where a labour man had been selected in Wellington and Otago, the trades and labour councils complained that the chosen individuals did not represent as many workers as the nominees they had submitted.[106] These protests had no direct impact for two reasons. First, a great deal of opinion, including within 'moderate' labour circles, blamed the lack of an Auckland and Canterbury representative on the failure of the labour representation committees to provide nominations, rather than

46 *Judges and juries*

on Allen's imposition of a selection criterion.[107] Second, the outspoken groups in these districts were far more concerned with contesting the overall legitimacy of conscription than with debating specifics like the boards' memberships.[108] As for Wellington and Otago, Allen argued he had only ever promised to consider the names put forward and had explicitly stated that individuals would not be appointed to represent particular interests.[109] This stance certainly did not appease everyone. However, whereas an opposition group in Britain only needed to influence a majority on the local council, it would have taken something far more widespread to cause the Minister of Defence to make changes that would have been reported nationally in New Zealand. Ultimately this eventuality never came close to occurring. Allen felt able to inform Massey that 'very little criticism' had been received, and there was no hint that any alterations to the boards' original constitutions were contemplated.[110]

Yet these events do appear to have influenced Allen's thinking when it became necessary to establish six additional boards in January 1917. Nominations were again received from a wide range of sources, but Allen continued to place more reliance on the recommendations of government ministers, and he further solicited the views of MPs and the current board members.[111] The previously agreed screening criteria remained in force, with there being only one elected figure among the new appointments, and it was also decided to retain the standard selection formula. This meant that each of the additional boards contained one member from the country, who was always a prominent or retired farmer. Although the inability of the Ministry of Justice to release more than three magistrates did necessitate the appointment of a king's counsel and two barristers, the policy of having legal professionals as chairmen was maintained.[112]

The most significant development concerned the urban members. The regret expressed over the lack of labour representatives on the First Auckland and Canterbury boards seems to have motivated Allen to place a working-class man on all the new appeal bodies. However, there was no change in the type of individual selected, as 'moderate' views and a support for the war effort were still essential prerequisites. Labour's representative on the Second Auckland Board was Arthur Rosser, the secretary of at least nine trade unions. His role as an active recruiter, member of the National Reserve, and supporter of conscription had made Rosser very unpopular in radical circles, but he chose to regard this criticism 'as a compliment to me as a Britisher'.[113] The labour members of the Second and Third Wellington boards had also distanced themselves from militancy. Frederick Curtice briefly resigned his presidency of the Wellington Waterside Workers Union in protest at its affiliation to the radical New Zealand Federation of Labour, while Matthew Mack had refused to associate the Amalgamated Society of Railway Servants with the 1913 Great Strike.[114] Rather less can be discerned about the two Canterbury labour members, Frederick Eldridge, foreman carpenter for the Christchurch City Council, and Henry Robbins, an agricultural implement worker, as even contemporary labour men were said to be not conversant with their views.[115] Nevertheless, it is certain that they were amenable to the provisions of the Act. So too was Robert Breen of the Second Otago Board, the secretary of the Otago Trades and Labour Council, who had rebuked members of the New Zealand Labour Party over their encouraging Australian workers to vote against the introduction of conscription.[116]

Criticism of these new appointments was virtually non-existent. By placing a working-class representative on each of the boards, Allen had effectively nullified the claim there were not enough labour members. The Auckland Labour Representation Committee repudiated the idea that Rosser stood for labour's interests, while the *NZ Truth* maintained that attempts to divide the working class by giving it a semblance of representation would not succeed, as the new appointees were regarded as having turned their backs on the labour movement.[117] Yet these appear to be the only instances of dissent. J. T. Paul, a Labour member of the Legislative Council, endorsed all the new appointments, and there is no evidence of dissatisfaction at the Wellington, Canterbury or Otago trades and labour councils.[118]

Like the tribunal members, the men appointed as military representatives in the division were a diverse and locally prominent group. Under authority delegated to him by the War Office, the choices were made by the General Officer Commanding-in-Chief Northern Command, and included a number of retired officers.[119] One of these was Lieutenant Colonel James Hewitt, attached to the Barnsley Borough and Barnsley Rural tribunals, who had raised and then commanded the 13th (Service) Battalion York and Lancaster Regiment, until he was forced to resign due to ill health.[120] Other military representatives were serving Territorial officers, such as Captain George Greenwood of the Whitwood and Castleford tribunals, who had been a member of 1/4th Battalion King's Own (Yorkshire Light Infantry) until July 1915, when he was transferred to the depot of the York and Lancaster Regiment at Pontefract.[121] Yet there were also many appointees who did not hold army commissions, and who were simply prominent citizens whose standing in the community would, it was believed, entitle them to respect. The chosen individuals not only differed by their level of involvement with the military, but also by their occupation. Hewitt was president of the Barnsley and District Colliery Owners' Association; H. D. Leather, responsible for the Spen Valley tribunals, was a chartered accountant; and Arthur Crosland at Huddersfield combined the callings of solicitor, wine merchant and manufacturer.[122]

The members of the division's advisory committees also possessed differing backgrounds, but considerable local stature. Like the military representatives, these bodies often served more than one tribunal. However, the nature of their brief, that of determining which men were entitled to exemption based on the local economic conditions, led to the appointment of personnel who reflected the major commercial and industrial concerns in a district. This produced substantial variations between them. A further point of difference was the position of organised labour, with the committees not being subject to the same regulation requiring working-class representation that was supposed to govern the constitution of the tribunals. Although trade union members were selected for a few of the division's advisory bodies, there were protests from several trades councils over a lack of labour men in their district.[123]

48 *Judges and juries*

New Zealand's military representatives were chosen primarily for their shared traits. The Defence Department decided to forgo current or retired regular army officers in favour of legal professionals who were also serving Territorial officers. However, the department did adhere to the concept of posting its representatives away from their district of residence. A typical appointee was Cuthbert Free, practising in Christchurch, who had suffered an accident that prevented him from going to the front. He was raised to the temporary rank of captain in the Canterbury Yeomanry Cavalry upon taking up his position as military representative to the First Otago Board.[124] Similarly, Captain John Conlan of the 13th Territorial Regiment was promoted major on leaving his Kaiapoi practice to become military representative to the First Auckland Board.[125]

This rigid and centralised New Zealand appointments process stands in sharp contrast to the locally driven methodology practiced in Britain. A crucial variable was that Britain's local authorities had almost total discretion to select whomsoever they wished to sit on their tribunals. With there being more than two thousand councils across the country, each with its own internal dynamics, and each presiding over a different set of local circumstances, it was inevitable that there would be disparities in the way these bodies carried out the task. There were commonalities in the resulting memberships, but not all the division's tribunal personnel were middle-class local government members, and there were additional variations in occupations and in attitudes towards conscription. When local labour organisations moved to protest the initial selections, some were rebuffed, whereas others managed to secure the appointment of additional working-class men. As for the military representatives and advisory committee members, these individuals too were chosen primarily for their knowledge of, and standing within, the local community. In contrast, New Zealand's appointments process hinged on centralised decision-making. Allen imposed detailed selection criteria for prospective members and determined that the boards' constitution should follow a uniform pattern. This led to appeal bodies that were nearly identical in terms of the occupations and attitudes of their members. The initial appointments did attract some criticism, but such dissent never came close to forcing any deviation from the desired formula. Likewise, the Defence Department first established the exact type of individuals it wanted as its military representatives, and then went about securing men who satisfied this prescription.

Despite these very different approaches, the personnel appointed to Britain's and New Zealand's exemption systems carried the same immense burden. For the next two or three years, they would be responsible for determining how their fellow citizens could best serve the nation in a time of profound uncertainty and crisis. Yet if the individuals sitting on the bench were faced with many difficult decisions, the same can be said for those who had the option of appearing before them.

Notes

1 Minutes, Golcar Urban District Council, 15 Nov. 1915, KMT 12/2/1/11, West Yorkshire Archive Service, Kirklees, Huddersfield (KA); Minutes, South Crosland Urban District Council, 16 Nov. 1915, KMT 38, KA.

Judges and juries   49

2 *Barnsley Chronicle (BC)*, 6 Nov. 1915, 7.
3 Minutes, Linthwaite Urban District Council, 1 Nov. 1915, 22 Nov. 1915 and 13 Dec. 1915, KMT 23/2/1/8, KA; *Colne Valley Guardian (CVG)*, 7 Jan. 1916, 2.
4 *CVG*, 14 Jan. 1916, 2.
5 Ibid.
6 *Worker (W)*, 29 Jan. 1916, 6.
7 Minutes, Birstall Urban District Council, 1 Nov. 1915, KMT 3/2/1/5, KA; *Dewsbury Reporter (DR)*, 6 Nov. 1915, 1.
8 *BC*, 6 Nov. 1915, 7.
9 Ibid., 13 Nov. 1915, 2.
10 Circular, LGB R. 1, 26 Oct. 1915, MH 47/142, NA.
11 *Ossett Observer (OO)*, 6 Nov. 1915, 8.
12 *W*, 27 Nov. 1915, 5; Minutes, Huddersfield and District Trades and Labour Council, 24 Nov. 1915, S/HTC/1/4, KA.
13 *Pontefract & Castleford Express (PCE)*, 19 Nov. 1915, 5.
14 *DR*, 20 Nov. 1915, 6 and 27 Nov. 1915, 7.
15 "The Military Service (Regulations) Order, 1916," 3 Feb. 1916, MH 47/142, NA.
16 Circular, LGB R. 36, 3 Feb. 1916, MH 47/142, NA.
17 Ibid.
18 *W*, 8 Jan. 1916, 7.
19 Minutes, Batley Borough Council, 22 Mar. 1916, KMT 1/2/2/15/4, KA.
20 Circular, LGB R. 36, 3 Feb. 1916, MH 47/142, NA.
21 *Wakefield Express (WE)*, 26 Feb. 1916, 5; *Barnsley Independent (BI)*, 12 Feb. 1916, 5; Minutes, Batley Borough Council, 9 Feb. 1916, KMT 1/2/2/15/4, KA; *1911 Census of Great Britain*.
22 Minutes, Huddersfield County Borough Council, 16 Feb. 1916, KMT 18/12/1/35, KA; Minutes, Dewsbury County Borough Council, 10 Feb. 1916, KMT 8/3/2/1/3-4, KA; *1911 Census of Great Britain*.
23 *WE*, 12 Feb. 1916, 6; Minutes, Lepton Urban District Council, 10 Feb. 1916, KMT 22/2/1/4, KA; *BC*, 12 Feb. 1916, 2; *1911 Census of Great Britain*.
24 *PCE*, 11 Feb. 1916, 6; *Huddersfield Chronicle*, 19 Feb. 1916, 7; *1911 Census of Great Britain*.
25 *PCE*, 11 Feb. 1916, 6.
26 *BC*, 11 Mar. 1916, 2; Minutes, Golcar Urban District Council, 10 Feb. 1916, KMT 12/2/1/11, KA.
27 *PCE*, 25 Feb. 1916, 1.
28 Minutes, Holmfirth Urban District Council, 7 Feb. 1916, KMT 16/6/1/20, KA; Minutes, Dewsbury County Borough Council, 17 Feb. 1916, KMT 8/3/2/1/3-4, KA.
29 *OO*, 19 Feb. 1916, 3.
30 *Holmfirth Express (HE)*, 12 Feb. 1916, 2.
31 *PCE*, 11 Feb. 1916, 6.
32 Ibid., 3.
33 Minutes, Leeds City Council, 17 Feb. 1916, LL 2/1/33, West Yorkshire Archive Service, Leeds; Mein, Wares and Mann, *St Albans*, 45.
34 Minutes, New Mill Urban District Council, 11 Feb. 1916, KMT 29/4/1/8, KA.
35 *HE*, 12 Feb. 1916, 2.
36 Pearce, *Comrades in Conscience*, 162.
37 *BC*, 12 Feb. 1916, 3.
38 Rae, *Conscience and Politics*, 56; Peacock, *York in the Great War*, 382.
39 Minutes, Batley Borough Council, 9 Feb. 1916, KMT 1/2/2/15/4, KA; Minutes, Ossett Borough Council, 14 Feb. 1916, WMT/5/2/1/1/3, West Yorkshire Archive Service, Wakefield.
40 *BC*, 19 Feb. 1916, 3.
41 *HE*, 19 Feb. 1916, 6 and 4 Mar. 1916, 6.

50   *Judges and juries*

42 Minutes, Huddersfield and District Trades and Labour Council, 9 Feb. 1916, S/HTC/ 1/4, KA.
43 *HEx*, 19 Feb. 1916, 7.
44 *Press (P)*, 16 Sep. 1916, 7.
45 See correspondence in AD 1 769 22/117, ANZ.
46 Scholes to Jennings, 20 Jun. 1916 and Robb to Allen, 14 Jun. 1916, AD 1 769 22/117, ANZ.
47 Gray to Fraser, 11 Sep. 1916, AD 82 2 1/11/1, ANZ.
48 Ibid.; Circular, LGB R. 36, 3 Feb. 1916, MH 47/142, NA.
49 *EP*, 14 Sep. 1916, 8.
50 Ibid., 27 Sep. 1916, 3.
51 Ibid.
52 James Watson, "Patriotism, Profits and Problems: New Zealand Farming during the Great War," in *New Zealand's Great War: New Zealand, the Allies and the First World War*, ed. John Crawford and Ian McGibbon (Auckland: Exisle, 2007), 535–36.
53 *Auckland Star (AS)*, 22 Sep. 1916, 4 and 13 Sep. 1916, 6.
54 Ibid., 14 Sep. 1916, 8.
55 Fraser to Gray, n.d., AD 82 2 1/11/1, ANZ.
56 Gray to Northcote, 16 Sep. 1916 and Allen to Giles, 18 Sep. 1916, AD 1 769 22/117, ANZ.
57 Stephen, "Tribunals," 384; *BI*, 1 Jan. 1916, 5.
58 Ernest Lockwood, *Colne Valley Folk* (London: Heath Cranton, 1936), 29; *BN*, 26 Aug. 1916, 6; Malcolm Clegg, *A History of Birstall: The Last 200 Years* (Batley: Malcolm Clegg, 1994), 149–54.
59 Lockwood, *Colne Valley Folk*, 44–47.
60 *W*, 4 May 1918, 2; Kelly's, *Kelly's Directory of the West Riding of Yorkshire, 1917* (Kelly's Directories, 1917).
61 Kelly's, *Directory of the West Riding*.
62 *WE*, 12 Feb. 1916, 6; Minutes, Holmfirth Urban District Council, 7 Feb. 1916, KMT 16/6/1/20, KA; *HE*, 11 Mar. 1916, 8.
63 Lockwood, *Colne Valley Folk*, 25.
64 *BI*, 13 Nov. 1915, 8.
65 E. A. Hilary Haigh, ed., *Huddersfield, A Most Handsome Town: Aspects of the History and Culture of a West Yorkshire Town* (Huddersfield: Kirklees Cultural Services, 1992), 541.
66 Lockwood, *Colne Valley Folk*, 19, 21–22, 27, 61; Kelly's, *Directory of the West Riding*; *CVG*, 29 Sep. 1916, 2; *W*, 6 Nov. 1915, 5.
67 *PCE*, 31 May 1918, 2; Kelly's, *Directory of the West Riding*.
68 *BC*, 4 Dec. 1915, 8.
69 K. W. Mitchinson, *Saddleworth, 1914–1919: The Experience of a Pennine Community during the Great War* (Saddleworth: Saddleworth Historical Society, 1995), 58; Ben Turner, *About Myself, 1863–1930* (London: Humphrey Toulmin, 1930); Ben Turner, *Short History of the General Union of Textile Workers* (Heckmondwike: Labour Pioneer and Factory Times, 1920), 160; Piercy to Hoyle, 30 Oct. 1915, Harris Hoyle Papers (HHP), S/NUDBTW/34, KA.
70 Andrew Bannister, *One Valley's War: Voices from a Yorkshire Community in the Great War and its Aftermath, 1914–1919* (Pudsey: Outremer, 1994), 77.
71 *OO*, 26 Aug. 1916, 3 and 26 May 1917, 7.
72 *The Times*, 2 Oct. 1942, 7; *Dewsbury District News (DDN)*, 22 Jan. 1916, 3.
73 Pearce, *Comrades in Conscience*, 257; *W*, 26 Feb. 1916, 5.
74 Long to Chairmen of County Councils, Lord Mayors and Mayors, 31 Jan. 1916, MH 10/80, NA.
75 Minutes, Huddersfield Branch of the General Union of Textile Workers, 3 Jul. 1914, S/NUDBTW/1, KA; Pearce, *Comrades in Conscience*, 257.

Judges and juries   51

76 *BN*, 2 Sep. 1916, 8.
77 *W*, 3 Feb. 1917, 2; Lockwood, *Colne Valley Folk*, 21–22; *BN*, 19 May 1917, 2; J. P. W. Mallalieu, *On Larkhill* (London: Allison and Busby, 1983), 3–8, 44; *WE*, 5 Jan. 1918, 5.
78 *AS*, 17 Jul. 1918, 7.
79 G. H. Scholefield, *Who's Who in New Zealand and the Western Pacific, 1925* (Napier: Venables, 1924), 51.
80 *NZG*, 1916, 3125; Scholefield, *Who's Who*, 232–33.
81 Scholefield, *Who's Who*, 67.
82 Barry Gustafson, *Labour's Path to Political Independence: The Origins and Establishment of the New Zealand Labour Party, 1900–19* (Auckland: University of Auckland Press, 1980), 161; Biographical Notes, "Edward Kellett," Herbert Otto Roth Papers (HORP), MS 6164-046, Alexander Turnbull Library, Wellington (ATL).
83 John McCaw, "Biography of My Life for the Benefit of My Children", 1929, MS 1164, ATL.
84 Minutes, Executive of the Wellington Branch of the Farmers' Union, 3 Feb. 1916, MSY 0296, ATL; Scholefield, *Who's Who*, 176.
85 E. C. Studholme, *Te Waimate: Early Station Life in New Zealand* (Wellington: A. H. and A. W. Reed, 1940).
86 Scholefield, *Who's Who*, 19.
87 *Waikato Times* (*WT*), 10 Apr. 1938, 8.
88 Keith Sinclair, *A Destiny Apart: New Zealand's Search for National Identity* (Wellington: Allen and Unwin, 1986), 173; *WT*, 15 Feb. 1917, 4; *NZH*, 23 Feb. 1917, 8; *EP*, 14 Jun. 1917, 2.
89 *Wairarapa Daily Times* (*WDT*), 13 Dec. 1916, 2; *Timaru Herald*, 6 Feb. 1917, 5; *Dannevirke Evening News* (*DEN*), 20 Mar. 1917, 3.
90 *Ohinemuri Gazette* (*OG*), 29 Sep. 1916, 2 and 2 Feb. 1917, 2; *Ashburton Guardian* (*AG*), 13 May 1918, 4 and 10 Jul. 1918, 4.
91 Gray to Fraser, 11 Sep. 1916, AD 82 2 1/11/1, ANZ; John McCaw, "Biography of My Life for the Benefit of My Children," 1929, MS 1164, ATL.
92 Peter Franks and Jim McAloon, *Labour: The New Zealand Labour Party, 1916–2016* (Wellington: Victoria University Press, 2016), 55–56; *EP*, 14 Jun. 1916, 2.
93 Biographical Notes, "Edward Kellett," HORP, MS 6164-046, ATL; *Maoriland Worker* (*MW*), 29 Nov. 1916, 3.
94 Minutes, Mirfield Urban District Council, 29 Mar. 1916, KMT 27/2/1/8, KA; *BN*, 1 Apr. 1916, 8.
95 Minutes, Huddersfield and District Trades and Labour Council, 22 Mar. 1916, S/HTC/1/4, KA; Minutes, Huddersfield County Borough Council, 11 Apr. 1916, KMT 18/12/2/37/17-18, KA.
96 Mitchinson, *Saddleworth*, 62–63.
97 Minutes, Heckmondwike Urban District Council, 13 Mar. 1916, KMT 14/2/1/12, KA; Minutes, Spenborough Urban District Council, 20 Mar. 1916, KMT 39/1/1/1, KA.
98 Minutes, Dewsbury County Borough Council, 17 Feb. 1916, KMT 8/3/2/1/3-4, KA.
99 *Goole Times* (*GT*), 10 Mar. 1916, 5.
100 Thomas, 80 Parl. Deb., H.C. (5th ser.) (1916), 2229; Long, 2229–30.
101 *GT*, 14 Apr. 1916, 6 and 19 May 1916, 6.
102 Hogan to Robin, 24 Aug. 1916 and Hogan to Allen, 5 Oct. 1916, AD 1 769 22/117, ANZ.
103 Minutes, "Meeting between Allen, O.C. Auckland District, the Group Commander and the Full Sub-Committee of the Recruiting Committee," 13 Oct. 1916, AD 1 769 22/117, ANZ.
104 *Southland Times* (*ST*), 26 Jan. 1917, 5.
105 Evans to Gray, 29 Jan. 1917, AD 1 769 22/117/1, ANZ.
106 *AS*, 27 Sep. 1916, 4, 7; Jones to Allen, 12 Oct. 1916, AD 1 769 22/117, ANZ.

52   *Judges and juries*

107 *AS*, 27 Sep. 1916, 7 and 3 Oct. 1916, 7.
108 Ibid., 13 Sep. 1916, 6 and 21 Sep. 1916, 2.
109 Allen to Jones, 19 Oct. 1916, AD 1 769 22/117, ANZ.
110 Allen to Massey, 29 Sep. 1916, AP, ALLEN 1 9, ANZ.
111 Allen to Barr, 18 Jan. 1917 and Allen to McLaren, 19 Jan. 1917, AD 1 769 22/117, ANZ.
112 *NZG*, 1917, 343–44.
113 Rosser to Allen, 12 Sep. 1916, AD 1 769 22/117, ANZ.
114 Biographical Notes, "Fred Curtice," HORP, MS 6164-017, ATL; Biographical Notes, "Matthew Joseph Mack," HORP, MS 6164-060, ATL.
115 *AG*, 24 Jan. 1917, 5; *AS*, 1 Feb. 1917, 8.
116 Biographical Notes, "Robert Breen," HORP, MS 6164-012, ATL; *MW*, 15 Nov. 1916, 6.
117 *AS*, 9 Feb. 1917, 4; *NZ Truth*, 3 Feb. 1917, 7.
118 *AS*, 1 Feb. 1917, 8.
119 *HE*, 1 Jan. 1916, 8.
120 *BI*, 20 Nov. 1915, 5.
121 *WE*, 6 Oct. 1917, 2.
122 *BC*, 22 Jan. 1916, 8; Leather to Gray, 10 Jan. 1916, Birstall Local Tribunal Files (BLTF), RD 21/6/2, KA; *HEx*, 24 Feb. 1948, 5.
123 *OO*, 22 Jan. 1916, 2; *GT*, 14 Apr. 1916, 6.
124 Free to Massey, 13 Jun. 1916, AD 1 769 22/117, ANZ; *Otago Daily Times (ODT)*, 8 Nov. 1916, 8.
125 Cosgrove to Quartermaster General, 23 Mar. 1917, AD 1 769 22/140, ANZ.

3 Willing and able to go?

In the only full-scale study of those men who were conscripted into the British Army, Ilana Bet-El completely underplays a critical aspect of their experiences. She maintains that, while volunteers took an active decision to join the colours, the enlistment of a conscript was a bureaucratic process 'marked by the lack of choice or control of the individual over his own fate'.[1] In fact, it was the voluntary system that allowed individuals to postpone a decision on whether they were willing and able to perform military service. The possibility of appealing for exemption from conscription required every eligible British and New Zealand man to weigh up his circumstances and reach a definite decision.[2] This was the one element of conscription over which the respective governments and militaries had no control, regardless of how they had configured their exemption systems. The authorities in both countries simply had to wait and see what proportion of men would chose to become appellants, and what attitudes those who did would express towards joining the army.

Anecdotal accounts from across Britain indicate that a vast number of appeals were lodged. As Mayor of Birmingham and chairman of its local appeal body, Neville Chamberlain wrote that serving on the tribunal had proven to be the 'most tiring' of his two roles, given that it sat 'three days a week from 10.30 to 1.30 & 2.15 till 6 or even 6.30'.[3] Likewise, Harry Cartmell, chairman of the Preston body, suggested the number of appellants had 'considerably exceeded the expectations' of the authorities and that 'the duties of the Tribunals in busy areas made very heavy demands upon the time of their members'.[4] This was undoubtedly the case at Leicester, where the local appeal body often found it necessary to sit for ten hours a day; in the Carmarthen Rural District of Wales, where a member quipped he had been 'sentenced to twelve months hard labour at the Tribunal'; and in the Metropolitan Borough of Hampstead, where Charles Repington asserted that he and his colleagues had 'worked like niggers'.[5] This overstretching of the tribunals' capacities led to consternation at the War Office, where it was believed that an inability to process men fast enough was contributing to the unsatisfactory flow of recruits into the army. A reporter for *The Times* observed the Director General of Recruiting's dismay at the tribunals having become 'encumbered and clogged with work', while the Adjutant General lamented that the appeal bodies 'cannot handle all the material satisfactorily at present'.[6]

54　*Willing and able to go?*

Statistical evidence supports the tenor of these observations. There is no source that indicates the overall rate of appealing in Britain for the whole of conscription, but combining the available information does provide some significant insights. The approximately 1.2 million call-up notices issued between January and July 1916 generated 748,587 appeals.[7] In one of these months, March 1916, 25,941 unattested men were taken into the army under the Military Service Act. Yet at the same time, 58,947 were exempted and another 18,079 had cases outstanding.[8] In other words, 74.81 percent of these men were appellants, alongside the enlistees who had their pleas turned down.

Examining the situation in individual districts yields similar results. As British men were called up by age 'group' or 'class' rather than by ballot, it is problematic to relate the number of appeals to the number of men who were summoned. An alternative is to calculate the number of appellants as a proportion of the approximate eligible population. This method gives an appeal rate for Leeds of 21.76 percent, Bristol 23.36 percent and Birmingham 28.51 percent.[9] Yet these figures greatly understate the likelihood of a claim being made, as they only relate to men whose cases came within the purview of the tribunals. With each government department being responsible for granting exemptions to its employees, and being permitted to direct that any war service badges issued under volunteering should now be treated as certificates of exemption, many prospective conscripts had no need to engage with the appeal bodies. The pressing need to maintain food and armaments production, and to supply essential goods to soldiers and civilians, prompted organisations like the Ministry of Munitions, the Board of Agriculture and the Board of Trade to safeguard vast numbers of their personnel. By October 1916, government departments had granted over 1.5 million exemptions, compared to 1.1 million issued by the tribunals.[10] This situation became even more pronounced by April 1917, with around 780,000 tribunal exemptions against nearly 1.8 million from other sources.[11] Given that Leeds, Bristol and Birmingham were all major industrial and administrative centres, many of their male residents would have been employed in war-related occupations.

A sizeable proportion of the division's eligible men also became appellants. The first public sitting of the Morley Tribunal lasted for twelve hours, as the members worked through one hundred and fifty cases, while the Huddersfield body regularly disposed of more than one hundred applications several times a week.[12] This intense schedule proved too much for some tribunal members, who were forced to resign after they found it impossible to both attend sittings and devote sufficient time to their own businesses.[13] Under conscription, claims relating to 519 individuals were lodged in the Urban District of Birstall, which had an approximate eligible population of 1,922, to give an appeal rate of 27 percent.[14] The figures for the Borough of Batley and the Urban District of Marsden were 33.95 percent and 36.54 percent, respectively.[15] Yet even these striking findings are eclipsed by what occurred in the County Borough of Huddersfield, where the local tribunal received 12,865 claims in 1916 alone, with the 1911 population of males aged ten to forty-four being only 29,651.[16] If these statistics are extrapolated, and taken alongside the fact many men would have already volunteered,

Willing and able to go?   55

been classed as medically unfit or been exempted as coal miners, ship builders, iron workers et cetera, then it 'must have been a rare individual who did not make a claim'.[17]

Appealing was much less common in New Zealand. Although the government did find it necessary to increase the number of boards from four to ten in January 1917, this was still far fewer per capita than the more than two thousand local tribunals in Britain. Furthermore, at the same time as tribunal members and the British military authorities were complaining of overwhelming case-loads, the Third Canterbury Board was never required to hold sittings and Allen was able to progressively abolish several other boards owing to a lack of work. The Second Otago body ceased its operations on 31 October 1917, followed by the Third Wellington Board four months later.[18] By February 1918, the Recruiting Board believed it could also move towards 'dispensing with' the Second Auckland, Second Wellington and Second Canterbury bodies, and only held off due to the need for a double ballot in response to the German Spring Offensive.[19]

Despite previous claims to the contrary, statistical evidence presents much the same picture. Baker's widely quoted figures on the rate of appealing in New Zealand are gathered from two sources. The first is a return prepared by the Adjutant General in April 1917, from which Baker calculates that 48.28 percent of first-ballot men appealed, before a gradual decline saw the proportion reach 34.72 percent by the fifth ballot.[20] Thereafter, he utilises a return on the work of the boards between 2 June 1917 and 7 September 1918 to argue the appealing rate then 'increased again, to average 51 per cent' during these months.[21] Baker therefore implies that just under half of the 134,632 balloted European men, or approximately sixty thousand, appealed overall.[22] Yet these figures greatly exaggerate the situation. Correspondence from Major General Robin points to four thousand men being drawn in the first ballot, with around one thousand seven hundred choosing to appeal.[23] While the Adjutant General's return cited by Baker gives a similar total of appellants, it relates this to the number of reservists who were 'available and under disposal', rather than the number balloted. As only 3,554 men were 'available and under disposal', the apparent rate of appealing is inflated. This proviso also applies to the Adjutant General's returns for ballots two to five.[24] Doubts over a 51 percent appealing rate between 2 June 1917 and 7 September 1918 arise from the return that Baker uses to reach this conclusion. The return states that 87,781 men were medically examined during these months and that 'the total number of appeals ... disposed of ... was 45,535'. However, it draws a distinction between the number of 'appeals' (45,535) and the number of 'appellants' (only 14,547).[25] This means 45,535 'appeals' actually refers to every occasion the boards delivered a verdict, even if it was for a case that had already been adjourned for further consideration, or where an application for a rehearing, or for additional leave, had been made.

Baker's implication is further undermined by a report compiled in March 1919 by the Director of Recruiting, Captain Cosgrove, which identifies 32,445 European appellants during conscription. This figure could be regarded as definitive, as Cosgrove would have had time to collate the relevant data after the

56   *Willing and able to go?*

Armistice. Nevertheless, the report is unclear as to whether it takes every appellant into account. In the early months of sittings, it emerged that time was being wasted on individuals appearing before the boards having already been classed as medically unfit.[26] To alleviate this difficulty, these men were 'asked to withdraw their appeals' before a hearing took place.[27] Although withdrawals undoubtedly occurred, the report's total of 32,445 appellants is only broken down into the outcomes of allowed, dismissed, adjourned *sine die* and not determined.

The numerical list of reservists does not completely resolve this issue, but it does permit a conclusion on the rate of appealing. Produced by the Defence Department after the war, this resource gives details on every balloted European man, including the outcome of any appeal. To determine what the figure of 32,445 appellants includes, each reservist was categorised according to his final medical classification and whether the final outcome of his appeal was a verdict or withdrawal. This approach demonstrates that the Director of Recruiting did omit appellants from his report, with the total in the list being 43,544, rather than 32,445. However, it is impossible to determine precisely which appellants were excluded, as the 4,264 withdrawals in the list do not make up the difference. This discrepancy can be attributed to the varied ways the boards reported appeal outcomes. In the list, hundreds of unfit reservists at a time are shown as having their appeals dismissed or adjourned *sine die*. As it is inconceivable that all these men would have failed to withdraw their case, the First Canterbury Board was not alone in reporting a verdict being delivered even though no formal hearing had taken place.[28] Certainly, 43,544 is the maximum number of European appellants. Given that the list was produced after the war and details every balloted reservist, there is no possibility of men being omitted. Moreover, it cannot be argued that the list only covered men who appealed to one particular agency, as the boards were specifically established to be the sole authority for awarding exemptions

These considerations render Baker's inference that nearly half of all balloted New Zealanders were the subjects of appeals unsustainable. The actual rate was much lower. Of 134,632 European men, 43,544 or 32.34 percent became appellants, which, when expressed as a proportion of the eligible male population, equates to 17.77 percent.[29] As Figure 3.1 demonstrates, this is a significantly lower figure than any of those identified in Britain.

New Zealand's appeal rate was also very low when compared to the other dominions of the British Empire. Although Australian voters rejected conscription in two referendums, from September 1916 single men and widowers without dependents were eligible for compulsory military training. In northeastern Victoria, John McQuilton finds that 75 percent of those classed as fit appealed, with a figure of 71 percent being identified for South Australia by Michael McKernan.[30] Even though New Zealanders were balloted for active service rather than just training, only 41.93 percent of fit men appealed.[31] Further comparisons can be drawn with Canada. In that dominion, appeals against being conscripted for overseas military service were lodged on the grounds of occupation, hardship, conscientious objections or obvious physical disability by fully 94.1 percent of class 1 men (those who were unmarried and aged twenty to thirty-four).[32] For

Willing and able to go? 57

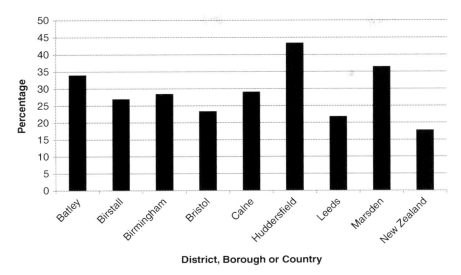

Figure 3.1 Appellants as a proportion of the eligible population

New Zealand, even treating all 75,406 unfit reservists as having appealed from an obvious physical disability still only gives an appeal rate of 74.56 percent when added to the 25,330 fit and not medically examined appellants.[33]

The disparity between the British and New Zealand rates did not result from greater approval for the British exemption system. In both countries, the appeal bodies came under sustained criticism from two distinct directions. On one side were those people who believed that exemptions were being granted too liberally. The War Office often asserted that a failure to meet its recruiting targets was partly due to the over-sentimentality and excessive localism of the tribunals. Indeed, the Adjutant General began describing the work of the appeal bodies as 'unsatisfactory' only two months after conscription came into force.[34] Members of the British Government also voiced this belief for much of 1916 and 1917, meaning the tribunals received a constant stream of instructions asking them to apply stricter standards.[35] Families who had lost several members, along with those who believed the nation's duty to send every fit man was going unfulfilled, also directed their anger towards the exemption systems. This came to a head in New Zealand during the early months of 1918, with the imminent mobilisation of the Second Division. Rioting broke out in Christchurch the first time married men were due to be sent into camp and, although such civil disobedience was widely condemned, there was still a sense of outrage that individuals with family responsibilities might be sent when thousands of singles remained at home. It was at this point that numerous local and sectional bodies took up the call for medical unfitness to become the only ground for exemption outside of being engaged in essential war work.[36]

58 *Willing and able to go?*

Yet there were also claims that exemptions were being unduly withheld. In the British Parliament, Long was continuously forced to deflect allegations of harsh treatment on the part of the tribunals. One MP likened the appeal bodies to 'recruiting sergeants' and 'the old press gangs'; another cited their relentless efforts at 'driving men into the army'; while a third lamented the 'very poor' hearings that were being accorded.[37] Such accusations were also voiced in the division. After the first few weeks of sittings, the *Dewsbury Reporter* concluded that the tribunals had decided to operate 'as the tool and instrument of the military'.[38] Likewise, the *Worker* suggested their members were endeavouring 'to press as many men as possible into the Army', and the Huddersfield Friendly and Trade Societies' Club opined that unless the appeal bodies began to show more consideration then 'there is likely to be serious shortage of farmers' production'.[39] The appellants themselves raised further grievances. Frank Lockwood bitterly resented the 'sarcastic remarks' he had been subjected to at the Linthwaite body and noted in his diary that 'tribunal' should be redefined as 'a collection of local celebrities who send other men's sons into the Army – & make bad jokes about it'.[40] Even more indignant was an appellant at Golcar, who greeted the appeal body's refusal to allow him further time by throwing his previous exemption certificate at the members and exclaiming 'I shall be shot before I go.'[41]

Some New Zealanders directed similar criticism at the boards. The *Round Table* asserted that the appeal bodies were regarding their 'whole function as being to get men for the reinforcements', while one appellant accused Chairman Bishop of the Second Canterbury Board of having turned him into a 'laughing stock'.[42] Particular displeasure was voiced where the 'last man' on the farm or the sole remaining son of a widow was taken for service. A member of the Taranaki branch of the Farmers' Union stated that the boards 'had no sympathy' with agricultural or pastoral claimants, and the *Dannevirke Evening News* described the Second Wellington body's decision to send the last of five sons in the Best family as a 'manifest inequality of sacrifice'.[43]

Being exposed to this double-edged censure was a constant source of exasperation to the appeal bodies and their administrators. The chairman of the Castleford Tribunal hastened to reassure his colleagues against the 'flood of abuse' they had received from individuals who apparently believed they were 'lacking in intelligence and full of partiality and prejudice, instead of being public businessmen who were sacrificing their time and energy in the conscientious performance of a somewhat unpleasant, if necessary, public duty'.[44] Similarly, when a mother complained to the Second Auckland Board about the number of cases that had been refused, the chairman wryly remarked that 'some people consider we grant too many'.[45] In the face of this persistent criticism, Long maintained he was at a loss over how to satisfy the many detractors who held that the system was too harsh, while simultaneously appeasing those who claimed it was too liberal.[46] For his part, Allen questioned how the public could demand the immediate conscription of all single men, yet be unwilling to give up any of the goods or services to which they were accustomed, by exclaiming 'you cannot have your cake and eat it'.[47]

Willing and able to go? 59

A second factor that does little to explain the differing appeal rates is the relative extent of conscription. Although the British Military Service Act of January 1916 covered only single men aged between eighteen and forty-one, a second Act applying to married men was passed four months later. All the single and married 'groups' and 'classes' were called up well before the end of the year, with subsequent statutes, regulations and instructions extending the age of eligibility to fifty, and providing for the 'combing out' of many men who had previously been safeguarded due to their occupation, or rejected due to their medical status.[48] Conscription in New Zealand not only started later, but also proceeded at a much slower pace. The first appeals came before the boards in November 1916 and, while all single men had been subject to the ballot by the close of hostilities, the calling up of the Second Division, which was carried out in sequence according to number of children, had only reached class C (married men with two children). This meant that around 16.4 percent of all European reservists were never balloted.[49] Had these individuals been required, the number of New Zealand appellants as a proportion of the eligible population would have increased and the difference with the British figures would not be as great.

Yet a substantial disparity would still exist. Despite James Belich's claim that married New Zealanders did 'everything possible to delay' their conscription, the numerical list of reservists indicates the calling of married men did not herald a significant rise in exemption claims.[50] Rather, the rate of appealing fluctuated throughout the boards' operations. The highest rate of 38.9 percent occurred for ballot twelve, which was the first time that members of the Second Division were drawn. However, appealing then quickly returned to its previous level, and the overall rate for ballots largely made up of the Second Division was very close to that for ballots that only included First Division reservists: 33.94 percent and 30.86 percent, respectively.[51] This situation could well have altered had conscription reached classes D (married men with three children), E (married men with four children) and F (married men with five children). Individuals with a higher number of dependents would have been more likely to prioritise the ties of their domestic situation than men with fewer or no children. Nevertheless, any increase in the appeal rate would surely not have been so large as to account for the vast difference between the New Zealand and British figures.

The third insufficient explanation is that the numerical list of reservists only covered men from New Zealand's European population. Due to administrative difficulties and concerns it would accelerate the decline of the race, conscription was not applied to Maori until mid-1918. Even then it was restricted to only those iwi and hapu living in the Waikato–Maniapoto Land District, which were perceived as having failed to supply enough volunteers for the Native Contingent.[52] Nonetheless, attempts to enforce military obligations in this region were met by a campaign of passive resistance. Local leaders, notably Princess Te Puea Herangi, denied the right of the European government to compel enlistment, particularly when settlers had inflicted decades of dispossession and poverty on Maori people.[53] Given such deep-seated antagonism, it might be supposed that adding Maori reservists to the official statistics would produce a higher overall appeal rate.

60 *Willing and able to go?*

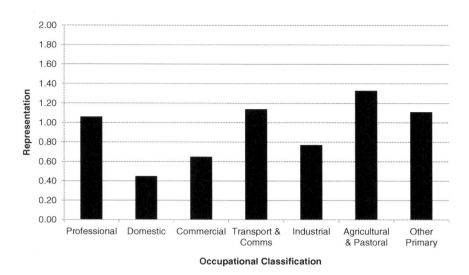

Figure 3.2 Representation of occupational classes among the New Zealand appellants

However, this is not the case. Four Maori ballots were held from May 1918, calling up a total of 552 men.[54] There is no return showing the proportion of these individuals who became appellants, but it is possible to make a reliable estimate by combining newspaper reports of the sittings of the specially constituted Native Military Service Board with correspondence that passed between the administrators of conscription. This approach reveals that 185 Maori men were the subjects of exemption claims, a proportion only slightly higher than that among New Zealand's European conscripts.[55]

A fourth variable that had limited significance was the more rural structure of New Zealand society. In 1911, approximately 11.42 percent of British males worked in agriculture, whereas the 1916 figure for New Zealand was 31.27 percent.[56] Although it is impossible to ascertain a comparable statistic for the division, given that it was a unit of administrative convenience rather than one possessing historical boundaries, only four of its sixty-three districts were classed as 'rural'. This disparity could be regarded as a meaningful contributor to the appeal rates. Catriona Pennell, David Silbey and Bonnie White have all found that predominately rural areas of Britain experienced lower levels of volunteering than those that were largely urban.[57] Likewise, the most detailed analysis of voluntary enlistment in New Zealand has discerned that 'farmers and farm employees' were 'under-represented' among those who joined the forces.[58] A reluctance to volunteer was not the same as deciding to appeal against conscription, but these findings at least suggest that rural men were more concerned, or came under more pressure, to remain at home than their urban counterparts.

Applying this theory to the measurable British districts produces only mixed results. Figure 3.1 shows the rate of appealing in the Wiltshire Rural District of

Calne was 29.14 percent, which was higher than in Birmingham, Birstall, Bristol and Leeds, but lower than for Batley, Huddersfield and Marsden. On the other hand, the proposition is strongly borne out by the New Zealand figures. Figure 3.2 divides the percentage of appellants from an occupational classification by the percentage of the dominion's employed male population it constituted. A result of 1.00 would mean proportionate representation, above would be an overrepresentation, and below an underrepresentation. Agriculturalists and pastoralists were easily the most overrepresented group. They made up 41.62 percent of the appellants, but only 31.27 percent of New Zealand's male workers, giving a representation of 1.33. In contrast, appeals concerning men employed in the predominately urban industrial and commercial sectors were much less common, their representation being 0.77 and 0.65, respectively. This finding becomes even more pronounced when eligibility for conscription is taken into account. The agricultural and pastoral category had the second lowest proportion of men in the ballot, with only 51.56 percent of workers being aged twenty to forty-six in 1916.

However, this significant overrepresentation of rural dwellers only makes New Zealand's relatively low appeal rate that much more striking. If there were a positive correlation between the proportion of men employed in rural occupations and the proportion of exemption claims, then one would expect it to have been New Zealand, rather than Britain, that had the greater incidence of appealing. These figures demonstrate the inclination *not* to claim exemption in New Zealand was so powerful that it outweighed the considerably greater tendency to appeal of New Zealanders engaged in agriculture, who were a much higher proportion of the eligible population than in Britain.

The relative distance of the two countries from the fighting was also of limited importance when it came to appealing. It could be argued that Britain's proximity to the Western Front would have made its young men more cognisant of the conditions and risks that soldiers had to endure, whereas the thousands of miles separating New Zealanders from their expeditionary force would have left them unaware of the war's realities. If this were indeed the case, it might well have been a significant factor in making New Zealanders less likely to appeal. Certainly, a greater proportion of the British population were exposed to soldiers who came home on leave, with several historians suggesting that these men were more candid about their battlefield experiences than has previously been claimed.[59]

However, there are compelling reasons for discounting distance from the frontline as a major factor. On the one hand, New Zealanders were not blind to the true nature of the conflict. The dreadful losses sustained during the 1915 Gallipoli Campaign were extensively reported, and graphic accounts of death and hardship were published in the newspapers. One soldier's submission to the *Press* stated 'I know what hell is like now ... All my mates were either killed or wounded', while the *New Zealand Herald* carried a letter that read 'what do I think of war? Well, it is kill, kill, kill. No one cares if you are the next to be shot'.[60] On the other hand, the influence of geographic remoteness can also be viewed from the opposite perspective. Several recent studies have shown that the outbreak of war did not prompt an immediate rush of British men to the colours.

62   *Willing and able to go?*

Instead, Adrian Gregory, Stuart Halifax and Pennell all assert that volunteering only surged following the publication of reports detailing the extent of the initial German advances into France and Belgium.[61] This indicates that the willingness of men to serve increased if they perceived their country's war effort was on the brink of disaster. When conscription was introduced in 1916, Britain was suffering from aerial bombing raids and the shelling of coastal towns, while German submarines were threatening its food supplies by decimating merchant shipping in the Atlantic. Moreover, there existed the continued spectre of an invasion by an unscrupulous and 'evil foe', whose army was widely believed to have committed a series of brutal atrocities in occupied Belgium.[62] In contrast, the prospect of New Zealand coming under direct attack had completely receded by November 1916. If proximity to the front could be regarded as giving British men an incentive to appeal, then it can also be perceived as making them more likely to want to fight for the protection of their homes and their way of life.

A final unsatisfactory explanation is the relative financial costs of joining the army. New Zealand soldiers were remunerated considerably better than their British counterparts, up to four or five times as much for the lower ranks.[63] Furthermore, the dominion offered a higher level of separation allowances, paid to the wives and dependents of servicemen, and, from January 1917, allowed men to apply for a grant under the Financial Assistance Scheme. This latter measure provided soldiers with up to £213 2s. a year for their wife, and £13 13s. for each child, to cover obligations incurred prior to the introduction of conscription, such as rents and mortgages.[64] When the scheme was first initiated, reservists were required to apply to the boards, who then made recommendations to Allen. However, this mechanism proved to be far too cumbersome, so a dedicated Financial Assistance Board of three businessmen was established in March 1917. By the end of May, the Financial Assistance Board had ruled on 679 cases and awarded a grant, averaging £26 per annum, in 510 of these.[65] If the pecuniary losses faced by New Zealand men were lower, it might be anticipated that this would make them more amenable to being conscripted. Certainly, the division's tribunals did hear many accounts of financial hardship, often regarding the support of parents, siblings, wives and children.

Yet there are several reasons for rejecting this as a significant factor. The first is that cases based on financial difficulties were heard in New Zealand as well. Edward Coffey argued both of his brothers were serving and that he contributed an essential one pound per week from his wages to support his elderly parents and three sisters.[66] Similarly, Alfred Hitchcock stated he was the sole support of both his wife and his widowed mother, who was in poor health, and objected that he would not be able to properly support them even with the assistance available.[67] A second consideration is that, while the number of financially based claims was not insignificant, they were outweighed by appeals lodged on occupational grounds. Indeed, the available evidence suggests the proportion of claims made for employment reasons was greater in Britain than in New Zealand. At the Birstall Tribunal in the division, 86.23 percent of appellants cited occupational factors as part of their case, whereas only 33.22 percent asked for financial, domestic or

Willing and able to go? 63

business hardship to be considered.[68] Likewise, Marjorie Levine-Clark's analysis of Stourbridge and Dudley in the Black Country has found that, where the grounds of appeal were readily apparent, occupational claims outnumbered those based on domestic factors by 72.42 percent to 20.43 percent.[69] Ascertaining a comparable figure for New Zealand is problematic, as the absence of any board minute books makes it necessary to rely entirely on newspaper reports. The varied level of detail in these accounts can render determining the basis of a case very difficult. Some state the grounds cited in terms of the Military Service Act, but others contain no information on the appellant's motivations. A lack of detail clearly makes it unfeasible to ascertain the basis of the claim, so only those 13,332 men whose motivations were reported as per the Act were considered. Using this approach reveals that public interest was raised by 51.73 percent of New Zealand appellants, against 35.98 percent who cited undue hardship.[70]

A more persuasive explanation for the differing appeal rates is the level of protection that the British system afforded to many industries. Government departments were not only permitted to issue exemptions directly, but could also safeguard men working in their 'sphere' by placing a calling on the list of certified occupations. The considerable scope of this document meant it came under frequent attack from the army and the War Office. Indeed, the Director General of Recruiting called for its total abolition as early as March 1916, while the concept of cancelling all exemptions held by men below a certain age was first mooted the following February.[71] During any appeal where the reservist's occupation appeared on the certified list, the tribunals was obliged to regard him as having *prima facie* grounds for exemption. Such a case could only be refused if the military representative raised an objection and the tribunal subsequently found it was not in the 'national interest' to retain the man in civil employment.[72] These stipulations would have encouraged certain appeals on the basis that their success was highly likely. By 15 October 1916, 473,000 men employed in certified occupations had received exemption from the tribunals alone.[73] Furthermore, the list effectively told the individuals it covered that their duty was to remain at home. At a time when many others had to weigh up their personal responsibilities against social pressure and the country's need for soldiers, these men were supplied with an answer as to whether they should appeal. Age limits were progressively applied to some of the certified occupations, while others were removed from the list entirely.[74] Nevertheless, in October 1918 the Ministry of National Service calculated that 2,574,860 men were still eligible for some form of protection by virtue of their employment.[75]

The situation in New Zealand was rather different. Its government did contradict the idea that each case would be judged solely on its merits by directing that coal miners, slaughtermen and merchant seamen should have their appeals granted, and by issuing ministerial certificates to essential individuals. However, these provisions safeguarded a far lower number of occupations, and a far lower proportion of men, than the British system. In 1917, the New Zealand Government sent out further instructions regarding the exemption of the 'last man' on the farm, with official approval also being given to a classification of industries, professions

64 *Willing and able to go?*

and occupations. Yet the onus of proof remained on the appellant or his employer in most cases. The 'last man' was tightly defined as only those individuals 'doing the whole of the work on his own farm, or the last son on the farm of parents who are unable ... to do the work themselves', while the classification of industries emphasised that no claim should be accepted unless the individual was irreplaceable.[76] Without the near certainty of success, or the same degree of official sanction, that many British men enjoyed, New Zealanders would have been less likely to appeal on occupational grounds.

Another significant variable was the social acceptability of appealing. Matthew Wright's assertion that overt conscientious objectors 'were the only ones targeted' in New Zealand for choosing to claim relief is contradicted by a wealth of evidence.[77] Even before hearings commenced, the Minister of Internal Affairs pleaded for the automatic exemption of farmers and industrial workers so that they could avoid the 'humiliation' of appealing, while a prospective claimant hoped he would not branded as a 'shirker' when he had crucial obligations at home.[78] These fears were to prove well founded. Newspapers invariably gave the full names and addresses of appellants, and endeavoured to cover as many cases as possible. Moreover, the *New Zealand Herald* took to reporting claims under the heading 'Reservists' Excuses', a label that would have been endorsed by the editors of the *Hawke's Bay Tribune*, who lamented that 'many of the appellants have no ground of appeal at all'.[79]

A lack of sympathy was also evident among the New Zealand public, members of whom thronged the galleries at many early sittings.[80] Board members and military representatives frequently mentioned letters they had received opposing appellants' testimony, and citing the 'feeling in the district' that had arisen against the exemption of certain individuals.[81] Correspondents to local newspapers could be particularly vitriolic. One described any unmarried individual who appealed as 'not worthy of the name of a man', while another lambasted those who were 'selfish and mean enough to offer paltry excuses to the Appeal Board to evade military obligations and take no part in defending our women and children'.[82] In response to this climate of opinion, Chairman Poynton of the Second Wellington Board repeatedly advised appellants to withdraw their claims on the grounds that 'it would be better to ... not have it recorded against him that he has appealed'.[83] Some men even considered it unbecoming to have their name associated with appeals. When writing to correct a report that listed him as claiming for an employee, Charles Laurie implied the very notion was a stain on his patriotism. He argued that he 'would not appeal for anybody', that he considered 'every fit man in my employ should go', and stressed that his son was presently returning home wounded from the front.[84]

This is not to suggest that appeals meet with universal approval from the British public. In her influential analysis of the home front, Nicoletta Gullace argues that, by 1916, the traditional benchmarks of responsible masculine citizenship had been supplanted by the performance of military service. Certainly, the widespread belief that the Germans had committed all manner of atrocities in occupied Belgium led some people to assert that only a coward would vacillate over defending his country from the same fate.[85] The charges of 'shirking' made in one anonymous letter were 'so serious' that the accused tracked down its author and forced him to apologise under threat of prosecution, while 'A "Stiff" From Huddersfield' wrote of his disgust at seeing 'the number of smart young fellows … chaffing with girls down Westgate'.[86]

However, there does seem to have been a greater tolerance of appealing overall.[87] Most newspapers in the division did not print the names or addresses of appellants, and often limited their coverage to a handful of the more 'interesting' or 'informative' cases from each sitting. Indeed, the *Colne Valley Guardian* refused to report on the tribunals' activities altogether, so that men who had exercised their legal right to claim relief would not be 'made the butt of idle and mischievous gossip'.[88] The accessible nature of the exemption system also raised the prospect of appellants being badgered during their hearings, but there are very few recorded instances of this taking place. On the contrary, many sittings in the division attracted few, or even no, onlookers, and any heckling that did take place was far more likely to be directed at the tribunal members than at the appellants.[89]

Debates around the exemption systems also tended to be orientated differently. Those New Zealanders who believed relief was being granted too freely tended to blame the duplicity of appellants, whereas British opinion was more apt to target protected occupations or the tribunals. Furthermore, if one excludes the War Office, it is relatively uncommon to find such an argument being voiced in Britain.[90] Instead, editorials, correspondence columns and parliamentary debates were full of complaints about the harsh treatment of appellants. Each of these observations is very much a matter of degree rather than a dichotomy. Nevertheless, the lower rate of appealing in New Zealand can partly be attributed to the way such claims were perceived.

If undertaking military service had become the essential prerequisite of masculine citizenship by 1916, one would expect most appeals for exemption to have originated from conscientious objectors. Yet this was not the case in either country. The highest proportion of claims identified as being made on conscientious grounds to a single British tribunal is the 6.56 percent before the Middlesex Appeal Tribunal.[91] However, given that conscientious objectors were the most likely appellants to be dissatisfied with their original verdicts, this figure exaggerates the general situation. Indeed, it could be considered an aberration, as only 1.56 percent of the cases taken to the Northamptonshire Appeal Tribunal were overtly lodged for religious or political reasons.[92] As for Britain's local tribunals, James Cranstoun in regard to East Lothian; Mike Fraser in regard to Berwick-upon-Tweed; Keith Grieves in regard to Leek; Christine Housden in regard to Kingston; Levine-Clark in regard to Stourbridge and Dudley; and Paul Rusiecki in regard to Essex have all found that cases based on conscientious scruples constituted a tiny fraction of the tribunals' workload.[93] More specifically, Ivor Slocombe asserts that objectors made up just 1.8 percent of all the appellants in Wiltshire, while Philip Spinks finds that they were 0.8 percent of the men who applied to the Stratford-upon-Avon Borough Tribunal, and 0.9 percent of those heard by the Stratford Rural body.[94] A recent study carried out by the local Home

66 *Willing and able to go?*

Front Project Group has revealed that conscientious objectors amounted to just 2 percent of the appellants who came before the St Albans City Tribunal.[95]

The evidence for the division conforms to this wider pattern. In his examination of wartime Saddleworth, K. W. Mitchinson finds that 'few' of the appellants to the local tribunal were conscientious objectors.[96] There were only six such men among 377 claimants to the Birstall Tribunal, and just sixteen overt objectors among 3,385 Batley appellants.[97] Even Cyril Pearce, who describes Huddersfield as 'a virtual citadel for the anti-war cause', admits that less than 1 percent of the cases before the local tribunal were explicitly based on religious or political sensitivities.[98] While John Rae's oft-cited figure of 16,500 conscientious objectors across Britain has recently been contested, even the highest estimate of 23,032 would still constitute less than 0.5 percent of all the men recruited during the war.[99]

It is more difficult to determine the exact proportion of conscientious objectors in New Zealand, but they were undoubtedly few. The official statistics only reveal that a total of seventy-three objectors had been granted exemption by the end of the war.[100] Otherwise, it is necessary to rely on the sample of 13,332 men whose motivations were reported in the newspapers as per the Military Service Act. Doing so indicates that 4.76 percent of the appellants cited conscientious grounds, a higher proportion than for any of the districts in the division. However, some significant provisos must be appended. The figure of 4.76 percent includes several individuals who appealed on all the available grounds, but who subsequently made no mention of conscientious scruples during their hearings. This suggests they either misread the appeal form or selected 'all grounds' by default. The evidence given by Arthur Longhurst of Wellington revolved entirely around undue hardship and, when questioned by the confused board chairman, he explained that he had left all the grounds in as he 'did not understand'.[101] Moreover, as conscientious objections were viewed as being so 'unusual', and therefore newsworthy, they tended to be reported in detail, whereas 'routine' undue hardship or public interest cases were much more likely to be omitted from the coverage. Even the decision to begin conscripting Maori from May 1918 did not increase the proportion of appellants who cited conscientious objections. In fact, only three Maori men did so, on the basis that the third article of the 1840 Treaty of Waitangi had guaranteed New Zealand's indigenous people the rights and privileges of British subjects.[102] The combined weight of these caveats suggests that overt conscientious objectors were just as rare in New Zealand as they were in Britain.

If so few men advanced moral or political objections, what reasons did they give for appealing? Most personal claims in the division were lodged on hardship grounds. The concept of the male provider had gained considerable standing in nineteenth-century Britain, and the testimony given during appeal hearings showcased its continued influence.[103] At Dewsbury, Norman Pontefract asserted he was the only one keeping his widowed mother out of the workhouse.[104] Likewise, an individual before the Barnsley Borough Tribunal claimed to be providing his invalid mother with an essential twenty-five shillings from his weekly wage.[105] Appellants tended to link these concerns to the responsibilities they had inherited after the enlistment or conscription of their siblings.

A thirty-one-year-old painter's labourer from Goole stated he was the last of four brothers at home, which made him vital to the upkeep of his mother and father.[106] The primary concern for most married men was continuing in their 'natural' role as head of the household. Andrew Coult explained his previous failure to volunteer by insisting it would 'have done his wife and children a great injustice', while Leonard Hartley had 'thought it my duty to stick to the obligations to my parents, and to look after my wife and children'.[107] Many other appellants rejected the notion that their wives should enter the workforce, arguing this was not a role women could, or should, be expected to fulfil. Similar ideals were expressed in business hardship cases. A saddler and harness maker told the Barnsley Borough Tribunal that he had spent his entire life savings on making the concern profitable. It would have to be closed down if he were conscripted, thereby ruining the prospects of his young family.[108] Similarly, the Birstall Tribunal heard from a joiner who forecast dire consequences if he were taken: 'the connection would go, the stock depreciate, the business be sold; and there would be nothing to come back to'.[109]

Enduring ideals of male citizenship were also used to support occupational appeals. The pre-war British working class was divided into skilled artisans, semi-skilled labourers and the unskilled, with very little movement, but a great many economic and social distinctions, between those categories.[110] Under conscription, employers from urban areas often emphasised their willingness to release unskilled or non-essential men, but only if they could retain a core of indispensables. The owner of a plumbing firm told the Barnsley Borough Tribunal he would have no option but to close down if any more men were taken, while the manager of Howden Clough Collieries based his appeal for Fred Broadhead on the grounds that the company had failed to secure another clerk by advertising, and had already been reduced to two-thirds of its pre-war output through releasing over one hundred men to the forces.[111] When an employer's appeal for Frank Percy, a bricklayer, was brought before the Featherstone Tribunal, he was described as indispensable for maintaining the company's coke ovens, which had to be kept operating at full capacity to meet their existing contracts.[112] Occupational claims were also common in rural areas, where farmers pleaded for the retention of their experienced personnel. One appellant to the Goole Rural Tribunal stated that he had exchanged all of his more recent employees for boys or pensioners. As a result, there was no way he could supply enough milk to the nearby towns if any of his leading hands were taken.[113]

When the appeal bodies' questioning turned to potential compromises, most employers refused to perceive men who were outside the military age as suitable replacements. The director of H. H. Holdsworth & Co. labelled the proposed use of fifty-year-olds as roving overlookers 'absurd', while a nurseryman exclaimed that 'he would go short' rather than employ school leavers.[114] An even stronger resistance greeted the suggestion of female labour. Taylor Yielding & Co., textile manufacturers, based several claims on the fact their materials and machines were simply too heavy for women to manage, and a furniture manufacturer argued that women lacked both the 'initiative' and the 'judgment' to replace his senior clerk.[115]

68 *Willing and able to go?*

Like their British counterparts, most New Zealand appellants who cited undue hardship did so on the basis of family responsibilities. George Cook maintained that his mother was in a weak state of health and asked for a period of 'grace' to enable the doctors to build up her strength, while Charles Howe stressed that having three brothers in the forces had temporarily left him as the only one able to look after their sisters and elderly parents.[116] For Colin Wild only total exemption would suffice, as his weekly wage was essential to the upkeep of an elderly mother and a delicate sister.[117] After the balloting of the Second Division began in November 1917, numerous appellants came forward to argue that conscription would leave their wife and children in difficulties. The language used during these cases indicates the widespread prevalence of a 'male breadwinner' culture.[118] John Casey insisted that his wife and child would be entirely unable to subsist without him, and many other individuals baulked at the idea of their spouses having to take on paid employment.[119] Such concerns were not solely financial, with several appellants asking for a short interlude to see their wife through a debilitating illness.[120]

Business concerns were another regular feature of hardship cases. Most of these appellants asserted that their enterprise would no longer be financially viable if they were taken, due to a lack of expertise or replacement manpower. William Hardwick claimed his Hataitai grocery shop was too large for his wife to run alone and that he would be forced to hand it over to the local Chinese, whose young men were not subject to conscription.[121] For William Hudner, there was no one else capable of carrying on his undertaking firm, as it was the oldest and largest of its kind in Hamilton.[122] Some appellants argued this situation was greatly compounded by having been found unfit when they had volunteered. Particularly unfortunate in this regard was Reginald Taylor, who informed the First Auckland Board that he had sent his wife to England and sold his home at a loss to enter camp with the 19th reinforcements. However, after undergoing four months' training, he had required an operation for appendicitis and been discharged. Believing this decision to be final, Taylor had brought his wife back to New Zealand and become a fruiterer, only to then be medically reclassified as C1, which made him liable for overseas service after training in a specially established camp.[123]

Most New Zealand farmers cited a combination of family and business concerns as the basis for their hardship appeals. In every case, the testimony revolved around how the farm would be carried on in the man's absence. Two frequent claims were that brothers could not take over as they had gone to the front and that fathers were too old or infirm for strenuous work. Percy Cramp explained that both his brothers were already serving, meaning he would have no choice but to sell his dairy stock if conscripted.[124] Likewise, a mother's appeal for George Fiddis centred on the fact one of his siblings was currently in camp and another had been killed at Gallipoli.[125] The common attitude towards female relatives was one of distrust in their competence, usually based on a belief that women were not cut out for the rigours of agricultural work.[126] Similar themes were evident when farmers discussed outside assistance: the war effort had caused a labour shortage

Willing and able to go? 69

and, even when they admitted men were available, farmers were often scornful about their quality. One told of a young boy who

> dried half my cows off, although it was in the flush of the season. Some days he milked them at 11, and on other days not at all. He also let them into the garden, and they ate all the shrubs round the house.[127]

Farmers argued these issues had left them in a perilous situation. If conscripted they would suffer a major decline in production or be forced to sell up altogether. Most included public interest as part of their appeal and a few emphasised they would no longer be able to supply food for the war effort. Peter Campbell 'thought he would be doing the country good service by remaining and working the farm', while Leslie Mohring postulated that 'the man who gave his life in the firing line was doing little more than the one who stayed at home and worked hard producing the country's needs'.[128] Yet most farmers prioritised the undue hardship that would result from losing their livelihood. Farms were portrayed as the only means an individual had of providing for his family, and were also seen as business enterprises, into which considerable time and capital had been sunk.[129] Thomas Mitchell summed up the attitudes of many farmer appellants towards having to relinquish their holdings: 'it would be bung; father would be ruined, the family would [be] ruined, and I would be ruined'.[130]

The ubiquity of public interest appeals in New Zealand primarily resulted from the high volume of cases brought by large-scale employers, or by trade union secretaries who were permitted to act as employers for the purpose of appeals.[131] Whereas Parsons contends that many such individuals 'declined to apply for mass exemptions', this is strongly contradicted by the evidence.[132] By May 1917, the Wellington secretary of the Seamen's Union had already appealed for 164 men, with many other merchant mariners having had claims lodged on their behalf by the major shipping companies.[133] Sittings in the cities or larger towns regularly witnessed policemen, clerics, civil servants, medical students, seamen, railway workers, coal miners, shearers, slaughtermen or watersiders being appealed for *en bloc*.[134] Indeed, the boards immediately became suspicious of anyone from these occupations who lodged only a personal appeal, as they believed a lack of employer endorsement meant the man could not be considered essential.

Most employers based their public interest appeals on two arguments. First, that their calling was fundamental to New Zealand's wartime society and second, that previous enlistments had reduced staff to a bare minimum and made replacements impossible to find. The Minister of Police argued that maintaining 'the safety of the public in New Zealand' required the exemption of every detective and constable.[135] Similarly, the Wellington manager of the Union Steamship Company stated that the loss of any more marine engineers would compromise his fleet's ability to continue operations that were of vital economic 'importance to the Dominion'.[136] The claims made by the owners of smaller firms also concentrated on these areas. Robert Duckworth's appeal on behalf of Patrick O'Gorman, a Dunedin baker, asserted five individuals from his company had already enlisted,

70   *Willing and able to go?*

leaving him with only two men and a boy. As O'Gorman was the only bread maker, taking him would compel the closure of that side of the business, as repeated efforts to obtain additional labour had proven fruitless.[137]

An unwillingness to join the army certainly extended beyond men who held moral or political qualms, but such resistance was rarely voiced at exemption hearings in the division. There were a few appellants who candidly admitted they had no wish to serve at the front. A master painter explained his failure to attest by stating 'he did not want to go', while a wheelwright told the Spenborough Tribunal he 'did not want to go into the Army if he could help it'.[138] The clear majority of men expressed a strong desire to fight for the national cause. Some accounted for their failure to act on this impulse by reference to an existing role in the wartime economy. Benjamin Thurman told the Batley Tribunal that he was 'doing more good to the State' as a painter and decorator, while a Spenborough watchmaker maintained that he was repairing the clocks that allowed munitions workers to arrive for their shifts on time.[139] Yet a much greater proportion of men who appealed on their own behalf drew the tribunals' attention to personal domestic or business obligations. One typical argument was that raised by a licensed victualler from Dewsbury, who assured the local tribunal that 'I don't mind going tomorrow, the only thing I worry about is the business and home.'[140] Most employers were also at pains to deny any selfish motives. They were considerably more likely to justify a claim by reference to the 'patriotic' needs of Britain or its empire than were individual appellants. One manufacturer insisted that his compliment of asbestos workers 'should not be interfered with in the interests of both Army and Navy', while a mill-owner argued that conscripting his carter and flour makers would restrict the supply of food to nearby cities.[141] But even employers often included more immediate concerns in their testimony, with the *Batley News* listing the 'familiar' grounds raised by large-scale textile firms as 'diminution in staff, difficulty in maintenance of output, and the scarcity of competent labour to fill vacancies'.[142]

Similar notions were espoused in New Zealand. Years of casualty lists and exposure to wounded soldiers meant that board sittings did not witness the excitement, or the expectation of glorious adventure, that had characterised many attitudes towards military service in 1914.[143] Yet the clear majority of appellants did assert a willingness to do their bit. A small number argued they could not determine whether the desire to serve outweighed their responsibilities at home, and had appealed so the boards could decide. John Walker submitted several petitions from local settlers testifying to the great importance of his chaff cutting plant for their farming operations. Yet Walker placed himself at the board's discretion, stating 'if it were decided he should go to the front he was ready to go'.[144] Some men who claimed they had been called up incorrectly also maintained that their appeals were not derived from a reluctance to serve. Albert Denham had been balloted while still only nineteen years old and appealed so that he could volunteer rather than being conscripted.[145] Easily the largest group of appellants were those who professed a desire to serve, if only they were not being held back by their existing obligations. There were those, particularly employers and some farmers,

Willing and able to go? 71

who based their claims around the work that they were already performing for country or empire. As a freezing works operator, Harry Blackie indicated his desire to help keep the works going, while Jeremiah King opined that he 'ought to stay on the farm in the interests of the milking industry'.[146] However, for the most part, appellants focused their arguments on personal domestic, business or employment matters.[147] Andrew Johnston told the Second Otago Board that he 'recognised it was up to him to do his bit for the Empire's cause' and would have enlisted months ago but for the delicate health of his mother.[148] Similarly, William Green stated that 'if it were not for his mother's sake he would be prepared to go away', while Charles Sneddon insisted 'it was only the way [he] was situated that prevented him from going to the front before the ballot', as he worked two farms, was married, and provided for his elderly parents.[149]

When assessing the credibility of these statements, Baker's suggestion that individuals might have concealed their unwillingness to serve cannot be entirely discounted. Both the tribunals and boards made it plain that they would be vigilant in their efforts to detect 'shirking', 'the slightest hint of which was the kiss of death for an appeal'.[150] In the light of this, some men could well have exaggerated, or even invented, difficulties to obtain exemption. At Preston, Chairman Cartmell noted how certain individuals tried to misrepresent their employment circumstances in an attempt to bring themselves within the list of certified occupations, while the chairman of the First Otago Board exclaimed that 'the women of New Zealand appeared to be a very frail lot', as 'almost every statement which appellants put in had to do with invalid mothers and delicate sisters able to do very little work'.[151] The authorities occasionally discovered that an appellant was definitely guilty of giving false evidence. Herbert Murgatroyd had been granted a conditional exemption by the Pontefract Borough Tribunal on the grounds he was the sole support of his mother, to whom he gave the whole of his wages. However, he was forced to undergo a rehearing in May 1916, at which he admitted that his mother had savings she could draw on to the value of 17s. each week.[152] A comparable case from New Zealand concerned Vernon Hunt, who originally obtained a *sine die* exemption by stating that, on his brother's enlistment, he had promised to care for their aged parents and tend their mother's farm.[153] Yet Hunt was back before the board a month later, when new evidence forced him to concede that he had been working for a farmer and hardly ever assisted his parents. Pressed for the reasons behind this deceit, Hunt stated 'as my brother had gone I wished to stay at home.'[154]

A more common practice would probably have been for appellants to conceal all, or part, of their true motivation for claiming exemption in favour of grounds that the appeal bodies would be inclined to accept. A baker who did not want to go could point out that he was supplying his customers, while a farmer could highlight the importance of maintaining food production. It is striking that of the 273 New Zealand conscientious objectors who were imprisoned at the Armistice, 'about a third' had lodged appeals only on the grounds of hardship or public interest.[155] Even four of the famous 'Fourteen' objectors who were forcibly transported to the Western Front did not raise their conscientious scruples before the boards.[156]

72 *Willing and able to go?*

A final consideration is that many men never had to state their grounds of appeal, as their employer or union secretary appeared on their behalf. Some coal miners, waterside workers or merchant seamen likely held political objections to fighting in a 'capitalist' war, but never came before the tribunals or boards for them to be disclosed.[157]

Ultimately, the extent of these factors is impossible to quantify. Baker is almost certainly correct that some appellants did conceal a reluctance to go in order to give themselves a better chance of exemption, but there is no way to determine how widespread this practice was. Clearly, it is far easier to discover what men did say, rather than what they left unsaid.[158]

Nonetheless, there are compelling reasons for believing that the majority of appellants in the division were genuinely willing to serve. Appointed by the War Office to safeguard the army's interests, and to oppose doubtful claims, the military representatives would surely have been quick to report any widespread tendency towards 'shirking'. This was not the impression given by Mr. Oddy, military representative to the Ossett Tribunal, who described the 'cheery words with which those who had to appear before them often came into the room', and who regarded most eligible men as 'true sportsmen'.[159] Similarly, Colonel Mellor, military representative at Holmfirth, heartily praised the district's employers for their patriotic attitude towards releasing men to the forces.[160] Another important consideration is that large numbers of appellants did not ask for absolute exemption, but for a period of 'grace' before they were required to mobilise. One Batley appellant stated that he was 'quite willing to go when it is time, but not while there are a lot of single men at home', while a Dewsbury coal merchant said he was 'as willing to go as the first man who "listed"' and only wanted a few months in which to train a manager to look after the business in his absence.[161] A man who was prepared to be conscripted at some point was considerably less likely to have been opposed to serving than one who did not wish to go at all.

The evidence suggests that most New Zealand appellants were also legitimately asserting their willingness to go to the front. On the one hand, around 20 percent of the 13,332 man sample were not appealing for total exemption, but merely for an interlude before they were required at camp. D. W. Robson of Paeroa asked only for a chance 'to arrange my affairs', while James Bennett of Turua stated that he just wanted three months to dispose of his property.[162] As this figure is restricted to the proportion of cases where such a plea was reported by the newspapers, the true number is almost certainly higher. Indeed, appeals for time to complete farm or contract work, or to sell a business at a good price, were so common that an exasperated member of the First Wellington Board remarked 'we will have to stop the war for a few months. They all want temporary exemptions.'[163] Many appellants who argued they had been placed in the wrong class of the Second Division were also likely to have been willing to serve. By choosing to cite this ground of appeal, these individuals were spurning exemption in favour of deferring their calling until a later date. Such appellants seem to have been motivated by the notion that, while they were prepared to go, they did not feel that they should have to do so before men with fewer children.

Willing and able to go? 73

What of those New Zealand appellants who asked for total exemption? At the end of the war, the board chairmen gave a unanimous appraisal of the individuals who had appeared before them. Frederick Burgess of the First Auckland body argued that the 'great majority' of appellants had been motivated by concerns of 'real or supposed hardship', and Howell Widdowson wrote that 'almost every case' dealt with by his First Otago Board had been made 'upon what was generally supposed to be good grounds'.[164] Likewise, James Evans said that most Canterbury appellants 'decidedly were not shirkers', while Frank Hockly of the Second Auckland Board identified a common recognition that it was 'the duty of every fit man of military age to "do his bit"'.[165] Admittedly, the chairmen might have been inclined to put a positive spin on matters now that the war was won and soldiers were no longer required for the army. Their assertions are somewhat contradicted by statements from board members during sittings, when the willingness of men to go was variously described as 'a pleasant change' and 'refreshing'.[166] However, as stipendiary magistrates, king's counsel or barristers, the chairmen were individuals with a vast amount of court experience whose job focused on determining the validity of testimony. They were thus well placed to comment on the appellants' motivations. Equally important are the views of the military representatives. Major Conlan asserted that very few Auckland appellants had exaggerated or invented their circumstances, while Major Gresson believed most of the men who claimed exemption in Christchurch and South Canterbury were 'prepared to do their duty and sought no more than time in which to put their affairs in order'.[167]

The right to claim exemption produced some similar and some different responses among the two sets of prospective conscripts. Most eligible British men opted to appeal, with the division's population strongly conforming to this wider pattern. In contrast, less than one-third of all balloted New Zealanders chose to come before the boards, far fewer than has previously been claimed. Degrees of confidence in the national appeal machinery, the varied scales of conscription, the omission of Maori appellants from official statistics, New Zealand's more rural population, the relative proximity of the two countries to the Western Front and the differing financial hardships of being conscripted all offer limited explanations for this discrepancy. Of much greater importance was the protection that the British system afforded to many occupations and the hostile reception that exemption claims generated among large sections of the New Zealand public. For both nations, the historiography's overwhelming focus on conscientious objectors has obscured the fact these individuals were very few, with the clear majority of claims being based on hardship or occupational grounds. Indeed, nearly every appellant asserted a definite willingness to be conscripted, but for their existing obligations. Although the possibility that some men pragmatically concealed a reluctance to serve cannot be discounted, there is strong evidence to suggest that many of them were genuinely prepared to go to the front if only they could get away.

Between them, the administrators of conscription, the individuals responsible for evaluating appeals and the appellants compromised the key participants in the

74 *Willing and able to go?*

British and New Zealand exemption systems. They all approached their roles with numerous concerns, but also with a degree of hope for what might be achieved. Whether it was the concerns or the hopes that came to be realised would ultimately depend on how the three parties interacted with each other.

Notes

1 Ilana R. Bet-El, *Conscripts: Lost Legions of the Great War* (Phoenix Mill: Sutton, 1999), 27.
2 Adrian Gregory, *The Last Great War: British Society and the First World War* (Cambridge: Cambridge University Press, 2008), 101.
3 Robert Self, ed., *The Neville Chamberlain Diary Letters*, vol. 1, *The Making of a Politician, 1915–20* (Aldershot: Ashgate, 2000), 110.
4 H. Cartmell, *For Remembrance: An Account of Some Fateful Years* (Preston: George Toulmin and Sons, 1919), 68.
5 F. P. Armitage, *Leicester, 1914–1918: The War-Time Story of a Midland Town* (Leicester: Edgar Backus, 1933), 169; *Carmarthen Journal*, 18 Feb. 1916, 4, quoted in Barlow, "Military Tribunals in Carmarthenshire," 12; Lieut.-Col. C. À Court Repington, *The First World War, 1914–1918: Personal Experiences of Lieut.-Col. C. À Court Repington* (London: Constable, 1921), 297.
6 Michael MacDonagh, *In London During the Great War* (London: Eyre and Spottiswoode, 1935), 98–99; Minutes, Cabinet Committee on the Co-ordination of Military and Financial Effort, 10 Apr. 1916, CAB 27/4, NA.
7 Brigadier-General Sir James E. Edmonds, *Military Operations: France and Belgium, 1916: Sir Douglas Haig's Command to the 1st July: Battle of the Somme* (London: Macmillan, 1932), 152.
8 Report, Cabinet Committee on the Co-ordination of Military and Financial Effort, 13 Apr. 1916, CAB 27/4, NA.
9 William Herbert Scott, *Leeds in the Great War, 1914–1918: A Book of Remembrance* (Leeds: Leeds Libraries and Arts Committee, 1923), 316; George F. Stone and Charles Wells, eds., *Bristol and the Great War, 1914–1919* (Bristol: J. W. Arrowsmith, 1920), 116; Reginald H. Brazier and Ernest Sandford, *Birmingham and the Great War, 1914–1919* (Birmingham: Cornish Brothers, 1921), 29; *1911 Census of Great Britain*.
10 Report, "Numbers of Men due to the Army and the Number of those Remaining in Civil Life," 24 Oct. 1916, CAB 17/158, NA.
11 *Statistics of the Military Effort*, 367.
12 *WE*, 11 Mar. 1916, 3; Minutes, Huddersfield Local Tribunal, KMT 18/12/2/52/1, KA.
13 Minutes, Batley Borough Council, 22 Mar. 1916, KMT 1/2/2/15/4, KA.
14 Sitting Agendas, BLTF, RD 21/6/2, KA; *1911 Census of Great Britain*.
15 Register of Cases, Batley Local Tribunal, KMT 1, KA; Sitting Agendas, HHP, S/NUDBTW/34, KA; *1911 Census of Great Britain*.
16 Minutes, Huddersfield Local Tribunal, 3 Jan. 1917, KMT 18/12/2/52/1, KA; *1911 Census of Great Britain*.
17 Gregory, *Last Great War*, 102.
18 Widdowson to Allen, 13 Dec. 1918, AD 82 2 1/11/2, ANZ; Secretary of Third Wellington Military Service Board to Cosgrove, 6 Mar. 1918, AD 82 2 1/5/2, ANZ.
19 Gray to Earl, 25 Feb. 1918, AD 82 1 1/3, ANZ.
20 Memorandum, "Observations on Returns of 14th April, 1917," AD 1 1038 64/12, ANZ; Baker, *King and Country Call*, 106.
21 Baker, *King and Country Call*, 106; *NZH*, 19 Sep. 1918, 6.
22 Report, "Recruiting 1916–1918," 31 Mar. 1919, AD 1 712 9/169/2, ANZ.
23 Robin to Allen, 16 Jan. 1917, AD 1 769 22/151, ANZ.

Willing and able to go? 75

24 Memorandum, "Observations on Returns of 14th April, 1917," AD 1 1038 64/12, ANZ.
25 *NZH*, 19 Sep. 1918, 6.
26 Report, "Recruiting 1916–1918," 31 Mar. 1919, AD 1 712 9/169/2, ANZ.
27 Allen to Cooper, 13 Mar. 1917, AD 82 1 1/3, ANZ.
28 Evans to Gray, 9 Dec. 1918, AD 82 2 1/11/2, ANZ.
29 Paul Baker, "New Zealanders, the Great War, and Conscription" (PhD thesis, University of Auckland, 1986), Appendix 25.
30 John McQuilton, "Doing the 'Back Block Boys Some Good': The Exemption Court Hearings in North-Eastern Victoria, 1916," *Australian Historical Studies* 31, no. 115 (2000): 239; M. McKernan, *The Australian People and the Great War* (Melbourne: Nelson, 1980), 197.
31 Numerical List of Reservists, AD 25 1/1, ANZ; Report, "Recruiting 1916–1918," 31 Mar. 1919, AD 1 712 9/169/2, ANZ.
32 Granatstein and Hitsman, *Broken Promises*, 84–85.
33 Numerical List of Reservists, AD 25 1/1, ANZ; Report, "Recruiting 1916–1918," 31 Mar. 1919, AD 1 712 9/169/2, ANZ.
34 Minutes, Cabinet Committee on the Co-ordination of Military and Financial Effort, 12 Apr. 1916, CAB 27/4, NA.
35 Circular, LGB R. 113, 20 Jan. 1917 and Circular, LGB R. 114, 20 Jan. 1917, MH 47/142, NA.
36 Baker, *King and Country Call*, 147–50; *WT*, 2 May 1918, 4; *NZH*, 4 May 1918, 7.
37 Lough, 80 Parl. Deb., H.C. (5th ser.) (1916), 951; Glanville, 81 Parl. Deb., H.C. (5th ser.) (1916), 125; Morrell, 80 Parl. Deb., H.C. (5th ser.) (1916), 2211.
38 *DR*, 4 Mar. 1916, 8.
39 *W*, 25 Mar. 1916, 4; *HEx*, 24 May 1916, 2.
40 Notes, "Written by Frank T. Lockwood," 3 Apr. 1916 and Mar. 1917, Frank Lockwood Papers, Documents 5744, IWM.
41 *HEx*, 16 May 1916, 4.
42 *Round Table*, Jun. 1917, 633-34; *AG*, 28 Jun. 1918, 4.
43 *HNS*, 21 Sep. 1917, 5; *DEN*, 1 Jul. 1918, 4.
44 *PCE*, 2 Jun. 1916, 6.
45 *WT*, 28 Nov. 1917, 4.
46 Long, 81 Parl. Deb., H.C. (5th ser.) (1916), 136–39.
47 *Poverty Bay Herald* (*PBH*), 4 May 1918, 7.
48 Notes, "Calling Up of Groups and Classes," 2 Feb. 1916, AsqP, MSS Asquith 29, BodL; Dearle, *Economic Chronicle*, 72, 76, 83.
49 Report, "Recruiting 1916–1918," 31 Mar. 1919, AD 1 712 9/169/2, ANZ; Baker, "New Zealanders," Appendix 25.
50 Belich, *Paradise Reforged*, 103.
51 Numerical List of Reservists, AD 25 1/1, ANZ.
52 James Cowan, *The Maoris in the Great War: A History of the New Zealand Native Contingent and Pioneer Battalion* (Auckland: Whitcombe and Tombs, 1926), 21–22.
53 Michael King, *Te Puea: A Life*, rev. ed. (Auckland: Reed, 2004), 82–96; P. S. O'Connor, "The Recruitment of Maori Soldiers, 1914–1918," *Political Science* 19, no. 2 (1967): 74–83.
54 Report, "Recruiting 1916–1918," 31 Mar. 1919, AD 1 712 9/169/2, ANZ.
55 *NZH*, 24 Jul. 1918, 6, 25 Jul. 1918, 6, 30 Jul. 1918, 7, 6 Aug. 1918, 4, 8 Aug. 1918, 6, 10 Aug. 1918, 9 and 21 Oct. 1918, 4; Correspondence in AD 83 1 R 6/11, ANZ.
56 Peter Dewey, *British Agriculture in the First World War* (London: Routledge, 1989), 36–37; *1916 Census of New Zealand.*
57 Pennell, *A Kingdom United*, 149; Silbey, *British Working Class*, 39; Bonnie White, "Volunteerism and Early Recruitment Efforts in Devonshire, August 1914–December 1915," *Historical Journal* 52, no. 3 (2009): 641–66.
58 Baker, *King and Country Call*, 54, 242.

76 *Willing and able to go?*

59 Joanna Bourke, *Dismembering the Male: Men's Bodies, Britain and the Great War* (London: Reaktion Books, 1996) 22; David Englander, "Soldiering and Identity: Reflections on the Great War," *War in History* 1, no. 3 (1994): 314–15; Gregory, *Last Great War*, 133.

60 *P*, 17 Jun. 1915, 11; *NZH*, 21 Jul. 1915, 9.

61 Adrian Gregory, "British 'War Enthusiasm' in 1914: A Reassessment," in *Evidence, History and the Great War: Historians and the Impact of 1914–18*, ed. Gail Braybon (New York: Berghahn Books, 2003), 80–81; Stuart Halifax, "'Over by Christmas': British Popular Opinion and the Short War in 1914," *First World War Studies* 1, no. 2 (2010): 104–08; Pennell, *A Kingdom United*, 52, 144–47.

62 Nicoletta F. Gullace, *"The Blood of our Sons": Men, Women, and the Renegotiation of British Citizenship during the Great War* (New York: Palgrave Macmillan, 2002), 113.

63 Richard Holmes, *Tommy: The British Soldier on the Western Front, 1914–1918* (London: Harper Perennial, 2005), xxvi–xxvii; Harper, *Johnny Enzed*, 16.

64 *NZH*, 30 Mar. 1917, 4.

65 Report, Soldiers' Financial Assistance Board, 3 Sep. 1917, AD 82 3 2/1, ANZ.

66 *EP*, 7 Dec. 1916, 7.

67 *AS*, 16 May 1917, 7.

68 Sitting Agendas, BLTF, RD 21/6/2, KA.

69 Marjorie Levine-Clark, *Unemployment, Welfare, and Masculine Citizenship: "So Much Honest Poverty" in Britain, 1870–1930* (Houndmills: Palgrave Macmillan, 2015), 126–27.

70 David Littlewood, "The Dutifully Reluctant: New Zealanders' Appeals for Exemption from Conscription, 1916–1918," *New Zealand Journal of History* 50, no. 2 (2016): 30–32.

71 Derby to Asquith, 14 Mar. 1916, Walter Long Papers, GB 190/497, Wiltshire & Swindon History Centre, Chippenham (WSHC); Report, Director General of National Service to the War Cabinet, 3 Feb. 1917, CAB 1/23/14, NA.

72 Circular, LGB R. 36, 3 Feb. 1916, MH 47/142, NA.

73 Memorandum, "Supply of Men Available for the Army and Navy," 20 Nov. 1916, CAB 37/160/24, NA.

74 Circular, LGB R. 75, 4 Apr. 1916, Circular, LGB R. 94, 7 Jul. 1916, Circular, LGB R. 118, 1 Feb. 1917 and Circular, LGB R. 136, 23 Jun. 1917, MH 47/142, NA.

75 *Statistics of the Military Effort*, 368.

76 Gray to Military Service Board Chairmen, 12 Oct. 1917, AD 82 2 1 1/5, ANZ; "Classification of Industries, Professions, and Occupations during the War Period," *AJHR*, 1917, H43-B.

77 Wright, *Shattered Glory*, 255.

78 Russell, 175 NZ Parl. Deb., H.R. (1916), 763; *EP*, 6 Oct. 1917, 7.

79 *NZH*, 17 May 1917, 4 and 23 May 1917, 8; *Hawke's Bay Tribune* (*HBT*), 19 Jan. 1917, 2.

80 *DEN*, 16 Jan. 1917, 5; *Bay of Plenty Times*, 17 Jan. 1917, 2; *WT*, 18 Jan. 1917, 4.

81 *EP*, 29 Jan. 1918, 6; *DEN*, 6 Jun. 1918, 8; *WT*, 2 Oct. 1918, 3.

82 *WT*, 6 Nov. 1917, 7; *HNS*, 23 Apr. 1918, 4.

83 *PBH*, 8 Mar. 1917, 2.

84 *AS*, 23 Apr. 1917, 6.

85 Gullace, *Blood of Our Sons*, 101–09, 113.

86 *W*, 17 Nov. 1917, 3; *HEx*, 8 Nov. 1916, 2.

87 David Littlewood, "Personal, Local & Enduring: Masculine Citizenship in First World War Britain," in *The Citizen: Past and Present*, ed. Andrew Brown and John Griffiths (Auckland: Massey University Press, 2017), 187–88.

88 *CVG*, 3 Mar. 1916, 4.

89 *WE*, 26 Feb. 1916, 6; *PCE*, 10 Mar. 1916, 6; *BN*, 6 May 1916, 8.

90 McDermott, *British Military Service Tribunals*, 1.

91 Minutes, Middlesex Appeal Tribunal, 21 Nov. 1918, MH 47/5, NA.

92 McDermott, *British Military Service Tribunals*, 40.
93 James G. M. Cranstoun, "The Impact of the Great War on a Local Community: The Case of East Lothian" (PhD thesis, Open University, 1992), 117; Mike Fraser, *"Does My Country Really Need Me?": The Work of the Berwick-upon-Tweed Military Service Tribunal* (Berwick-upon-Tweed: Blue Button, 2015), 47; Keith Grieves, "Military Tribunal Papers: The Case of Leek Local Tribunal in the First World War," *Archives: The Journal of the British Record Association* 16, no. 70 (1983): 146; Christine Housden, "Researching Kingston's Military Tribunal, 1916–1918," *Occasional Papers in Local History* 2 (2004): 6; Levine-Clark, *Unemployment*, 127; Paul Rusiecki, *The Impact of Catastrophe: The People of Essex and the First World War (1914–1920)* (Chelmsford: Essex Record Office, 2008), 97.
94 Slocombe, "Recruitment," 111; Spinks, "War Courts," 214; Philip Spinks, "First World War Conscientious Objection in South Warwickshire," *Local Historian* 42, no. 4 (2012): 286.
95 Mein, Wares and Mann, *St Albans*, 47.
96 Mitchinson, *Saddleworth*, 66.
97 Sitting Agendas, BLTF, RD 21/6/2, KA.
98 Pearce, *Comrades in Conscience*, 15, 138.
99 Ibid., 143; Rae, *Conscience and Politics*, 71.
100 "Defence Forces of New Zealand," *AJHR*, 1918, H-19, 15; "Defence Forces of New Zealand," *AJHR*, 1919, H-19, 15.
101 *EP*, 7 Dec. 1916, 7.
102 *NZH*, 8 Aug. 1918, 6.
103 Wally Seccombe, "Patriarchy Stabilized: The Construction of the Male Breadwinner Norm in Nineteenth-Century Britain," *Social History* 11, no. 1 (1986): 54; John Tosh, *A Man's Place: Masculinity and the Middle-Class Home in Victorian England* (New Haven: Yale University Press, 1999), 1–2.
104 *BN*, 19 Jan. 1918, 1.
105 *BC*, 4 Mar. 1916, 1.
106 *GT*, 12 May 1916, 4.
107 *PCE*, 21 Jul. 1916, 5 and 14 Jul. 1916, 3.
108 *BC*, 3 Jun. 1916, 6.
109 Ibid., 22 Jul. 1916, 6; *BN*, 1 Jul. 1916, 3.
110 Simmonds, *Britain and World War One*, 3.
111 *BC*, 4 Mar. 1916, 1; Howden Clough Collieries to Gray, 9 Mar. 1916, BLTF, RD 21/6/2, KA.
112 *PCE*, 21 Jul. 1916, 5.
113 *GT*, 15 Sep. 1916, 3.
114 *WE*, 5 Aug. 1916, 7; *HEx*, 11 Jan. 1917, 3.
115 Yielding to Gray, 28 Feb. 1916, BLTF, RD 21/6/2, KA; *BC*, 8 Apr. 1916, 1.
116 *EP*, 29 Dec. 1916, 3; *AS*, 20 Feb. 1917, 6.
117 *NZH*, 2 May 1918, 2.
118 Melanie Nolan, *Breadwinning: New Zealand Women and the State* (Christchurch: Canterbury University Press, 2000), 13.
119 *NZH*, 4 Dec. 1917, 6.
120 *Manawatu Evening Standard* (*MES*), 14 Mar. 1918, 3; *EP*, 18 May 1918, 7; *WDT*, 14 Aug. 1918, 5.
121 *EP*, 3 Jul. 1918, 7.
122 *AS*, 26 Jun. 1917, 3.
123 *NZH*, 10 Jan. 1918, 4.
124 *Rodney and Otamatea Times, Waitemata and Kaipara Gazette* (*ROT*), 21 Mar. 1917, 5.
125 *ODT*, 7 Feb. 1917, 6.
126 *WT*, 21 Dec. 1916, 4; *HBT*, 30 Jul. 1917, 6.
127 *WC*, 30 Oct. 1917, 4.

78 *Willing and able to go?*

128 *NZH*, 13 Jan. 1917, 8; *AS*, 23 Feb. 1917, 6.
129 *EP*, 23 Nov. 1916, 8; *WC*, 24 Oct. 1918, 5.
130 *EP*, 8 Feb. 1917, 8.
131 Allen to Marment, 4 Dec. 1916, AD 1 1046 66/8, ANZ.
132 Gwen A. Parsons, "The Christchurch Community at War 1914–1918: Society, Discourse and Power" (master's thesis, University of Canterbury, 2003), 104.
133 *AS*, 2 May 1917, 4.
134 *Grey River Argus* (*GRA*), 3 May 1917, 4; *EP*, 10 May 1917, 8 and 4 Jul. 1918, 7; M. J. Kelly, *Military Board Appeals: Otago Witness, Dec 1916 to Feb 1917* (Auckland: Old News Publications, 1993), 47–48.
135 *WC*, 4 Dec. 1916, 4.
136 *EP*, 18 Apr. 1917, 8.
137 *ODT*, 2 Feb. 1917, 3.
138 *GT*, 14 Jul. 1916, 7; *Cleckheaton & Spenborough Guardian* (*CSG*), 5 Oct. 1917, 3.
139 *BN*, 30 Sep. 1916, 5; *CSG*, 24 Mar. 1917, 3.
140 *BN*, 22 Jul. 1916, 6.
141 *CSG*, 24 Mar. 1917, 3; *GT*, 7 Apr. 1916, 5.
142 *BN*, 15 Apr. 1916, 1.
143 Harper, *Johnny Enzed*, 19–27.
144 *WT*, 15 Mar. 1917, 5.
145 *EP*, 14 May 1917, 7.
146 *WC*, 15 Jun. 1918, 4; *Taranaki Herald* (*TH*), 20 Dec. 1916, 4.
147 Parsons, "Many Derelicts," 41.
148 *ODT*, 21 Mar. 1917, 7.
149 *AS*, 23 May 1917, 6; *WC*, 21 May 1917, 4.
150 Baker, *King and Country Call*, 106.
151 Cartmell, *For Remembrance*, 70–71; *EP*, 13 Jun. 1917, 8.
152 *PCE*, 26 May 1916, 2.
153 *WDT*, 10 Jan. 1917, 5.
154 *MES*, 1 Mar. 1917, 6.
155 Tate to Director of Personnel Services, 27 Feb. 1918, AD 1 733 10/407/3, ANZ.
156 Draft, Statement to be made by Allen, 28 Feb. 1918, AD 1 733 10/407/3, ANZ.
157 Cyril Pearce and Helen Durham, "Patterns of Dissent in Britain during the First World War," *War & Society* 34, no. 2 (2015): 144.
158 Loveridge, *Calls to Arms*, 52–53.
159 *OO*, 16 Mar. 1918, 3.
160 *HE*, 17 Jun. 1916, 5.
161 *BN*, 10 Jun. 1916, 1, 5.
162 *OG*, 10 Jan. 1917, 2 and 21 Feb. 1917, 2.
163 *EP*, 27 Dec. 1916, 7.
164 Burgess to Gray, 5 Dec. 1918 and Widdowson to Allen, 13 Dec. 1918, AD 82 2 1/11/2, ANZ.
165 *Marlborough Express* (*ME*), 20 Dec. 1918, 3; Hockly to Allen, 9 Jan. 1919, AD 82 2 1/11/2, ANZ.
166 *EP*, 4 Dec. 1917, 8; *HNS*, 17 Mar. 1917, 5.
167 *NZH*, 4 May 1918, 8; Gresson to Gray, 19 Mar. 1919, AD 1 1046 66/57, ANZ.

4 Autonomy or compliance?

During conscription, the tribunals and boards worked alongside several different agencies. Both were subject to official instructions and had attached military representatives. In addition, the British system contained advisory committees and higher appeal bodies, and afforded government departments the power to grant exemptions, while New Zealand witnessed the establishment of a National Efficiency Board (NEB) and large numbers of local trustee boards in early 1917. The participation of these other actors was designed to facilitate a division of labour. Rather than investigating claims from the beginning, the tribunals and boards would instead be presented with all the relevant facts at appeal hearings, thereby allowing them to concentrate on reaching the 'correct' decisions. However, what sounded an ideal arrangement in theory also created the prospect of friction and dispute. Each of the agencies would expect to have their say, and none of them were likely to remain passive if they felt their views were being ignored.

The British exemption system came under considerable pressure from an early stage. Although some government ministers believed the Military Service Act would automatically provide enough men to meet the army's demands, it actually served to hinder that aim. Compulsion brought voluntary recruitment to an end, while the availability of single attestees and conscripts failed to compensate for the fact married men were not yet being summoned.[1] The immediate shortfall was further enhanced by exemptions. Under the Derby Scheme, men in reserved or 'starred' occupations had been immune from service, whereas individuals whose callings appeared on the list of certified occupations under conscription were not protected until they made an appeal. The strains placed on domestic and business arrangements by calling up all the single 'groups' and 'classes' within two months also prompted a vast number of hardship claims.[2]

As most of these initial cases concerned men who were entitled to relief, the rate of success was extremely high. Between January and March 1916, 189,918 attested men were obtained for the army, against 829,667 who were postponed, badged or found to be in certified occupations. The situation concerning their unattested counterparts was no better. During April, 25,941 of these individuals joined the forces, but another 158,338 received exemptions.[3] In desperation, the government ordered the calling up of all the attested married 'groups' between 7 April

80   *Autonomy or compliance?*

and 13 June, only to be confronted with yet more exemptions, along with the anger of men who argued it was palpably unfair for them to be summoned before those who had refused to signify their willingness to serve.[4] A sense of betrayal was also apparent among the army's generals, who maintained that the government's half-hearted introduction of conscription, and the over-sentimentality of the tribunals, was holding back the men necessary for the sixty-seven-division force they had been promised.[5]

These complaints had significant repercussions for the exemption system. In May 1916, the Military Service Act (Session 2) extended conscription to all married men aged between eighteen and forty-one, and permitted the tribunals to stipulate that any period of exemption would be 'final', i.e. there could be no application for renewal.[6] Long used the passage of this legislation to provide the appeal bodies with further guidance. He insisted that food supplies should be preserved by retaining crucial agricultural workers, that other essential home industries 'should not be materially impaired', and that sole heads of business should be not taken if it would lead to their concern being closed. However, the import of these statements was reduced by several qualifiers, which indicated they should not be regarded as definite rules.[7] Changes were also made to the list of certified occupations. Several callings were removed entirely, while the protection afforded by employment in many of those that remained became subject to age limits. Upon losing his certified status, a man's occupational exemption was automatically cancelled.[8]

When these measures failed to solve the recruiting shortage, additional pressure was brought to bear on the tribunals. All the married 'classes' were called up in June 1916, but any manpower gains were more than offset by the disastrous losses sustained during the Battle of the Somme. With another major offensive planned, the Army Council calculated it would require 940,000 men for the first nine months of 1917, at a time when the British Army on the Western Front numbered around 1.5 million, and its overall strength was around 3.3 million.[9] Meeting this target would require a significant improvement on the previous twelve months where only 809,272 recruits had been obtained.[10] To co-ordinate labour allocation so that more men could be released, the government first established a Man-Power Distribution Board, and then a Department of National Service. Neither of these measures proved successful, but they did have some important ramifications for the exemption system. The first was the introduction of the Trade Card Scheme, intended to halt a groundswell of industrial unrest, which empowered certain trade unions to grant exemptions to their members.[11]

The second was several instructions that more closely defined the certified occupations, and that urged the release of younger men in the higher medical categories, subject to their being replaced by older or lower category substitutes.[12] On 1 December 1916, the LGB informed the tribunals that all category A ('general service') men under twenty-six would be 'of more value to the country with the Forces than … in civil employment', unless they were employed in a certified occupation or were 'irreplaceable' to other work of national importance.[13] This formula was extended one month later to include category A and B1 men up to the

Autonomy or compliance? 81

age of thirty-one.[14] Finally, in March 1917, the tribunals were ordered to review the certificates of all men under thirty-one outside the certified trades, and not to grant a renewal unless there were 'strong reasons which make the case clearly exceptional'.[15] The only industry excluded from these directives was agriculture, where concerns over the nation's ability to feed itself led to a virtual moratorium on recruitment between October 1916 and 1 January 1917, extended to 1 April for those engaged in milk production. However, the tribunals were still permitted to dismiss the appeals of young men for whom substitutes were available, and, in late January 1917, the War Cabinet determined that thirty thousand 'general service' men should be taken from the land.[16]

This 'combing-out' of available manpower underpinned most government initiatives for the remainder of 1917. Only agriculture was again afforded special treatment. From 24 July, county agricultural executive committees were permitted to issue protection vouchers to any man who had been working the land since 31 March. These documents automatically made their recipients immune from call-up, with the tribunals' jurisdiction being limited to those few individuals whose retention was deemed to not be in the national interest.[17] Elsewhere, the emphasis remained on getting as many recruits as possible. In April, the Military Service (Review of Exceptions) Act allowed the Army Council to order men who had previously been rejected or discharged on medical grounds to attend a re-examination. If passed fit for service they became eligible for call up, but with a right of appeal to the tribunals.[18] The following month, the Military Service (Convention with Allied States) Act provided for the conscription of Allied citizens living in Britain. Beyond these legislative enactments, the government continued targeting men who had previously been granted exemption. To rationalise the use of labour in essential war work, the system of badging was abolished and replaced by a schedule of protected occupations. Only individuals fulfilling vital munitions requirements, or who were engaged in shipping or on the railways, would be eligible for new scheduled occupations certificates, or protection certificates issued by Munitions Area Recruiting Officers (MARO).[19] There were also significant cuts to the list of certified occupations and continued requests for the tribunals to adopt a 'strict standard' when reviewing exemptions.[20]

After these initiatives proved no more successful than their predecessors, government policy underwent a significant change. Whereas the military had demanded 940,000 soldiers for 1917, most of whom were to be category A, the 'comb-outs' and deluge of instructions to the tribunals only obtained 820,646 men of all classifications.[21] Angered by these statistics, the generals again put forward heavy demands for the coming year. However, the government, its faith shaken by the losses sustained during the Third Ypres Campaign, and aware that the nation's manpower reserves had reached critical levels, determined military needs should no longer take precedence.[22] In November 1917, control over recruitment passed to the new Ministry of National Service under Auckland Geddes. Tasked with controlling manpower allocation in its entirety, Geddes concluded that the army should have no greater priority than food production, shipbuilding or munitions, and that the haphazard 'comb-out' approach should be replaced by a more

82   *Autonomy or compliance?*

systematic 'clean-cut'.[23] To this end, the Military Service Act, 1918, passed in February, allowed for the cancellation of any exemption granted on occupational grounds without reference to the tribunals.[24] Having chosen not to use these new powers at first, the government obtained sufficient recruits by making sweeping cuts to the list of certified occupations, and by placing tighter age limits on the schedule of protected occupations.[25]

This promising situation was undone by the initial success of the German Spring Offensive. As repeated blows threatened a complete collapse of the British front, emergency measures brought the army back to the top of the manpower agenda. On 20 April 1918, a royal proclamation cancelled all occupational and hardship certificates held by men under twenty-three who were in medical grades I and II, or categories A, B1 and C1, except in agriculture, where only 'general service' men were included.[26] A few days later, a Ministry of National Service order withdrew the right to occupational exemption from all fit individuals in certain industries, and 'general service' men below specified ages in others.[27] Believing even such a strong use of its existing powers was insufficient, the government also secured the passage of the Military Service (No. 2) Act, 1918, which increased the military age to fifty-one. Accompanying instructions stipulated that occupational or hardship exemptions could no longer be granted for more than six months, and implored the tribunals to recognise 'the need for men ... is now greater than ever, and the standard must therefore be stricter than ever.'[28] This flurry of activity came to a close on 22 June, after a second royal proclamation withdrew all the certificates held by grade I and II eighteen-year-olds, and a second decertification order the occupational exemptions of men below certain ages in a further set of non-essential callings.[29]

The war's final months witnessed only a partial reduction in pressure on the tribunals. There was no more legislation or 'clean-cuts', while in September the list of certified occupations was largely restored to its January 1918 extent.[30] Government instructions reduced in number and those that were issued tended to encourage a slight relaxation of standards. From 11 June, the power to exempt many classes of farm workers on occupational grounds was transferred from the tribunals to the county executive committees, with this being extended to all agricultural cases in September.[31] Nevertheless, the appeal bodies were still asked to review the certificates of non-essential men, to process cases as rapidly as possible, and to secure for the army any individual who failed to make a strong claim to exemption.[32]

In contrast, reinforcement of the New Zealand Expeditionary Force declined during conscription. After June 1917, when the rate peaked at 15 percent, or approximately 2,200 men per month, several factors prompted a re-assessment of the dominion's commitments.[33] The first was the imminent balloting of the Second Division, an event that would increase expenditure on separation allowances, disrupt family units and potentially cause unrest among men who were asked to leave their wives and children.[34] A second was the growing 'reductionist' movement. Although divided over its precise aims, this body of opinion argued the costs of the war effort had become unjustified. Not only was New Zealand

Autonomy or compliance? 83

reinforcing at a relatively high rate, but the United States' entry into the conflict meant the Allies could also call on millions of additional troops.[35] The final issue was a fear that current obligations would see the country run out of men, forcing it into the embarrassing position of having to break up the New Zealand Division.[36]

These considerations acted as a strong incentive to reduce reinforcement. Allen approached the Army Council in July 1917 and negotiated a decrease to 12 percent.[37] Yet this proved insufficient to halt the rise of 'reductionism', particularly when news of the losses sustained during Third Ypres arrived. In December, further pressure led to the rate being slashed to 6.5 percent, or 1,000 men per month. While the retreats forced on the British Army in March and April 1918 prompted a reluctant decision to raise reinforcement back to 13 percent, it was scaled down to 6.5 percent again as soon as the German advance petered out.[38] These various reductions had a significant impact, with New Zealand sending only 12,995 men in 1918, compared to 26,022 the previous year.[39]

The government's policy of curtailing reinforcement meant the boards came under relatively little pressure to obtain recruits. Not one piece of legislation or regulation extended the scope of conscription, or reduced the grounds for, or the validity of, certain appeals. Indeed, the only substantive change to the Military Service Act was an effort to make the conditions of exemption more acceptable to conscientious objectors. The boards also received few instructions urging them to dismiss appeals. Their initial activities were subject to an ambiguous and rarely stated intimation that men were more important than production.[40] However, several directives that called for more exemptions to be granted swiftly contradicted this philosophy. Thereafter, the boards were told to adopt strict standards on only two occasions. The first was in July 1917, with instructions to review all *sine die* exemptions granted to First Division reservists in essential industries, and to award further time only where an individual was irreplaceable.[41] Although this measure was designed to reduce the number of exemptions, its import was mitigated by the fact the boards would have been unlikely to grant relief in the first place if a man could be spared. The other instance of pressure was during the German Spring Offensive, when the boards were asked to reconsider all *sine die* exemptions and to rehear cases where men had been given periods of leave before they were required in camp. This was the one point where the appeal bodies were decisively told that the needs of the army should override all other considerations.[42] Nonetheless, by May the government was stating no more *sine die* men could be taken without significant economic disruption, and in June the boards were informed their new priority was to maintain production 'as near as possible at present standard' to enable the dominion to meet its growing war expenditure.[43]

Although the boards were subject to few demands for soldiers, this did not mean the government granted them a free hand. Instead, the executive took numerous steps to secure the exemption of certain occupational groups. Allen had gained the Catholic Church's acquiescence to conscription by promising that its priests, teachers and theological students would receive ministerial certificates recommending their exemption, and a subsequent misunderstanding had given the impression that the boards were obligated to accept these documents.[44]

84 *Autonomy or compliance?*

This prompted fury among the Catholic hierarchy when the Third Wellington Board dismissed the appeals of two theological students on 16 February 1917. Accused of deception, Allen insisted the qualifier in the regulation, to grant exemption unless they saw 'good reason to the contrary', permitted the boards to reject a certificate.[45] Rather than accepting this explanation, the bishops viewed it as an incitement for other bodies to follow suit, a charge given added weight by the dismissal of two more students' appeals by the First Otago Board in March.[46]

Allen was now caught at a crossroads. Had he been committed to preserving the boards' independence, he would have continued to defend their right to overrule certificates. Instead, he endeavoured to have the decisions reversed. Mobilisation of the students was postponed so the Solicitor General could draft regulations to establish the Final Appeal Board with authority to overturn verdicts. The Recruiting Board then approached the cabinet for approval to proceed, only to be rebuffed.[47] Allen's next move was to arrange a conference with the board chairmen to bring their 'decisions into line'.[48] On 27 April 1917, it was agreed that future procedure would be to grant *sine die* exemptions to all clergymen, all religious teachers whose schools would close in their absence and all theological students who were in the final four years of training.[49]

Yet the crisis did not end here. When awarding *sine die* exemptions, several boards signalled their intention to review these decisions before the calling up of the Second Division. By June 1917, the imminence of this re-assessment raised fears that more Catholic appeals might be dismissed, a concern given added impetus when another conference, including all the boards' members rather than just their chairmen, failed to ratify the April agreement.[50] The government now decided that definite measures were required. The Expeditionary Forces Amendment Bill would have provided for the statutory exemption of ministers, men in holy orders and all teachers, but was rejected by the Legislative Council. With this failure, the government reverted back to directing the boards. In November 1917, a conference with their chairmen resulted in an agreement to 'co-ordinate New Zealand with Imperial practice' by granting *sine die* exemptions to all ministers and members of holy or religious orders. While the meeting again failed to define a policy over theological students, the chairmen did consent to suspend the hearings of these individuals after being informed that not one of their number had yet been required to mobilise.[51] The final acts in the Catholic exemption question came in May and August 1918, when the First and Second Wellington boards dismissed appeals from six more theological students.[52] In response, the Recruiting Board simply determined the men would not be taken into camp.

Alongside the government's attempts to enforce the exemption of Catholic clergymen were its instructions regarding essential industries. A crucial move came during February 1917, when the NEB was constituted to help develop policies for the maintenance of production. In June, the government approved a classification prepared by the NEB that divided industries into 'most essential', 'essential', 'partially essential' and 'non-essential'. This measure was taken further three months later, by grading the significance of different positions within each occupation.[53] These classifications were sent to the boards for their

Autonomy or compliance? 85

'guidance'. However, in practice, the government insisted 'appeals should be considered strictly in accordance' with them.[54] The NEB also conducted a constant review of the ability of industries to release men. Its findings were submitted to the government, which forwarded them on to the boards with instructions to implement any necessary changes in their approach.

The government also persisted in its efforts to protect the 'strategic unions'. Having directed the boards to exempt any seaman with twelve months' experience and all *bona fide* slaughtermen, the executive left these instructions in place for the remainder of conscription. Its only intervention came during January 1918, when the Second Wellington Board dismissed the appeals of several slaughtermen. Allen sent a letter stating that official policy had not changed and that the men's union had been promised its members would be exempted. The board was ordered to rehear the appeals, with a firm intimation it was expected to 'give effect to the Government's policy'.[55]

Official direction over coal miners was more pro-active. During February 1917, Allen learned that a recent downturn in output was due to a co-ordinated 'go-slow' action. He wanted miners exempted to ensure adequate production, but could hardly justify their retention if they were not working to capacity. Proceeding with caution, Allen instructed the boards to warn the men that a failure to increase output would forfeit their exemptions.[56] This game of brinkmanship continued until 24 April, when the crisis was apparently ended by an agreement that saw all of the unions end their 'go-slow'. However, two days later, miners at Runanga and Paparoa struck again over local economic issues. Feeling he had been duped, Allen directed the First Canterbury Board to dismiss the appeals of all the men involved.[57] While this was a decisive action, it was one that Allen, fearing a renewed coal shortage, quickly regretted. The board was first told to halt the dismissal of men who had not been balloted at the time of the second strikes, and then to stop refusing cases altogether. In addition, the appeal body was informed that men who had their claims turned down would be allowed to return to the pits as 'soldier–miners'.[58] At this point the government's involvement largely ended. The only exception was an extension of the 'soldier–miner' provision to reservists whose cases were dismissed for low productivity. By September 1918 there were around one hundred 'soldier–miners', a situation the Recruiting Board justified by stating it did 'not want to precipitate a coal crisis and would prefer to wink at evasions within limits'.[59]

The greatest volume of official direction concerned men who were working the land. During the early months of conscription, the government came under attack over the boards' allegedly harsh treatment of these cases, with several organisations demanding the automatic exemption of all farmers.[60] To stave off this criticism, Allen pressured the boards to act 'much more circumspectly'.[61] On 16 March 1917, they were informed that it was no part of official policy to force men to give up their holdings; if there was any question over an individual's ability to obtain labour then he should be exempted.[62] The government also gave its sanction to the establishment of local trustee boards consisting of three farmers or businessmen. Over the next few months, the appeal bodies were told that all

86   *Autonomy or compliance?*

doubtful cases, particularly those concerning the 'last man' on a farm, should be referred to the trustees for a report.[63]

These measures did not prevent the government coming under fire over the supposed willingness of several boards to flout its directives. Allen dispatched a new memorandum on 12 October stating that

> in no case should the man who is doing the whole of the work on his own farm, or the last son on the farm of parents who are unable ... to do the work themselves, or skilled agricultural labourers, be taken for military service, unless, with respect to the last named, efficient labour is available to replace them.[64]

A literal reading of this instruction would have required the exemption of the first two categories of men regardless of the circumstances. However, the government quickly confirmed that, while the need to retain 'last men' and keep up production should be adhered to, the boards should still investigate each case to prevent deliberate 'shirking'.[65] Except for the change during the German Spring Offensive, this was the approach advocated in all future directives.

The East Central Division's tribunals were largely receptive to instructions urging them to refuse the appeals of young single men in the higher medical categories. As early as April 1916, the Spenborough Tribunal required an employer to release one of his two coal carters, both of whom were under thirty, because 'we keep getting instructions to tighten up with regard to the single men'.[66] A few months later, the Heckmondwike body maintained that the military's need for unmarried individuals meant it had no option but to reject the plea of a fruit-and-fish salesman, even if it meant the closure of his business.[67] As government pressure increased, so did the number of cases in which its instructions were cited. In March 1917, the Batley Tribunal refused to renew the certificate of the only man capable of driving a company's lorry, after being directed not to exempt twenty-five-year-olds, and then rejected a plea for two electrical engineers due to the 'urgent demand for men under 31'.[68] When the manager of a local co-operative society appeared before the ECAT to argue 67 out of his 118 eligible employees had already gone to the front, all five of his appeals were rejected upon the chairman stating 'we are asked to send all men under 31'.[69] A similarly definitive acceptance of official policy came at Wakefield Borough, where the chairman asserted 'all "A" men must serve and ... there was no way of any of them getting off'.[70]

Most tribunals were willing to adopt more rigorous criteria generally. After twice being called together by the military hierarchy to learn of the army's urgent requirements, many appeal bodies used their next sitting to advertise an intention to tighten up. Typical in this regard was the Birstall Tribunal, whose chairman affirmed that 'everything possible should be done to assist the military in obtaining sufficient men'.[71] The tribunals also displayed little resistance to reviewing exemptions, with this often being carried out as soon as the instructions were received. Indeed, many of the statements referring to the need to grant fewer

Autonomy or compliance? 87

claims were made while these re-appraisals were taking place. The strongest evidence of the appeal bodies' compliance is in the attitudes of the military representatives. Had there been any perceived laxity, these individuals would surely have protested during sittings and referred many decisions to the appeal tribunal. Yet the division's representatives were usually satisfied. Some verdicts were questioned and criticised, but there were few instances of a more general discontent. Similarly, while cases were taken to the ECAT individually or in small groups, there were none of the mass appeals against local exemptions that have been identified elsewhere in Britain.[72] Comprehensive statistics on the matter are no longer extant, but of the 338 verdicts delivered by the Marsden Tribunal in 1917, the military representative challenged only ten.[73]

Nonetheless, some tribunals did resist instructions that were perceived as threatening local interests. One such instance concerned the removal of fettlers from the list of certified occupations. Compelled to regard these men as being less entitled to relief, the tribunals operating in the division's textile-dominated districts asserted that fettling work was too heavy for women, and that efficient running of the mills necessitated the retention of trained personnel. Rather than carrying out their instructions, the appeal bodies instead played for time by granting adjournments or temporary exemptions so that a deputation, including several tribunal members, could attend the Reserved Occupations Committee to request that fettling be recertified. While it is unclear how much influence these approaches had, the occupation was restored to the protected list the following month.[74] A more prolonged opposition to government policy came from the farmers sitting on the Barnsley Rural Tribunal. When the military representative read out instructions stating that single reservists under twenty-five should not be granted exemption, a member moved that the needs of the district required all farmers and farm labourers to be retained during the harvest. Although this proposal was narrowly defeated, the objections revolved around its likely ineffectiveness rather than its justification, and the very next case saw an eighteen-year-old farmer's son given exemption for three months. Thereafter, the members continued to grant appeals from single agricultural workers under twenty-five whenever they thought the productivity of a holding required it.[75] A further occurrence of dissent involved the Goole Urban and Rural tribunals. In late 1916, the military representative criticised these bodies over the fact their exemption rates were nearly double that of any other appeal body in the region. This intervention failed to achieve the desired results. At Goole Urban, it was rebuffed when a member stated his 'conscience did not prick him' as 'he only voted for exemption where he considered it was deserved'. In a more detailed defence of their record, the Rural Tribunal members noted theirs was an agricultural district and one that required an unusually large labour force due to the prevalence of potato growing. As taking more men would doom the harvest and necessitate a drastic change in their policies, the Goole Rural Tribunal resolved to 'abide by their previous decisions'.[76]

Such direct resistance was exceptional, but many tribunals were inclined to protest three other limitations on their autonomy. The first was that some eligible men were placed outside their jurisdiction by being badged or otherwise

88 *Autonomy or compliance?*

protected by government departments. A second was the way their dismissal of certain cases was subsequently annulled. This occurred when government departments awarded exemption to workers they did not want to lose, when individuals obtained work in protected occupations after their cases had been rejected, or when the military authorities failed to call up refused men. The final source of resentment was the appeal tribunal's ability to overturn any local verdict. This sometimes concerned the exemption of men whose cases had been dismissed, but more commonly resulted from the ECAT's acceptance of a military representative's application for a certificate to be revoked. Although comprehensive figures are no longer extant, the appeal tribunal was quite prepared to exercise its amending powers. During conscription, there were fifty-six appeals against verdicts reached by the Marsden Tribunal, with the ECAT choosing to overturn nineteen of these.[77] Moreover, the ECAT's chairman responded to another local tribunal's displeasure at having its decisions varied by arguing it would be 'completely ridiculous' for his body to render itself nothing more than an 'automaton or a registering machine', as its role was to 'rectify mistakes' made at a local level.[78]

Some of the unrest generated by these practices stemmed from the restrictions they placed on the local tribunals' power to determine cases finally. While the exemption system clearly allowed for decisions to be overturned, certain appeal bodies perceived this as a challenge to their position as judicial authorities. On learning that a young eligible whose claim they had dismissed was still at large, the Holmfirth Tribunal wrote a letter of protest to the local recruiting officer, with one member stating that if the man was not called up 'he would move that the Tribunal go on strike'.[79] A similar impasse occurred at Horbury, after it was discovered that the local MARO had awarded protection certificates to three men whose exemptions had been withdrawn. Expressing their 'indignation' at being overruled, the members resolved to not adjudicate on any further cases until a reasonable justification came to hand.[80] Local tribunals also criticised the 'autocratic' attitude of the ECAT and the way their verdicts were 'constantly rudely over-ridden' by that body.[81] Being undermined was galling enough in itself, but the members pointed out that attending seemingly fruitless sittings required the neglect of their own businesses. When the Birkenshaw Tribunal was informed that the dismissal of two appeals had been nullified by the Ministry of Munitions, several members suggested their efforts were being turned into a 'waste of time' and that they could better spend their energies elsewhere. After resolving to adjourn until a 'satisfactory' justification was received, no more cases were heard at Birkenshaw for six months, the longest strike action undertaken in the division.[82] The members' outside responsibilities also increased their sensitivity in another way. Being community leaders, employers and union secretaries, these were individuals who were used to having their decisions respected. When verdicts were upset, therefore, the members were variously 'staggered', 'disbelieving' and 'disgusted', a 'humiliating' feeling of novelty that must surely have contributed to their discontent.[83]

Yet the local tribunals' protests often went beyond questions of authority. When criticising the protection afforded by government departments, members argued it was palpably wrong for them to be instructed to send eligible men who had major

Autonomy or compliance? 89

domestic or financial responsibilities, while others who were better able to go were being held back. The Goole Urban Tribunal objected when a local shipyard replaced some of its overage staff with workers brought down from Scotland, who then received exemptions from the Admiralty. Councillor Hill argued this was doubly unfair. Long-serving locals were being thrown out of employment and the Scottish men who were 'coming in and escaping' were young and single at a time when the tribunal was being urged to refuse married business owners.[84] More direct action was taken by the Heckmondwike body, which granted exemption to a forty-year-old weft scourer with four children specifically to protest at being required to take individuals like him while youths of eighteen were being issued with protection certificates.[85]

The tribunal members' anger was often stoked by witnessing injustices at first hand. When lambasting the undue retention of munitions workers, a member of the Wakefield Borough Tribunal recounted having 'four fine young fellows sitting in front of me in church', while Sir William Raynor of the Huddersfield body was motivated by seeing several young men from a local chemical works 'walking about the town'.[86] The most vigorous dissent was that mounted by Councillor Haigh of the New Mill Tribunal. In January 1917, he determined the holding back of single men had become so inequitable that he had no choice but to vote for the exemption of every married appellant.[87] After consistently carrying out this policy, Haigh brought matters to a head in July 1918 by moving the adjournment of sittings until several refused individuals who had 'walked past him' in the street were called up. Failing to gain the support of his colleagues, Haigh informed the tribunal clerk 'that he had no need to summon him to any further meeting' and stormed out of the building.[88] This was certainly one of the more extreme expressions of disgruntlement, but there was a notable increase in protests over the protection of young single men after the military age was raised to fifty-one.[89]

Local tribunals also baulked when the other actors in the exemption system appeared to threaten the local economy. Members often remonstrated at being required to take the best workers from industries under their jurisdiction, when at the same time firms enjoying official protection could keep whomever they pleased. In June 1917, the Whitwood Tribunal protested over having to strip all but the older and less able men from local farms, while thousands of fit individuals were carrying out menial jobs in mines or 'making "Johnny Walker" whisky bottles'.[90] Correspondingly, several New Mill members argued the retention of single young men in government offices was forcing them to jeopardise the production of local farms by leaving only the 'riff-raff' behind.[91] At Castleford, the chief complaint was that the tribunal's stricter policies were crippling long-established businesses, and yet vast numbers of non-essential individuals were still at large because the government did not wish to antagonise their trade unions.[92]

Despite being residents of the division, the ECAT's members could also be branded as unsympathetic 'outsiders'. After learning that the appeal tribunal had overturned several of their decisions, the Hemsworth Rural body claimed they 'knew the local circumstances better than any other' and passed a resolution urging that only a local tribunal should deal with local cases.[93] At Marsden, the

90   *Autonomy or compliance?*

ECAT was rebuked for cancelling the certificate of a beamer whom the local body considered essential to the woollen trade. The members argued they were trying to protect what they knew to be the requirements of the district, only to have these efforts set at naught by men who did not understand the circumstances.[94]

A final motivation behind the local tribunals' unrest was the positions their members held in the community. Being predominantly elected councillors, these were individuals who would have been deeply concerned with public perceptions of the exemption system. Indeed, the members came to believe that any injustices done to local men, or any damage done to the local economy, by other agencies could adversely affect their own standing by association. Some bemoaned that having decisions overturned was making them look 'rather ridiculous' or 'foolish', or even turning them into a 'laughing stock'.[95] Yet a more regularly expressed fear was the level of discontent certain actions generated. At Spenborough, the tribunal chairman asserted a failure to call up refused single men had caused 'great dissatisfaction locally', with another member lamenting that 'the public judged them' when they saw young eligibles remaining at home at the expense of married men over forty.[96] Equally, the appointment of a refused individual as local substitution officer was said by the Knottingley Tribunal to have prompted 'indignation in the town' against all those involved in the appeals process.[97] Sometimes the odium directed at members could be an even more immediate problem. The Marsden chairman recounted that the ECAT's decision to rescind the exemption of a 'pivot man' employed at his own firm had led to him being personally 'blamed by the applicants'.[98]

This concern with local sentiment is illustrated further by the manner of the tribunals' protests. Grievances that could have been ventilated in correspondence were instead raised at the start of sittings, or in comments made while cases were being heard. By adopting this approach, the members ensured their views would reach a wide audience through the newspapers, thereby allowing any blame to be appropriately allocated. The local tribunals also tended to draw clear distinctions between their own actions and those of the subjects of their censure. The Heckmondwike body wanted to make it 'well known' that the retention of refused single men in the district was 'not the fault' of the tribunal, but 'rested entirely with the military authorities at Bradford'.[99] Analogous wording was used at Birstall when complaining that the ECAT had released a co-operative society butcher from carrying out thirty hours' of munitions work each week. Alderman Flynn argued that his body had 'treated all alike' by applying this stipulation to every butcher's certificate, but equality had now been undermined by the ECAT, which had unilaterally placed the co-operative in a 'preferential position'.[100] The last facet of the tribunals' protests reinforced this 'us and them' dichotomy. In referring to their local knowledge and understanding of local needs, the members deliberately situated themselves as part of the community and as being uniquely sensitive to its concerns. The logical inference, sometimes explicitly stated, was that leaving matters to the local tribunals would have prevented injustices from occurring. By targeting often anonymous outsiders 'at Bradford', 'at Wakefield' or 'in London', the members emphasised that any problems were being caused by

Autonomy or compliance? 91

the structure of the appeal mechanism and the way it was being administered, not by the earnest efforts of local men.

Like the division's local tribunals, the boards were prepared to contest some of their official instructions. Although most clergymen, religious teachers and theological students were issued with ministerial certificates advocating their exemption, certain appeal bodies refused to accept these documents out of hand. The chairman of the Third Wellington Board epitomised this stance by maintaining it was his body's duty to 'investigate every case which comes before us', as that was the only way they could be sure exemption was justified.[101] Appeals from Catholic seminarians and teaching brothers were dismissed, and the board members consistently refused to implement a blanket exemption of theological students. Another point of resistance was the claims of some men employed in essential industries. After beginning to act on Allen's directive to refuse all miners who had struck after the April 1917 agreement, the First Canterbury Board was dismayed by his subsequent climb down. Despite several requests to halt the dismissals, the board continued rejecting the claims of 'second-strikers' over the following months.[102] Further discord occurred over the October 1917 memorandum regarding farmers. The chairman of the First Wellington Board lamented that this document 'wholly stultified' his body's independence, and would leave them unable to distinguish between genuine 'last men' and individuals who had only become such by sub-dividing farms.[103]

The appeal bodies also intermittently objected to working with the other actors in the exemption system. In March 1918, the Recruiting Board felt moved to remind the boards that 'appeals should be considered strictly in accordance' with the classification of industries.[104] A few months later, after complaints from the NEB that its scheme was still not being followed, Allen stated 'he would see that the Military Service Boards were again warned upon that point'.[105] A more widespread friction occurred between the boards and the farmers' trustees. One of the main criticisms farming organisations and MPs made of the appeal bodies was that they 'studiously disregarded' the expert counsel the trustees could provide. Dissent occurred in Otago when the Second Board refused to allow a trustee to speak on behalf of an appellant.[106] Then, in July 1917, the First Wellington Board twice took umbrage when a group of trustees gave it a recommendation on how to determine an appeal. The board members argued that the trustees' role was to ensure they were fully informed of a man's circumstances, not to advise them whether he should be exempted.[107] Likewise, the chairman of the First Canterbury Board complained when the Marlborough trustees began carrying out investigations on their own initiative, rather than waiting for the appeal body to refer cases to them.[108] Canterbury seems to have been a particularly fractious province in this regard, with the military representative of the Second Board suggesting there was 'hardly any co-operation' between the boards and trustees, and that 'sometimes there was hostility'.[109]

Yet the boards' resistance to official directions was limited in both scope and extent. While several bodies investigated Catholic appeals despite the granting of ministerial certificates, most of these cases were ultimately successful. Outside of

92 *Autonomy or compliance?*

theological students, no clergyman and only one Marist Brother were refused exemption, with the latter decision being reached after the bishop making the appeal admitted the man's school would not close if he were taken.[110] Within the essential industries, a handful of coal truckers and ship's pursers whose indispensability was in question were the only reported instances of ministerial certificates being rejected. Such responsiveness is even more evident over the appeals of seafarers. During their early sittings, several boards considered these cases in detail to ascertain the requirements of the mercantile marine.[111] Nevertheless, they quickly adopted the policy of exempting all seamen with twelve months' experience. Typical was the wording of Chairman Moorhouse, who indicated that his Third Wellington Board would 'take notice' of the directive 'except in case of special circumstances'.[112] Similar compliance occurred regarding slaughtermen's appeals. An initial review was again conducted into the industry's requirements, while regular discussions were held with freezing works employers to see if any of their men could be spared.[113] Yet the boards were careful to state that these appraisals were not a rejection of the government's instruction: 'we only want to know whether these men are bona fide slaughtermen'.[114] That the executive was so quick to admonish the Second Wellington Board for dismissing a small number of appeals indicates how sensitive it was to the potential for industrial unrest. However, this criticism was both the first and last of its kind, suggesting the boards' approach was otherwise in accordance with official policy.

Further evidence contradicts the claim that some 'maverick' boards refused to follow instructions regarding farmers.[115] In mid-1917, when criticism of the 'mavericks' was at its fiercest, Allen defended their conduct. He asserted that all the boards were carrying out the request for 'last men' to be exempted if they could not be replaced. He also maintained that the supposedly renegade bodies were justified in refusing to accept some who claimed to be 'last men', as the testimony showed they had only achieved that status by sub-dividing farms.[116] Of course, Allen might have felt compelled to re-assure farmers they were not being victimised. Yet his assertions are probably genuine, as he repeated them in private correspondence with Massey, Ward and the commander of II ANZAC Corps, Lieutenant General Alexander Godley, where such circumspection was not required.[117] The appeal bodies certainly put forward no stated resistance to the government's policies prior to the October memorandum. In regard to that document, the First Wellington Board was alone in criticising the implications of its literal interpretation. The other boards either signalled their willingness to comply, or remained silent until the government clarified that only irreplaceable farmers and farm workers should be exempted.[118] With this guarantee of discretion, the First Wellington Board dropped its opposition, and there were few protests over 'last man' instructions for the remainder of conscription.

Rather than resisting the government's involvement, the boards regularly approached it for extra guidance. The Third Wellington Board adjourned many appeals from the Railway Department to wait for an official policy on reducing services.[119] Similarly, the chairman of the First Otago Board requested the government's advice on how to deal with appeals received from medical

Autonomy or compliance?   93

students.[120] When the 'go-slow' crisis was in progress, the First Canterbury Board was in constant communication with Allen over how to handle striking miners. Chairman Evans emphasised his board's desire to know the 'mind and opinion of the Government' on the question and stressed they did not wish to act 'except in full concurrence with yourself'.[121] These three bodies joined the others in requesting general advice on the approach they should adopt. During the German Spring Offensive, the First Otago Board and both Auckland boards petitioned the government over how its directive that soldiers were now more important than production should affect the appeals of 'last men'. Then, in May, Allen divulged that all the boards had asked for 'a declaration of policy in regard to essential industries'.[122]

Even more striking is that the boards made scarcely any complaints when refused men were subsequently held back. The only exception concerned the First Canterbury Board. In November 1917, Chairman Evans wrote to protest at the retention of Arthur Sparrow as a 'soldier–miner'. He explained that the appeal had been dismissed after Sparrow admitted leaving his farm for work as a coal trucker in a deliberate attempt to avoid military service. Unhappy such a man was to be protected, Evans asked whether it was now the government's policy to retain all men who entered the mines 'ipso facto'.[123] In May 1918, another member of the board, James Milton, wrote to further question the executive's willingness to allow all dismissed men to become 'soldier–miners'. Citing individuals who had stopped work or taken unauthorised absences, he cautioned that his other colleague, Edgar Studholme, had threatened to resign unless defaulters were set to rights. Although there is a lack of confirmation on whether the two events were linked, it is surely no coincidence that Studholme left his position three weeks later.[124]

These actions were notable protests, but their apparent strength was mitigated by several factors. No member of the First Canterbury Board ever challenged the validity or justification of the 'soldier–miner' policy, only the way it was being applied. Moreover, Studholme's threatened resignation was not designed to force a major change in the government's approach. Instead, he simply asked that 'a few of the glaring cases shall be taken out of the mines'.[125] When Allen rather brazenly replied that the Recruiting Board preferred to allow recalcitrant men to evade their duties rather than risk industrial unrest, Studholme was the only one who gave up his post. Elsewhere, the boards proved considerably more acquiescent when their verdicts were upset. No complaints followed the revelation that the military authorities had been keeping back all theological students and Marist Brothers, while the government's instruction to rehear the appeals of dismissed slaughtermen resulted in those individuals being exempted.[126] None of the boards ever refused to hold sittings, while Studholme was the only member who resigned for anything other than personal reasons.

The boards also enjoyed a better relationship with the other actors in their exemption system. Certainly, the executive reproved the appeal bodies over their perceived failure to make full use of the classification of industries. Yet this resulted from differing perceptions. The classification explicitly stated that 'each and every man' employed in the 'most essential' occupations should not

94   *Autonomy or compliance?*

automatically be entitled to exemption, but rather that relief should only be given to those who were irreplaceable.[127] While the boards adopted this philosophy, there were inevitably occasions when their notion of irreplaceable differed from the government's. However, the fact the boards were admonished very infrequently demonstrates that they followed the classification and reached acceptable decisions most of the time.[128] The appeal bodies also adapted their approach in line with the NEB's investigations. Allen outlined that reports on the ability of a range of industries to release men had been forwarded to the boards and that they had been 'acting on the recommendations'.[129] During their valedictory reports, the board chairmen praised the NEB's efforts and commented on how essential its guidance had been.[130]

Friction did occur between some boards and the farmers' trustees, but there are several reasons for qualifying its extent. Most appeal bodies maintained a harmonious relationship with the organisations working in their district. The Second Auckland Board in particular was singled out for praise over the level of its co-operation, which even extended to permitting trustee members to give testimony during sittings.[131] Despite being accorded a high profile, instances of appeal bodies criticising trustees or coming into dispute with them were rare. Those boards that did complain were quite correct to maintain that the trustees' proper function was to report on an appellant's circumstances, not to recommend whether he should be exempted. This division of powers was not only stated in the documents that sanctioned the trustees' formation, but was also accepted by the NEB and even by many of the trustees themselves.[132] Moreover, all the boards, even those that most jealously guarded their position, were prepared to utilise the trustees' services. By mid-April 1917, the First Auckland Board had referred forty-three claims for investigation, while the two Otago bodies had sent 117 between them.[133] In June, the NEB confirmed that most appeal bodies were adjourning nearly every farmer's claim for a report, and in April 1918 Allen asserted that all cases were being directed to the trustees unless the 'correct' determination was immediately obvious.[134]

The boards' greater passivity was partly the result of their being the only body in New Zealand that could award or withdraw exemptions. Around 140 refused miners and theological students were subsequently held back, but these men constituted a tiny fraction of the total appellants, and all of them were technically soldiers and subject to military discipline after having their appeals dismissed.[135] When considering his response to the initial rejection of appeals from Catholic theological students, Allen prophesied that altering the regulation to make ministerial certificates binding would 'lead to the resignation' of the boards concerned.[136] If this forecast is combined with Studholme's actual resignation over the automatic use of the 'soldier–miner' provision, and the First Wellington Board's opposition to any blanket exemption of 'last men', then there likely would have been more protests by boards had their powers been subject to the same restrictions as the tribunals'.

A second factor was that the boards came under far less pressure to refuse appeals. On a human level, it must have been more palatable to be asked to let men stay at home, rather than being instructed to send ever increasing numbers of them off to face the prospect of death or injury. Furthermore, the individuals that the boards were being told to exempt were, for the most part, those whose occupation was of clear importance to the war effort. New Zealand needed coal, food and an efficient rail network, while sailors were required to transport soldiers and goods, and farm produce was helping to keep Britain in the conflict. Whether such considerations made up the government's entire motive or not, the boards could rationalise most of their instructions, and the need to work with the NEB and trustees, within the framework of protecting vital industries. When the appeal bodies did mount resistance, it was over the relief of miners who were not working to capacity, farmers who were not essential to production and Catholic students whose indispensability was at least questionable.

The boards' acquiescence also stemmed from a lesser sensitivity to local interests. Appointed by the government, often operating away from their place of residence, and mostly occupying positions that did not require an electorate's favour, the boards were far more likely to view exemptions from a national perspective. This, in turn, made them more open to official guidance. In writing to request a steer over the appeals of 'last men', the chairmen of the two Auckland bodies stated that 'the Military Service Boards are bound ... to make their determinations harmonise with the policy of the country, for which the Government and not the Boards are responsible'.[137] This sentiment was shared by the chairman of the First Otago Board, who described the declaration of official instructions as 'necessary and proper'.[138] Even while protesting against the government, the boards did not question its right to issue directives. When arguing the October 1917 memorandum placed too great a limit on his board's discretion, the chairman of the First Wellington Board stated that it would be 'absurd' for his body to take 'exception to the Government declaring a national policy'.[139] Likewise, after previously refusing to cease the dismissal of 'second strikers', the prospect of further industrial unrest in October 1918 prompted the First Canterbury Board to adjourn all coal miners' cases on the grounds that how to deal with them was a question 'of Government policy'.[140]

This centralist inclination also defined the boards' attitudes towards the other actors in the exemption system. Their criticism of the farmers' trustees was often explicitly motivated by a belief that those bodies were too concerned with local interests. In challenging the practice of offering unsolicited recommendations, Chairman Evans asserted that the Marlborough trustees 'were only human', which made it 'quite natural to suppose that they would be subjected to local sympathies'.[141] Similarly, the Second Otago Board refused to allow trustees to testify during appeal hearings once it had elicited that they were bodies of local farmers, which had been set up to protect the interests of local farmers.[142] This suspicion of localism explains why the boards generally enjoyed a better relationship with the NEB than with the trustees. For the chairman of the First Otago Board, the usefulness of the former body lay in the fact it was a disinterested central agency. In contrast, the trustees were 'not independent' of the appellants and were, therefore, 'unconsciously biased'.[143]

96   *Autonomy or compliance?*

There was usually a robust degree of co-operation between the division's tribunals and their attached military representatives and advisory committees. Some appeal bodies were prepared to accord considerable weight to the recommendations these War Office appointees made, and only delivered contrary verdicts when very strong evidence was brought forward. Indeed, a few tribunals simply accepted all the suggestions they received without conducting any further inquiries. This practice had a significant influence at Huddersfield, where fully 84.6 percent of the total decisions came from adopting recommendations *en bloc*.[144] When a formal hearing was deemed necessary, the tribunals usually valued the military representatives' input. There were few large-scale appeals to the ECAT and several tribunals allowed the military representatives to remain with them while they were discussing what verdict to deliver. The Goole Urban and Dewsbury tribunals did not require their representatives to leave the room on any occasion before September 1916 and January 1917, respectively.[145] Furthermore, when a solicitor before the Heckmondwike body in May 1917 asked that Mr. Richmond should withdraw at the same time as himself, the military representative replied 'it was a thing he had never been asked to do before at any of the Tribunals which he had attended'.[146] The comments and actions of some appeal bodies also point to a feeling of camaraderie. When it was suggested that specially trained barristers might replace the current military representatives, the Spenborough Tribunal came out in strong opposition on the basis that Mr. Richmond had their 'entire confidence'.[147] Likewise, the Marsden body expressed regret over the resignation of Captain Bradbury, who had always been 'fair and courteous' towards them; the Ossett members described working alongside Mr. Oddy as a 'pleasure'; and the members of the Castleford Tribunal were not only invited to Captain Greenwood's wedding, but also presented him with a dinner service as a gift.[148]

Nonetheless, the relationship between tribunals and their attached military representatives and advisory committees could become strained. Although some appeal bodies placed great importance on the recommendations they received, others quickly signalled a determination to make up their own minds. The members of the Cudworth Tribunal used their first sitting under the Military Service Act to assert that the local advisory committee would have 'nothing to do' with them and that they would be 'actuated and guided' only by their 'own conscience'.[149] Somewhat less heatedly, the Birstall Tribunal refused to automatically accept the recommendations made by their committee on the basis they might be wrong, while the members of the Goole Urban body opted to hear all future appeals themselves after finding that the military representative had exempted several shipping workers who were not essential.[150] Such views gained a wider currency as conscription progressed. The Slaithwaite Tribunal abandoned its policy of automatic acceptance in May 1916, when an investigation into twelve cases assented to by the advisory committee revealed that six of them should have been opposed.[151] That same month, the Spenborough Tribunal hesitated to allow their military representative and advisory committee to make further arrangements with local firms, and only acquiesced after obtaining a guaranteed right

Autonomy or compliance? 97

of rejection.[152] By 1917, the majority of the division's tribunals were auditing all the recommendations they received, and many were denying some of these on a regular basis.

There were also instances of tribunals opposing military representatives during and after hearings. In March 1916, the Golcar Tribunal took exception to Major Tanner's complaint that there had only been one refusal all day, asserting they had judged each case on its merits.[153] Seven months later, the same body resisted Captain Bradbury's contention that forty-two claims from a woollen firm should be determined on the basis that all men under thirty were needed at the front. Pointing out this would mean the loss of fully half those appealed for, the Golcar Tribunal instead ordered only twelve of them into the army.[154] Faced with a similar situation, the Marsden Tribunal provoked Captain Mallalieu's displeasure by refusing to cancel all the certificates held by fifteen single mill workers.[155] If disputes of this kind were uncommon, a more frequent point of conflict was the military representatives' ability to review exemptions and to take any decision before the ECAT. The Linthwaite body rebuked Mr. Quarmby for contesting the certificate awarded to the 'main man' at a dyeing works, while the Pontefract Borough Tribunal criticised Major Renny for his consistent refusal to accept the exemption of local tradesmen.[156] In Parliament, the MP for Elland argued the consistency with which the West Riding's military representatives were challenging 'most of the decisions of the local tribunals' was causing considerable 'discontent'. He instanced the fact that at one ECAT sitting, verdicts delivered by the Barnsley Borough Tribunal were upset in twenty-one cases out of twenty-four.[157]

These disputes partially resulted from the perceived threat that the military representatives and advisory committees posed to the tribunals' autonomy. One reason why most of the division's appeal bodies came to reject simply signing off on recommendations was a belief that they, as judicial authorities, had been established to determine all the cases submitted. The Spenborough body argued that allowing the War Office appointees to have the final say would amount to 'interference with the powers of the Tribunal' and the loss of its most essential function.[158] Likewise, the Goole Urban body held that the military representative's desire to make his own arrangements with large firms was 'wrong in principle', as the tribunals were tasked with reviewing claims in detail in order to reach considered decisions.[159] Some local tribunals also maintained that the military representatives' ability to review certificates was a 'waste of time', and portrayed the willingness of those individuals to take cases to the ECAT as an underhand way of bypassing adverse verdicts. At Pontefract Borough, it was asserted that the military representative's retrospective challenging of several decisions had left the tribunal feeling as though they were not 'treated with due respect'.[160] Using comparable logic, the Hemsworth Rural body alleged that an appeal against the exemption of a local co-operative society member, made at the same time as certain refused men were not being called up for service, smacked of a 'suspicious' and 'indirect' subversion of their intentions.[161]

Yet the tribunals usually went beyond matters of authority to cite the difference between knowledgeable locals and uncaring 'outsiders'. Three considerations

98 *Autonomy or compliance?*

could produce this type of response. The first was that military representatives and advisory committees were often assigned to more than one area. For example, the Spen Valley Advisory Committee, and H. D. Leather as military representative, served the tribunals at Birstall, Birkenshaw, Heckmondwike and Spenborough.[162] Drawn from across these four districts, Leather and his committee were, therefore, not strictly 'local' in all the cases they dealt with, nor always conversant with specific local industries. This distinction could carry significant weight, with a more harmonious relationship tending to exist between tribunals and War Office appointees who were from the same community. There were virtually no complaints made by the Huddersfield Tribunal about Arthur Crosland, and the recommendations he presented after consultation with the county borough's dedicated advisory committee were always adhered to. In contrast, the refusal of the Birstall body to automatically grant exemption in cases where Leather and his committee had indicated their assent arose from a belief that the tribunal members' greater 'local knowledge' could well lead them to reject certain appeals.[163] As a Barnsley resident, Lieutenant Colonel Hewitt enjoyed a comfortable relationship with the local Borough Tribunal, but was constantly at loggerheads with the farmer members of the Barnsley Rural Tribunal. When Hewitt accused these latter individuals of being biased towards agricultural cases, he was told that they 'knew better than he how many men it took to work a farm'.[164] Likewise, Councillor Naylor criticised the qualifications of the advisory committee serving at Ardsley by alleging it had incorrectly recommended the exemption of several employees at Rylands glassworks. After questioning why the committee had been delegated to visit the works 'when they did not understand the trades', Naylor argued that he was familiar with the glass-making process 'from the beginning to the end'. In complete agreement, the tribunal arranged for Naylor to visit Rylands himself with a view to producing new recommendations.[165]

A second catalyst was the replacement of a local military representative with someone from outside the district. When Captain Featherston resigned as military representative for Goole in July 1916, the members of the Urban Tribunal 'acknowledged the assistance' he had supplied and trusted that 'the same amicable relationship would continue' with his successor.[166] This was to prove a forlorn hope. Within a month of Lieutenant Neal's appointment, the tribunal had accused him of a 'lack of courtesy' for taking cases to the ECAT, and criticised his willingness to challenge their verdicts even when they clearly believed a man was essential.[167] Tensions came to a head in late August when the members questioned Neal's entreaty for the review of nine conditional exemptions. A heated argument then broke out between Neal and Councillor Porter, with the military representative citing that member's reluctance to revisit the claims as evidence of 'a biased mind'. Outraged, Porter condemned Neal's lack of local knowledge and lambasted the way 'a stranger comes down and begins talking about change of circumstances'.[168] Over the following months, the Goole Urban Tribunal had several more altercations with Lieutenant Neal, and never again developed the same comfortable relationship they had enjoyed with Captain Featherston. Analogous difficulties occurred at Dewsbury following Lieutenant Strachan's appointment.

Autonomy or compliance? 99

After co-operating well with his predecessors, the tribunal quickly took issue with this new military representative over his perceived lack of concern for local firms. Then, in January 1917, several members claimed that Strachan had gone behind their backs in approaching the Postmaster General for evidence with which to oppose an exemption. During this exchange, one member pointedly referenced the fact Strachan and the postmaster were 'outsiders' by labelling them 'good Scotch and bad Irish'.[169] Further disagreements occurred throughout Strachan's tenure, with the chairman remarking that the tribunal had 'not always seen eye to eye' with its military representative.[170]

The third possible reason behind a tribunal's criticism was the belief a military representative or advisory committee had forfeited their status as local men by proxy. It was occasionally noted that the tribunals had been established by local authorities, whereas the War Office appointees had been chosen by a military man who was not even a resident of the division. Those tribunal members who refused to work with the advisory committee for Cudworth explicitly cited its appointment by 'outsiders'.[171] A more common assertion was that any local understanding possessed by the military representatives was automatically negated by their willingness to treat central directives as binding. Captain Greenwood was the subject of considerable censure by the Castleford Tribunal after asserting that his orders left him with no choice but to appeal every exemption given to men in the higher medical categories. According to the members, this inflexibility not only subverted their local knowledge, but also made irrelevant all the consideration given to such cases at a local level.[172] Similarly, Mr. Baines' determination to appeal against every exemption given to grade 1 men so exasperated the Ossett body that one of its members stormed out of a sitting, and another accused the representative of talking 'piffle'.[173] Military representatives could also compromise themselves through their willingness to work with the ECAT. Outrage was expressed at Whitwood when the higher appeal body revoked the certificate awarded to John Rooke, a blacksmith, who had been exempted on the grounds he was carrying out essential work for the district's farmers. Arguing they 'had local knowledge which the Appeal Tribunal did not possess', the Whitwood members accused the military representative of undertaking a 'backstairs movement' to get their unanimous determination overturned, and threatened to suspend sittings if he did so again.[174]

Some disputes did take place between the boards and their military representatives, with members occasionally implying a failure to acknowledge cases of genuine hardship. Once John Condon's appeal had been presented to the First Otago Board, Captain Free asserted that sending him to the front would result in no financial difficulties. However, the chairman countered that the case should turn on 'the mother's welfare' and Condon was granted an indefinite period of relief.[175] Another military representative achieved little satisfaction after lamenting that all twenty-two claims heard at a sitting of the First Auckland Board had resulted in exemptions. One member noted that most of the cases concerned men who already had several brothers serving in the forces, and another went on to contend it was 'only fair that some consideration should be given such appellants'.[176] Differences

100   *Autonomy or compliance?*

also arose when the boards felt the military representatives had not appreciated that appellants were crucial to their occupation. When Captain Walker argued that the wages commanded by wool pullers would make a replacement easy to find, William Perry of the First Wellington Board opined that they were well worth the expense, as their skilled work made them essential.[177]

However, the boards generally enjoyed very amicable relationships with their military representatives. Arguments during sittings were extremely rare. The members and representatives nearly always focused their questioning around the same pieces of evidence and adopted similar attitudes towards the appellants' testimony. Recommendations made by the representatives were usually adhered to, while they in turn rarely felt moved to complain about the boards' verdicts. Major Gresson gratefully noted that the Second Canterbury Board had treated him 'as a fourth member' by allowing him to 'deliberate with them' and by according a great deal of 'weight' to his opinions, all practices that were the rule rather than the exception.[178] Moreover, the few ructions that occurred over individual cases are the only recorded disputes. There were seemingly no criticisms of the way in which the representatives went about their investigations, of how they handled matters after hearings had finished, or of the general attitudes they adopted. The strongest indication of amicability came in March 1918, when Adjutant General Tate wrote to the board chairmen asking for their views on a proposal to hand the military representatives' role over to the military group commanders. Only one chairman supported this idea, and on the basis that the post itself was unnecessary, rather than due to any fault with an individual's conduct.[179] Otherwise there was vigorous opposition to interfering with the status quo and strong praise for the manner in which the military representatives had conducted themselves. One chairman expressed his earnest 'hope [that] no change is contemplated', while another labelled the idea of doing away with the representatives as 'absurd'.[180]

This greater cordiality partly resulted from the lesser pressure that the New Zealand exemption system placed on the boards' autonomy. There were no advisory committees to make recommendations and the powers of the military representatives were far more circumscribed than those of their British counterparts. They had no formal right to indicate their views on claims before a sitting took place, could not request the review of exemption certificates and, most importantly of all, could not refer cases to a higher appeal body. In the face of an adverse decision, the most a New Zealand military representative could do was apply to the Commandant of the Defence Forces for a rehearing, but even here the final decision on whether a new appraisal should take place was always in the hands of the relevant board.[181]

New Zealand's rate of reinforcement was another important factor. Its military representatives operated in a climate where proportionally fewer soldiers were required, and received their instructions from a Defence Department whose head spent a great deal of time encouraging the boards to grant more exemptions. They could therefore be more circumspect over pressing for men. This is the certainly the impression supplied by the board chairmen, with Burgess asserting that Major Conlan gave 'fair and impartial treatment' to all those who came before him;

Autonomy or compliance? 101

Cooper commenting on the way Captain Walker had 'handled the appeals from their military aspect with great fairness'; and Day claiming he did not recall any case where Captain Barrett 'strove unduly to have an appeal dismissed'.[182]

The board members' lesser sensitivity to perceived community interests was a third contributor. Having been appointed as 'impartial' and often detached actors themselves, the boards were not concerned with local knowledge or sentiment, but simply wanted assistance in drawing out all the relevant facts. The praise their chairmen gave to the military representatives derived from a belief that this criterion had been well met. They strongly supported the use of solicitors for the role, given that 'a professional Soldier' would have been 'strongly biased against all appellants', while the use of inexperienced laymen might well have led to unnecessary 'friction' over legal rulings and procedure.[183] Similarly, the chairmen endorsed the deliberate selection of 'outsiders' rather than men resident in the district, who would have been 'subject to influence for various reasons'.[184]

These three considerations are crucial to explaining why, overall, the autonomy of the division's local tribunals came under greater threat than that of the New Zealand boards, and why the British appeal bodies proved much more likely to oppose any perceived challenges. The tribunals received a vast number of official directives, mostly asking them to obtain more men for the army. While the division's appeal bodies often accepted the need to grant fewer exemptions, this passive attitude only went so far. Many members came to resent the position the executive's ever-growing demands placed them in, particularly when they considered government departments were unduly protecting young single men, and when decisions they came to were subsequently overturned. Issues of authority played a role in these protests, but they mainly occurred when the tribunals felt that their informed attempts to balance the army's interests with those of the local area had been undermined by 'outsiders'. Likewise, the sometimes cordial relations that the appeal bodies enjoyed with their military representatives and advisory committees were frequently soured by a perception that the War Office appointees were too willing to utilise the powers given to them by the exemption system, and not responsive enough to the needs of the district. A very different situation prevailed in New Zealand. That country's declining rate of reinforcement meant there were no measures to limit the grounds of appeal and very few directives to tighten the exemption criteria. On the contrary, official instructions tended to focus on securing the exemption of politically important groups. For their part, the boards had some disagreements with the farmers' trustees, but these were overshadowed by their acceptance of nearly every government policy, and by the strong relationships they maintained with the NEB and the military representatives. This amicable position was partly due to the lesser requirements of the army and the more limited checks that had been placed on the boards' powers. Yet another critical influence was the board members' natural inclination to look towards the centre, and their conviction that localism was a quality to be avoided, rather than encouraged, when dealing with exemptions.

The involvement of outside agencies could, therefore, prove to be a tremendous help, or a considerable hindrance, to the tribunals' and boards' operations.

102 *Autonomy or compliance?*

However, the contact between these different groups was only ever intended as a means of facilitation. The course that the two exemption systems ultimately followed would depend on what happened when the appeal bodies and the appellants came face-to-face.

Notes

1   A. J. P. Taylor, *English History, 1914–1945* (Oxford: Clarendon Press, 1965), 55–56.
2   Circular, LGB R. 36, 3 Feb. 1916 and Circular, LGB R. 48, 10 Feb. 1916, MH 47/142, NA; Notes, "Calling Up of Groups and Classes," 2 Feb. 1916, AsqP, MSS Asquith 29, BodL.
3   Minutes, Cabinet Committee on the Co-ordination of Military and Financial Effort, 13 Apr. 1916, CAB 27/4, NA.
4   Dearle, *Economic Chronicle*, 76, 83.
5   Minutes, Cabinet Committee on the Co-ordination of Military and Financial Effort, 12 Apr. 1916, CAB 27/4, NA.
6   Military Service Act, 1916 (Session 2), 6 & 7 Geo. 5, c. 15, sec. 4(2).
7   Circular, LGB R. 84, 1 Jun. 1916, MH 47/142, NA.
8   Circular, LGB R. 74, 4 Apr. 1916 and Circular, LGB R. 75, 10 Apr. 1916, MH 47/142, NA.
9   Memorandum, "Supply of Men for the Army," 28 Nov. 1916, CAB 37/160/25, NA; Charles Messenger, *Call-To-Arms: The British Army, 1914–18* (London: Cassell, 2005), 277.
10 *Statistics of the Military Effort*, 83–84.
11 Circular, LGB R. 112, 22 Dec. 1916, G3 226/8, WSHC.
12 Circular, LGB R. 102, 29 Sep. 1916, Circular, LGB 105, 20 Nov. 1916 and Circular, LGB R. 117, 1 Feb. 1917, MH 47/142, NA.
13 Circular, LGB R. 107, 1 Dec. 1916, MH 47/142, NA.
14 Circular, LGB R. 114, 20 Jan. 1917, MH 47/142, NA.
15 Circular, LGB R. 122, 1 Mar. 1917, MH 47/142, NA.
16 Circular, LGB R. 102, 29 Sep. 1916 and Circular, LGB R. 119, 30 Jan. 1917, MH 47/142, NA.
17 J. K. Montgomery, *The Maintenance of the Agricultural Labour Supply in England and Wales during the War* (Rome: International Institute of Agriculture, 1922), 16–17.
18 Circular, LGB R. 127, 28 Mar. 1917, MH 10/81, NA.
19 Circular, LGB R. 133, 8 Jun. 1917, MH 47/142, NA.
20 Circular, LGB R. 136, 23 Jun. 1917, Circular LGB R. 136 (Revised), 8 Sep. 1917 and Circular, LGB R. 133, 8 Jun. 1917, MH 47/142, NA.
21 The War Cabinet: Report for the Year, 1917, Cd. 9005, at viii.
22 Adams and Poirier, *Conscription Controversy*, 212–16.
23 Geddes, 101 Parl. Deb., H.C. (5th ser.) (1918), 72–74.
24 Military Service Act, 1918, 7 & 8 Geo. 5, c. 66, sec. 2.
25 Dearle, *Economic Chronicle*, 180.
26 "Statutory Rules and Orders, 1918, No. 459: Military Service," 20 Apr. 1918, MH 47/142, NA.
27 "Order Under the Military Service Act, 1918: Section 2," 9 Apr. 1918, MH 47/142, NA.
28 Circular, LGB R. 184, 25 Apr. 1918, MH 47/142, NA.
29 Circular, LGB R. 208, 4 Jun. 1918, MH 10/82, NA; Circular, Ministry of National Service R. 53, 10 Jun. 1918, MH 47/142, NA.
30 Circular, LGB R. 136 (Revised), 26 Sep. 1918, MH 47/142, NA.
31 Circular, LGB R. 207, 3 Jun. 1918 and Circular, LGB R. 139 (Revised), 24 Sep. 1918, MH 47/142, NA.
32 Circular, LGB R. 220, 13 Jul. 1918, MH 47/142, NA.

Autonomy or compliance? 103

33 Allen to Godley, 6 Feb. 1917, AP, ALLEN 1 2 M1/15/4, ANZ.
34 Baker, *King and Country Call*, 142.
35 *NZH*, 6 Jun. 1917, 8; *ODT*, 10 Jul. 1917, 6 and 22 Aug. 1917, 5.
36 Allen to Godley, 23 Jul. 1917, AP, ALLEN 1 2 M1/15/4, ANZ.
37 Liverpool to Bonar Law, 17 Jul. 1917 and 17 Aug. 1917, AP, ALLEN 1 M1/57, ANZ.
38 Allen to Birdwood, 10 Apr. 1918, AP, ALLEN 1 9, ANZ; Massey, 182 NZ Parl. Deb., H.R. (1918), 65.
39 Lt.-Colonel John Studholme, *New Zealand Expeditionary Force: Record of Personal Services during the War of Officers, Nurses, and First-Class Warrant Officers; and other Facts Relating to the N.Z.E.F.: Unofficial, but based on Official Records* (Wellington: Government Printer, 1928), 373–76.
40 *Akaroa Mail and Banks Peninsula Advertiser*, 14 Apr. 1917, 2; M. J. Kelly, *Military Board Appeals: Otago Witness, March 1917 to July 1917* (Auckland: Old News Publications, 1994), 27–28.
41 Gray to Military Service Board Chairmen, 10 Jul. 1917, AD 82 2 1/11/1, ANZ.
42 Gray to Military Service Board Chairmen, 17 Apr. 1918, AD 82 2 1/11/1, ANZ.
43 Gray to Allen, 20 May 1918, AD 1 736 10/512, ANZ; Gray to Military Service Board Chairmen, 12 Jun. 1918, AD 82 2 1/11/1, ANZ.
44 Allen to Massey, 19 Dec. 1916, AP, ALLEN 1 9, ANZ; Allen to Coffey, 21 Mar. 1917, AD 82 4 5/1, ANZ.
45 O'Shea to Allen, 17 Feb. 1917 and Allen to O'Shea, 26 Feb. 1917, AD 82 4 5/1, ANZ.
46 Coffey to Allen, 16 Mar. 1917, AD 82 4 5/1, ANZ.
47 Gray to Tate, 27 Mar. 1917, AD 82 4 5/1, ANZ.
48 Allen to Massey, 28 Apr. 1917, AP, ALLEN 1 9, ANZ.
49 Minutes, Conference of Military Service Board Chairmen, 27 Apr. 1917, AD 1 765 20/43, ANZ.
50 Minutes, Conference of Military Service Boards, 2 Aug. 1917, AD 82 7 46/7, ANZ.
51 Minutes, Conference of Military Service Boards, 29 Nov. 1917, AD 82 7 46/1, ANZ; Gray to Cosgrove, 10 Jun. 1918, AD 82 4 5/1, ANZ.
52 *Dominion*, 17 May 1918, 7; *EP*, 7 Aug. 1918, 3.
53 "Classification of Industries, Professions, and Occupations during the War Period," *AJHR*, 1917, H43-B; Allen to Massey, 18 Sep. 1917, AP, ALLEN 1 11, ANZ.
54 Gray to Military Service Board Chairmen, 30 Jul. 1917 and 5 Mar. 1918, AD 82 2 1/11/1, ANZ.
55 Gray to Poynton, 15 Jan. 1918, AD 82 1 1/4, ANZ.
56 Evans to Gray, 16 Feb. 1917 and Gray to Evans, 17 Feb. 1917, AD 82 7 28/1, ANZ.
57 Gray to Evans, 30 Apr. 1917 and 1 May 1917, AD 82 7 28/1, ANZ.
58 Gray to Evans, 14 May 1917 and 25 Jun. 1917, AD 82 7 28/1, ANZ.
59 Tate to General Officer Commanding, 2 Sep. 1918, AD 1 736 10/483, ANZ; Gray to Milton, 6 Jun. 1918, AD 82 7 28/1, ANZ.
60 *Farmers' Union Advocate*, 9 Dec. 1916, 5; Minutes, Wellington Branch of the Farmers' Union, 29 Mar. 1917, MSY 0296, ATL; *WT*, 23 Mar. 1917, 4.
61 Allen to Massey, 17 Mar. 1917, AP, ALLEN 1 9, ANZ.
62 Gray to Military Representatives, 16 Mar. 1917, AD 82 2 1/11/1, ANZ.
63 Gray to Military Service Board Chairmen, 23 Mar. 1917, 31 Mar. 1917 and 5 May 1917, AD 82 2 1/11/1, ANZ.
64 Gray to Military Service Board Chairmen, 12 Oct. 1917, AD 82 2 1/11/1, ANZ.
65 Gray to Walker, 26 Oct. 1917, AD 82 1/3/7, ANZ.
66 *CSG*, 14 Apr. 1916, 2.
67 Ibid., 23 Jun. 1916, 3.
68 *BN*, 24 Mar. 1917, 1.
69 *CSG*, 4 May 1917, 3.
70 *WE*, 9 Dec. 1916, 5.
71 *BN*, 21 Oct. 1916, 2.

104 *Autonomy or compliance?*

72 McDermott, *British Military Service Tribunals*, 75.
73 Report, Work of the Marsden Tribunal from January to December 1917, n.d., HHP, S/ NUDBTW/34, KA.
74 *HEx*, 18 Apr. 1916, 2; *BN*, 22 Apr. 1916, 1, 3 and 6 May 1916, 8.
75 *BC*, 22 Jul. 1916, 7, 23 Sep. 1916, 3 and 10 Feb. 1917, 3.
76 *GT*, 29 Sep. 1916, 6 and 6 Oct. 1916, 8.
77 Report, Statistics on the Work of the Marsden Tribunal, 17 Dec. 1918, HHP, S/ NUDBTW/34, KA.
78 *WE*, 13 Jan. 1917, 2.
79 *HEx*, 12 Oct. 1916, 3.
80 *WE*, 9 Jun. 1917, 6 and 28 Jul. 1917, 6.
81 *GT*, 15 Jun. 1917, 5.
82 *CSG*, 9 Nov. 1917, 5 and 31 May 1918, 1.
83 *PCE*, 24 May 1918, 2; *GT*, 22 Apr. 1917, 4; *CSG*, 12 Jun. 1918, 2.
84 *GT*, 29 Sep. 1916, 6.
85 *CSG*, 6 Jul. 1917, 3.
86 *WE*, 30 Sep. 1916, 6; *W*, 16 Jun. 1917, 3.
87 *HE*, 13 Jan. 1917, 6.
88 *HE*, 27 Jul. 1918, 3.
89 *CSG*, 14 Jun. 1918, 2 and 21 Jun. 1918, 2.
90 *PCE*, 15 Jun. 1917, 3.
91 *HE*, 13 Jan. 1917, 6.
92 *PCE*, 24 May 1918, 2.
93 Ibid., 16 Jun. 1916, 3.
94 *HEx*, 27 Mar. 1917, 4.
95 *GT*, 1 Sep. 1916, 4; *OO*, 13 Jul. 1918, 4; *PCE*, 14 Dec. 1917, 2.
96 *CSG*, 18 Aug. 1916, 2 and 21 Jun. 1918, 2.
97 *PCE*, 24 Aug. 1917, 3.
98 *HEx*, 17 Apr. 1917, 2.
99 *CSG*, 9 Mar. 1917, 7.
100 *BN*, 11 Nov. 1916, 7.
101 *EP*, 20 Mar. 1917, 7
102 Gray to Evans, 14 May 1917, 25 Jun. 1917 and 4 Jul. 1917 AD 82 7 28/1, ANZ; *GRA*, 19 Jun. 1917, 3, 18 Jul. 1917, 3 and 15 Aug. 1917, 4.
103 Cooper to Gray, 15 Oct. 1917, AD 82 1 1/3, ANZ.
104 Gray to Military Service Board Chairmen, 5 Mar. 1918, AD 82 2 1/11/2, ANZ.
105 Ferguson to Gray, 4 Aug. 1918, NEB 1 16 703, ANZ.
106 W. H. Field, 178 NZ Parl. Deb., H.R. (1917), 480; *ODT*, 19 Apr. 1917, 4.
107 *MES*, 2 Jul. 1917, 5, 23 Jul. 1917, 5 and 24 Jul. 1917, 2.
108 *ME*, 14 Dec. 1917, 2 and 28 Mar. 1918, 2.
109 Gresson to Gray, 19 Mar. 1919, AD 1 1046 66/57, ANZ.
110 Gray to Tate, 7 Mar. 1918, AD 1 736 10/477, ANZ.
111 *EP*, 30 Dec. 1916, 6, 31 Jan. 1917, 7 and 18 Apr. 1917, 8.
112 *EP*, 14 Feb. 1917, 8.
113 *New Zealand Times*, 20 Apr. 1917, 7; Minutes, Conference regarding Freezing Industry Employees, 6 Oct. 1917, AD 82 8 74, ANZ.
114 *EP*, 20 Apr. 1917, 7.
115 Baker, "New Zealanders," 258–62.
116 *AS*, 7 Mar. 1917, 8; Allen, 178 NZ Parl. Deb., H.R. (1917), 480, 482, 824, 833.
117 Allen to Massey, 17 Mar. 1917, AP, ALLEN 1 9, ANZ; Allen to Ward, 21 Aug. 1917, AD 82 2 1/11/1, ANZ; Allen to Godley, 27 Mar. 1917, AP, ALLEN 1 2 M1/15/4, ANZ.
118 *ODT*, 31 Oct. 1917, 2–3; *Colonist*, 6 Nov. 1917, 2; *ST*, 7 Dec. 1917, 4.
119 *EP*, 17 Feb. 1917, 5 and 17 Mar. 1917, 6.
120 Kelly, *Military Board Appeals, Dec 1916 to Feb 1917*, 47–48.

Autonomy or compliance? 105

121 Evans to Allen, 13 Mar. 1917, AD 82 7 28/1, ANZ.
122 Gray to Allen, 20 May 1918 and Burgess and Earl to Gray, 27 May 1918, AD 1 736 10/512, ANZ; *EP*, 23 May 1918, 8.
123 Evans to Gray, 16 Nov. 1917, AD 82 7 28/1, ANZ.
124 Milton to Gray, 28 May 1918 and 4 Jun. 1918, AD 82 7 28/1, ANZ; Report, Members of the Military Service Boards, n.d., AD 82 2 1/11/1, ANZ.
125 Milton to Gray, 4 Jun. 1918, AD 82 7 28/1, ANZ.
126 *WDT*, 7 Jun. 1918, 6.
127 "Classification of Industries, Professions, and Occupations during the War Period," *AJHR*, 1917, H43-B.
128 Martin, "Blueprint for the Future," 522–23; Parsons, "Many Derelicts," 44.
129 Allen, 178 NZ Parl. Deb., H.R. (1917), 833–34.
130 Cooper to Gray, 10 Dec. 1918, AD 82 3 1/22, ANZ; Day to Ferguson, 29 Aug. 1917, NEB 1 16 703, ANZ; Widdowson to Allen, 13 Dec. 1918, AD 82 2 1/11/2, ANZ.
131 *WT*, 16 Mar. 1917, 2; *AS*, 23 May 1917, 6.
132 *ODT*, 13 Apr. 1917, 2; *WT*, 8 Jun. 1917, 5; *MES*, 29 Jun. 1917, 6.
133 *NZH*, 20 Apr. 1917, 6; *ST*, 14 Apr. 1917, 2.
134 *AS*, 13 Jun. 1917, 10; Gray to Allen, 11 Apr. 1918, AD 82 7 18/1, ANZ.
135 Tate to General Officer Commanding, 2 Sep. 1918, AD 1 736 10/483, ANZ; Report, "Recruiting 1916–1918," 31 Mar. 1919, AD 1 712 9/169/2, ANZ.
136 Allen to Massey, 27 Feb. 1917, AP, ALLEN 1 9, ANZ.
137 Burgess and Earl to Gray, 27 May 1918, AD 1 736 10/512, ANZ.
138 Widdowson to Allen, 13 Dec. 1918, AD 82 2 1/11/2, ANZ.
139 *EP*, 20 Oct. 1917, 4.
140 Evans to Gray, 24 Oct. 1918, AD 82 7 28/1, ANZ.
141 *ME*, 14 Dec. 1917, 2.
142 *ST*, 14 Mar. 1917, 5.
143 Widdowson to Allen, 13 Dec. 1918, AD 82 2 1/11/2, ANZ.
144 Minutes, Huddersfield Local Tribunal, 10 Jan. 1916 to 21 Oct. 1918, KMT 18/12/2/52/1, KA.
145 *GT*, 1 Sep. 1916, 4; *BN*, 6 Jan. 1917, 6.
146 *CSG*, 18 May 1917, 3.
147 Ibid., 13 Apr. 1917, 4.
148 *HEx*, 30 May 1916, 4; *OO*, 16 Mar. 1918, 3; *WE*, 6 Oct. 1917, 2.
149 *BC*, 11 Mar. 1916, 3.
150 Leather to Gray, 10 Jan. 1916, BLTF, RD 21/6/2, KA; Minutes, Birstall Local Tribunal, 18 Jan. 1916, BLTF, RD 21/6/2, KA; *GT*, 17 Mar. 1916, 4 and 9 Jun. 1916, 3.
151 *HEx*, 19 May 1916, 4 and 2 Jun. 1916, 4.
152 *CSG*, 19 May 1916, 3.
153 *HEx*, 29 Feb. 1916, 4.
154 Ibid., 31 Oct. 1916, 2.
155 Ibid., 23 Nov. 1916, 3.
156 *W*, 11 Aug. 1917, 3; *PCE*, 20 Apr. 1917, 1
157 Trevelyan, 109 Parl. Deb., H.C. (5th ser.) (1918), 1092–93.
158 *CSG*, 19 May 1916, 3.
159 *GT*, 9 Jun. 1916, 3.
160 *PCE*, 20 Apr. 1917, 1.
161 Ibid., 15 Jun. 1917, 2.
162 *CSG*, 24 Dec. 1915, 2.
163 Minutes, Birstall Local Tribunal, 18 Jan. 1916, BLTF, RD 21/6/2, KA.
164 *BC*, 17 Jun. 1916, 7.
165 Ibid., 22 Jul. 1916, 2.
166 *GT*, 14 Jul. 1916, 7.
167 Ibid., 4 Aug. 1916, 4.

106 *Autonomy or compliance?*

168 Ibid., 1 Sep. 1916, 4.
169 *BN*, 6 Jan. 1917, 6.
170 Ibid., 29 Sep. 1917, 5.
171 *BC*, 11 Mar. 1916, 3.
172 *PCE*, 24 May 1918, 2.
173 *OO*, 13 Jul. 1918, 4 and 27 Jul. 1918, 4.
174 *PCE*, 23 Mar. 1917, 5.
175 *ODT*, 12 Nov. 1917, 7.
176 *AS*, 25 May 1917, 2.
177 *MES*, 14 Feb. 1917, 4.
178 Gresson to Gray, 19 Mar. 1919, AD 1 1046 66/57, ANZ; Baker, *King and Country Call*, 116.
179 Earl to Tate, 25 Mar. 1918, AD 1 769 22/140, ANZ.
180 Burgess to Tate, 23 Mar. 1918 and Widdowson to Tate, 25 Mar. 1918, AD 1 769 22/140, ANZ.
181 New Zealand Military Service Act, 1916, 7 Geo. 5, no. 8, sec. 26(3).
182 Burgess to Gray, 5 Dec. 1918, AD 82 2 1/11/2, ANZ; Cooper to Tate, 20 Mar. 1918 and Day to Tate, 19 Mar. 1918, AD 1 769 22/140, ANZ.
183 Moorhouse to Tate, 16 Mar. 1918 and Day to Tate, 19 Mar. 1918, AD 1 769 22/140, ANZ.
184 Widdowson to Tate, 25 Mar. 1918, AD 1 769 22/140, ANZ.

5 Army first?

Despite being appointed according to very different criteria, and despite receiving very different sets of official instructions, the British and New Zealand appeal bodies were charged with the same essential task. They had to convene hearings at which all the available evidence was presented, a thorough questioning of the appellant and any additional witnesses was undertaken, and a decision finally reached on how the prospective conscript could best serve his country during a time of 'total war'. The attitudes that tribunal and board members adopted during these proceedings depended on what they saw as the exemption system's fundamental purpose. Did they believe that their primary responsibility was to meet the army's demands, or did they endeavour to balance the need for soldiers against a range of other factors and imperatives?

The East Central Division's tribunals displayed a virtually unanimous resistance towards exempting certain types of appellant. They believed men should join the army in a prescribed order, with an individual's position on the hierarchy being partly determined by his domestic responsibilities and capacity to serve. It was on this basis that appeals concerning single men were frequently subjected to criticism. During the claim of a work's chemist at New Mill, Councillor Roebuck questioned why the tribunal was being asked to exempt an unmarried individual on the grounds he was indispensable when there were numerous men with families scheduled for hearing.[1] Using analogous logic, the Goole Urban body informed the employer of a single carter that such men 'were wanted in the Army', and that he would simply have to do his best to find a replacement.[2] Disapproval was also voiced when the appellant was of a young age. For suggesting one such individual deserved exemption, a solicitor before the Barnsley Borough Tribunal was curtly reminded that 'if the young ones do not go we shall have to take those between 40 and 45'.[3] At Spenborough, a director's plea that his firm had not appealed for anyone prior to their leather workman was also rejected, with the chairman declaring that they had no intention of relieving men who were only twenty-seven years old.[4] A third factor that was almost guaranteed to provoke ire was the prospective conscript having been classed fit for 'general service'. When a firm argued that one of its employees should be given time to sit for an exam, the chairman of the Pontefract Borough Tribunal replied that they had sent barely suitable forty-year-olds to the front and could not be expected to exempt those who were in perfect

108 *Army first?*

fighting condition.[5] The same sentiment was voiced by the Spenborough body, which told a painter's employer that 'the first thing we have got to do is to get fit A men for the Army'.[6]

The tribunals were even less tolerant of men from families who were not represented in the forces. In these instances, it was often contended that the household had not only neglected its responsibilities previously, but that the decision to appeal revealed a continued willingness to let others fight on their behalf. When Mr. Arrand appeared before the Hemsworth Rural Tribunal to plead for his twenty-year-old son, the case quickly foundered once he admitted that his other four boys were still at home. Councillor Burns stated it was a 'positive waste of time discussing the matter further', Councillor Beach scathingly remarked 'you have five sons, and not one serving the country', while Mr. Jagger enquired how they might get their hands on the sons who were still at large.[7] Similarly, after the New Mill body had heard several cases relating to untouched households, Councillor Gill insisted that 'every family with sons of military age ought to be represented in the forces'.[8]

Some employers also received short shrift, especially when the tribunals perceived a reluctance to make sacrifices. When a tailor intimated that the Barnsley Borough Tribunal should allow him additional time to prepare for the loss of his cutter, the chairman replied 'the war has been on nearly two years. You have already had time'.[9] Likewise, the Spenborough body habitually dismissed appeals from firms that had not offered their staff any incentives to enlist, with the chairman stating that such enticements were the only 'absolute proof that they were doing all they could to stimulate recruiting'.[10] The tribunals further expected employers to seek out overage, unfit or female substitutes. When a firm of flock and horse clothing manufacturers appealed for Edgar Munns, they were informed that the Batley Tribunal had 'no sympathy' for companies which had not endeavoured to replace their eligible employees.[11] Alleged laxity also prompted the refusal of a painter's appeal at Golcar, once he admitted that he had failed to look for a medically rejected man to take over from his sign-writer, while a Barnsley firm of glass bottle manufacturers were relieved of their bookkeeper after the manager stated he had 'no convenience for women'.[12] Lest any employer think to make only a token search, the tribunals were careful to investigate exactly what measures had been adopted. To bolster his claim for a carter, a co-operative society director told the Linthwaite body he had made repeated attempts to secure a man through advertising. However, this argument came to nothing after it was revealed that the proposed wages had been set too low to attract any potential applicants.[13]

Equally disagreeable were individuals who exaggerated their circumstances. A market gardener before the Honley Tribunal managed to gain some favour by explaining that he had a widowed mother to support. However, this amicable mood evaporated as soon as the members discovered that the man had an active sister living at home.[14] Similarly chastised was a Slaithwaite appellant who claimed to make only 26s. each week with which to support his blind father. After a consultation with the man's employer had disclosed the wage was in fact 46s., the chairman remarked that the tribunal 'wouldn't stand deliberate lying'.[15] Occasionally,

Army first? 109

the appeal bodies decided to make an example of those who attempted to deceive them. When the case of Alfred Byram was heard at Batley, he claimed to be providing shoes for over fifty horses and to be averaging twenty jobs completed each week. Unconvinced, and with dissenting police evidence to hand, the tribunal members demanded to see Byram's workbook. Satisfied that several of the entries therein were fraudulent, the tribunal promptly dismissed the appeal and referred it to the military authorities for remedial action.[16]

Yet these few similarities in the tribunals' approach were overshadowed by a much greater degree of discrepancy. Indeed, the members were severely divided over the fundamental purpose of their work. When a Spenborough employer argued he could not run his scribbling machines without fettlers, the chairman retorted that his body's 'first duty' was to the army.[17] Elsewhere, Mrs. Tinker of the New Mill Tribunal told a head teacher that 'we must send all the men we can', and a Mirfield member justified his opposition to the case of a yarn warehouseman by proclaiming the tribunal had its 'duty to do' in securing recruits.[18] If such language denoted the prevalence of an 'army first' mindset, then that used at other tribunals was considerably more nuanced. Referring to their 'two-fold object', Councillor Saxton of the Barnsley Rural body argued that although he and his colleagues had to keep the military in mind, they should always be prepared to accept 'a clear and honest case for exemption'.[19] Equally, Councillor Simmonds described the Holmfirth Tribunal as a 'sort of escape valve' where military imperatives were weighed up against the circumstances of each appellant, and the Birstall members asserted that they would grant every individual a 'fair chance' to prove his claim.[20]

The division's tribunals also varied in their attitudes towards certain types of appeal. During hardship cases, some members focused entirely on objective calculations of domestic or financial strain, and refused to consider more intangible factors like loss or suffering. When a man supporting a widowed mother and a frail sister appeared before the Birstall Tribunal, his claim was refused on the basis that an army separation allowance would bring in more money than his current wages.[21] Using the same rationale, the Barnsley Borough Tribunal turned down Joseph Smeaton despite the fact his father's chronic bronchitis had left him as the sole provider for a mother and three young siblings.[22] This determination to resist 'sentiment' could even be applied to families who possessed stout records of service. Appealing at Batley, Thomas Ramsden's mother explained that she already had four sons serving in the army. Although the tribunal acknowledged the family had 'done very well', it ultimately concluded that the degree of financial pressure was insufficient to justify exemption.[23]

In contrast, other appeal bodies were determined to avoid causing significant hardship. Appearing at Huddersfield in October 1917, a butcher was exempted because his mother suffered from mental troubles and would probably be sent to an asylum without his constant care.[24] Two months later, the Wakefield Borough Tribunal was deeply moved by the appeal of a joiner's apprentice, the son of a widow who had already lost two sons in action, had another who was missing and had a fourth who was suffering from gas poisoning. In granting conditional

110 *Army first?*

exemption, the chairman said they were 'bound to let their feelings have a little play' given the 'appalling circumstances'.[25] Similarly reprieved was a family that boasted one of the most remarkable service records in the division. Speaking before the Goole Rural body, Mrs. Cowling divulged that she already had six sons in the firing line, with another on his way over from Canada. Delighted with this fulsome evidence of sacrifice, the chairman immediately granted conditional exemption to her remaining son, Frank, and announced 'Mrs. Cowling has done her share' to a resounding chorus of 'hear, hear'.[26]

Further disparities emerged over cases based on business or industrial dislocation. Some members were determined to obtain the maximum number of soldiers, regardless of how great the resulting interference promised to be. The chairman of the Wakefield Borough Tribunal, in dismissing an appeal from a window-cleaning firm, remarked that 'we must go with our windows dirty if necessary. We have got to beat the Germans.'[27] Likewise, Mr. Dennison warned prospective New Mill appellants that 'if you think more about your business than about your country then the war will have to drag on'.[28] Even the probable closure of an enterprise could be deemed insufficient to warrant exemption, with the Batley Tribunal refusing the claim of a theatre owner on the basis that 'tens of thousands' of more important concerns had already been shut down.[29] Some employers' claims also came up short. In March 1916, the Holmfirth Tribunal conducted a detailed investigation into the requirements of local textile mills. While the findings suggested that production would decline if any more men were taken, the members still opted to refuse several appeals because of the army's urgent need for reinforcements.[30] One year later, the Stanley Tribunal countered a colliery owner's plea of having already released 440 employees with the assertion that having sent 4,040 would still not absolve him from providing more given the military situation in France.[31]

Other tribunals proved far more amenable to cases made on business grounds. The Featherstone body exempted Eric Cooper, manager of two fruit shops, after he pleaded that both his former assistants were serving at the front.[32] Likewise, the Goole Urban body awarded a six-month certificate to G. H. Thompson, ironmonger, arguing it would be 'a serious matter' to close his 'well-established' business.[33] Cases lodged on behalf of skilled and essential workers were also favourably received. The Shepley body granted all the appeals made by a quarry manager who outlined the importance of his operation to the local economy, while substantial praise, and a conditional exemption, was afforded to a contractor claiming for his son, who informed the Normanton Tribunal that three of his other boys, and thirty-five out of his eighty-six workers, had already joined the forces.[34]

Appeals based on medical grounds were another point of inconsistency. The fifth exemption criteria, that of 'ill-health or infirmity', was intended to cover dissatisfaction with the examinations conducted on all prospective recruits. Throughout 1916, evidence was brought forward showing that the army medical boards were passing men who should have been rejected outright, and classifying men with obvious ailments as fit for 'general service'. The tribunals were undoubtedly aware of this criticism. In September, the government appointed a Central Medical Board to adjudicate on cases where civilian doctors contradicted

Army first? 111

the military examiners' findings.[35] In addition, the appeal bodies were confronted by an ever-increasing number of appellants who claimed that inadequate procedures had led to their being wrongly assessed. Despite this growing indication of poor practice, several of the division's tribunals persistently rejected all medical claims. In September 1916, the Wakefield Borough body conceded that some men who had been passed fit would likely break down at the front, but still refused to question the findings of the army doctors.[36] The following month, the Batley Tribunal tersely dismissed the claim of John Hepworth, who was using crutches for his hip disease and had a crushed ankle, while the Mirfield chairman cut short a money-lender's claim of unfitness by stating 'that is not for us, but for the Medical Board to say'.[37] Such outright rebuttals did decline after May 1917, when evidence surfaced of inadequate re-examinations being carried out under the Military Service (Review of Exceptions) Act, but several tribunals still remained reluctant to grant exemption on medical grounds.

Other bodies quickly moved to safeguard the appellants' interests. As early as March 1916, the Huddersfield Tribunal granted absolute exemption to a warehouseman who submitted a doctor's certificate showing that he suffered from chronic dyspepsia and fits.[38] A week later, the same body lodged a formal protest after hearing from a man whose examination by the Halifax Medical Board had lasted only two minutes.[39] This loss of faith was not an isolated incident. By the end of 1916, many tribunals were referring all doubtful cases for re-examination, while the Pontefract Borough body had begun indefinitely adjourning every appeal where a man had not been properly assessed the second time around.[40] In November 1917, the government re-allocated the responsibility for conducting medical evaluations to civilian medical boards operating under the Ministry of National Service.[41] While those tribunals that had adopted a pro-active stance appreciated the resulting improvement, they were still willing to challenge any further instances of poor practice.[42]

A particularly divisive issue among the division's tribunals was whether to impose military obligations on exempted men. Established at the war's outbreak to resist a possible German invasion, the Volunteer Training Corps (VTC) was destined to play a significant role under conscription.[43] By making involvement with their local branch a condition of exemption, the tribunals could ensure that conscripts would have already completed part of their military training before any subsequent drafting. This stipulation was applied in the months following April 1916 by several appeal bodies. At Linthwaite, it was held that undertaking drills would allow men to 'remain at their work and at the same time be training for the army'.[44] Less charitably, a member of the Knottingley Tribunal described the condition as a means of forcing young singles who were 'shirking behind their occupation' to commence military service.[45] After January 1917, the VTC was re-organised into several sections. The most important for the tribunals was section B, whose members were required to serve for the remainder of the war and to attend a prescribed number of drills each month. If an exempted man did not join section B, he was only obligated to perform drills as stated by his appeal body.[46] Some tribunals immediately took advantage of this new provision.

112 *Army first?*

The Ossett body began requiring nearly all exempted men to join section B, while the Horbury Tribunal imposed the condition on anyone who had been medically classed A, B1 or C1.[47] Then, in March 1917, the Slaithwaite Tribunal became the first in the division to cancel an exemption certificate over a man's failure to attend the requisite number of drills.[48]

These wide-ranging procedures were not adopted everywhere. The two Goole tribunals resisted employing any version of the VTC condition until February 1917, and the Birstall members were still holding out that September.[49] In addition, the Wakefield Borough body firmly rebuked their military representative for merely advising appellants to join section B, while the Dewsbury Tribunal temporarily cut all ties with the local corps after learning that its officers had browbeaten men into signing a form that bound them to serve for the duration.[50] A more common approach was to impose obligations in a selective manner. Numerous bodies automatically absolved men who were over a certain age, who were working long hours, or who would have to travel large distances.[51] Conversely, other bodies applied the VTC condition in most instances, but were quite willing to compromise if the appellant could prove that it was too much of a burden.[52]

Substantial disparities also occurred over matters of impartiality. One troublesome issue was whether appeal hearings should be conducted in public or behind closed doors. Privacy was the norm everywhere during the Derby Scheme, but a myriad of approaches emerged once conscription came into force. The pertinent regulation stated that 'all applications to the Local Tribunal shall be heard in public', unless the interests of the parties required otherwise.[53] Most tribunals immediately admitted onlookers to their sittings, except when sensitive personal or business information was being disclosed. Indeed, the chairman of the Meltham body specifically stated that 'cases were to be heard in public, and subject to certain reservations it would be all right for the public to attend'.[54] Yet this was not the practice throughout the division. At Honley and the two Pontefract tribunals, it was left open for any appellant to request a private sitting.[55] Even more extreme was the policy adopted by the Castleford, Goole Urban and Wombwell bodies, which resolved to exclude all outsiders from their early meetings.[56] Most of these tribunals reverted to public hearings after just a few months, but the South Crosland members continued to insist that journalists should not identify which of them had asked particular questions.[57] Furthermore, the Goole Urban body was still probing every appellant on their desire to be heard *in camera* as late as June 1916, despite a series of objections from the *Goole Times* and the local military representative about such 'hole and corner proceedings'.[58]

Uniformity was also lacking over the potential encroachment of class bias. There were numerous allegations that the tribunals routinely favoured men of a high social standing. One delegate to the Huddersfield and District Trades and Labour Council suggested that 'the tribunals were packed by middle-class men, who looked after middle-class interests', while a New Mill appellant reacted to the dismissal of his appeal by exclaiming 'if I had been a man of money you would have given me three months, perhaps six months'.[59] Several historians have given considerable credence to these assertions, and there is certainly supporting

Army first? 113

evidence from parts of the division.[60] In December 1916, William Bruce, the owner of a blind-making business, asked the Batley Tribunal for a temporary exemption. Stating that his enterprise would come to a standstill if he were taken, Bruce maintained this would put one hundred men out of work and prevent completion of the many orders his firm had received. Initially, the chairman seemed poised to dismiss the case. He noted Bruce was only twenty-eight years old and had made no effort to sell his concern, both factors that had ruined the chances of many previous appellants. However, after further consideration, the tribunal awarded a three-month exemption due to the business being 'an extensive one'.[61] A similar incident occurred at Wakefield Borough, when the military representative challenged the certificate held by the director of a local textile mill, who was thirty-six and had been passed fit for 'general service'. For unstated reasons the case was heard in private, resulting in the man's exemption being continued. This decision contrasts strikingly with that in the very next claim, where a thirty-three-year-old woollen warehouseman, classed B1 and described by his employer as 'absolutely indispensable', had his exemption revoked.[62]

Many other tribunals actively resisted the lure of class sentiment. One of the few aristocratic appellants in the division was Cassandra, Countess of Rosse, who appealed for several members of her household staff to the Pontefract Rural body. Although her testimony was enough to secure three men conditional exemptions, the tribunal decided to send two more of them into the army.[63] Similarly treated was Charles Edward Fox, the twenty-seven-year-old son of George Fox J. P., a former Mayor of Dewsbury and the head of an architectural and surveying firm. This case had previously resulted in a conditional exemption, awarded so the military representative could find a suitable substitute. However, Lieutenant Strachan now informed the tribunal that he had sent five prospective candidates to the firm, only for Fox senior to reject them all as unqualified. Regarding this as unwarranted obstruction, the appeal body chose to cancel Charles's exemption forthwith.[64]

There was no unanimity either as to how the tribunals should deal with claims made by their own personnel or their families. The regulations regarding the latter stated that members should withdraw from any case in which they were 'personally interested'.[65] Yet this was not always carried out. In October 1916, the Goole Urban Tribunal, after reviewing several exemption certificates, informed the watching journalists that their sitting had concluded. However, the members then remained behind to hear one last case in private, that of F. W. Porter, a thirty-two-year-old timber importer's foreman. After a lengthy discussion, Porter was awarded conditional exemption ostensibly because he was carrying out skilled work and was the only experienced employee left in the firm. However, given that he was single and had been passed fit for 'general service', these secretive proceedings make it difficult to look past the fact Porter was also the son of one of the appeal body's members.[66] The hearings of tribunal personnel proved even more awkward. Although Long had advised the local registration authorities not to appoint men of military age, some councils promptly ignored this guidance, while other members became eligible after being medically re-classified, or after the raising of the military age in 1918. At Ossett, Alderman Wilson was

114 *Army first?*

repeatedly supported in his re-election as mayor by the other councillors on the appeal body, despite having taken up the position at the age of forty. When he finally resigned from the tribunal and claimed exemption in June 1918, Wilson was not only granted a six-month exemption, but also excused from joining the VTC and told that his relief was conditional on him standing for mayor again that November.[67]

In contrast to these highly dubious practices, some tribunals endeavoured to uphold strict standards of impartiality. At Batley, Alderman Blackburn recused himself while several cases from his firm were heard, and raised no objection when the appeal body ordered his son, Fred, to the front.[68] Likewise, Councillor Banks retired from a sitting of the Castleford Tribunal to watch his son, George, be told he must join the Army Ordnance Corps.[69] While there were seemingly no instances in the division of a tribunal member having his appeal dismissed, several did step down on principle once they had been re-classified as fit or had come within the extended military age.

Another contentious matter of impartiality was whether members should rule on appeals concerning their own employees. Again, some bodies ignored the regulations, particularly when local council personnel were being dealt with. In August 1917, the Spenborough Tribunal granted conditional exemption to the corporation's accountant, with all the councillors present casting a vote.[70] Likewise, a scavenging foreman was afforded relief at Whitwood after the tribunal chairman pledged himself 'on behalf of the Council' to try and find a replacement.[71] When the military representative pointed out that the Central Tribunal had ruled local authority members should not vote in the claims of their own staff, the chairman of the Featherstone body argued that they 'had been appointed by the Government to sit on the Tribunal, and had had no intimation they were not to sit in such cases, and so long as he was a member, he should continue to adjudicate'.[72] The regulations were also disregarded for other employees. When the Normanton body reviewed the certificates held by five members of the local butchers' association, a unanimous vote decided that Councillor Butler, who was president of that association, 'should not vacate the Chair'.[73]

Yet some of the division's tribunals acted with scrupulous fairness. The Barnsley Borough body heard several appeals relating to employees of the Worsborough and Hoyland Nether local authorities, after the councillors sitting in those districts had decided they could not judge the claims of their own staff.[74] Elsewhere, when the Slaithwaite and South Crosland tribunals found they would have insufficient numbers to form a quorum if all the councillors recused themselves, it was decided to ask for the appointment of additional personnel.[75] Outside of council interests, Alderman Holton always retired at Birstall when cases from his firm were being considered, with the same procedure being followed by members of the Knottingley, New Mill and Ossett bodies, among others.[76]

Differences in outlook also occurred between the members of individual tribunals. This usually involved a tribunal's labour representatives taking a minority stand for exemption. At Huddersfield, Joseph Pickles, national secretary of the Painters' Union, and Councillor Taylor, secretary of the Postmen's Federation,

Army first?   115

often voted for the relief of men whom their colleagues wished to refuse, while Councillor Brook, a member of the ILP, walked out of a meeting of the New Mill Tribunal when it decided to make VTC drills obligatory.[77] However, some working-class members were at the forefront of demands to send more men to the army, and the fault-lines within other appeal bodies' did not reflect political allegiances. In January 1917, Chairman McCann criticised his Dewsbury colleagues' apparent predilection towards leniency by arguing 'our business is to get men into the Army'. This reasoning was swiftly countered by a second non-labour member, who maintained their primary responsibility was 'to hold the balance' between the appellants and the military.[78] At Heckmondwike, Councillor Clarke and Mr. Atkin resisted the exemption of forty textile mill employees by arguing the tribunal had 'as much interest in getting men as the military representative', but were challenged by the chairman on the basis that the appeal body had been established 'as a safeguard' for the appellants' interests.[79] Regarding specific cases, Councillor Jagger, a factory manager on the Honley Tribunal, consistently found himself in the minority when he voted for the exemption of widows' only sons, and Councillor Armitage, a chartered accountant, resisted the Huddersfield chairman by advocating for an appellant whose care was the only thing keeping his mother out of a workhouse.[80] From the opposite perspective, one Hemsworth Rural member exclaimed that he was 'openly against the leniency shown' to many appellants by his colleagues.[81]

One reason for this variation in attitudes was the sheer volume of guidance that the division's tribunals received. The LGB alone dispatched 244 circulars, including notes on those 103 cases heard by the Central Tribunal that were considered to establish a precedent. In addition, the local tribunals were subject to: the six Military Service Acts and their associated regulations; the frequently revised list of certified occupations and schedule of protected occupations; Army Council instructions; correspondence from the War Office; and circulars from the Board of Education, Board of Agriculture, Ministry of Munitions, Department then Ministry of National Service and Man-Power Distribution Board. It is little wonder that one handbook designed to keep the tribunals abreast of all this information opined that it would require 'the brain of a Philadelphian lawyer to cope with accumulated mass of Terminological Government Literature'.[82]

As well as being overwhelming in their extent, the tribunals' directions were frequently ambiguous. When attempting to clarify what should constitute 'serious hardship' under the Act, Long sent out a list of five questions for the appeal bodies to consider, each of which contained various sub-questions.[83] Likewise, the tribunals were told to impose the VTC condition only in cases where it was 'reasonable', a word that could be construed in any number of different ways, and were asked to evaluate the standing of a man's occupation against such nebulous criteria as 'work of national importance' or 'manifestly irreplaceable'.[84] The fact the appeal bodies' instructions derived from a multitude of different sources meant they could even be contradictory. As early as April 1916, the Spenborough chairman lamented that 'things seem to be getting into a fearful muddle'.[85] A few months later, the Whitwood chairman complained 'there were so many

116 *Army first?*

committees that they scarcely knew where they were', and the Barnsley Borough chairman told his military representative that 'I wish we could place confidence in the Government ... but they change their mind so often'.[86]

Receiving a mass of vague instructions might have been less problematic if the tribunals had possessed a ready means of consulting with the government. Yet this was not the case. The appeal bodies frequently complained that their letters to the LGB either went unanswered or received a *pro forma* reply.[87] Moreover, there was not a single instance where a member of the government travelled to visit the division's local tribunals. The appeal bodies were asked to send representatives to meet with General Lawson in Leeds during October 1916, and to a further session with General Maxwell in June 1917.[88] Yet these gatherings did not include all the tribunals' members, were focused only on the War Office's view of the exemption system, and were followed by numerous complaints along the lines of 'I do not think the outcome of the meeting is likely to be of benefit to anyone'.[89]

Another cause of discrepancy was the large number of tribunals and members. With there being sixty-four appeal bodies in the division alone, inconsistencies were always highly likely, if not inevitable. Moreover, each tribunal was staffed by personnel who differed from their counterparts on at least a few, and possibly many, of the other appeal bodies in terms of their occupation, political allegiance, eligibility for service and beliefs about the war and conscription. Just one of these variables could profoundly affect a member's views, and thereby impact on the approach of his or her entire tribunal. This issue was further compounded by the size of many of the appeal bodies. The involvement of up to eleven members, each voicing their own opinions, meant reaching a verdict sometimes proved extremely difficult and time consuming. While around four hundred tribunal personnel were appointed in the division at the outset, a combination of additions, deaths, re-assignments, resignations and absenteeism meant the total number during conscription was probably closer to six hundred. Across Britain it has been estimated that a staggering forty thousand men and women served on tribunals.[90]

The final contributor to the tribunals' divergent approaches was the localism of their personnel. No member would have completely disregarded the national context of exemptions; nearly all of them were desperate to win the war, while maintaining food or industrial production obviously held wider implications. Yet, above all, these were individuals who had been appointed for their knowledge of, and standing within, the local community. Indeed, one of the few beliefs the division's members did share was that the unique circumstances of their district had to be taken into account. Such thinking was inherently opposed to uniformity. In November 1916, the Marsden body informed their military representative that they would refuse to take any more men from beleaguered local textile mills so long as similar facilities in Slaithwaite were able to maintain a full schedule of day and night work.[91] That same month, the Slaithwaite Tribunal protested that they had utilised the VTC condition far more extensively than the Marsden body, thereby placing an unequal burden on local men and causing a greater strain to the local economy.[92] The logic of the members' position also hindered uniformity in another way. As local, and often elected, figures, they proved highly responsive to

Army first? 117

the community feeling that arose around certain cases or issues. Yet by adjusting its approach to appease unrest, a tribunal could take itself out of alignment with the others. When the Dewsbury body cut ties with the VTC following allegations men had been bullied into joining section B, it became one of the few in the division to not impose drill on at least some exempted appellants. Similarly, the public allegations of bias made against the Castleford Tribunal prompted its members to start recusing themselves whenever they had even the most tenuous connection to an appellant or his place of employment.[93]

There was a degree of inconsistency in the attitudes adopted by the New Zealand boards. This primarily concerned the amount of proof they required before exempting men from essential industries. Some bodies accepted ministerial certificates that recommended relief out of hand, whereas others looked in detail at the circumstances of every case. By July 1917, the secretary of the Federated Seamen's Union had become so frustrated at the differing types of corroborative information stipulated by the three Wellington boards that he exclaimed 'I don't want to be messed about any longer'.[94] Similarly, most of the appeal bodies were prepared to exempt shearers or slaughtermen on the assurance of a union secretary that they were *bona fide* and essential, but a few insisted on local testimony being given in each claim.[95] Fears over what these variations might mean for the boards' reputation were expressed by the Canterbury member of the NEB, William Frostick. He asserted that although the two appeal bodies in his military district were always following official instructions, the fact they were interpreting these slightly differently meant the public perceived that some form of 'injustice' was taking place.[96]

Yet in contrast to the division's tribunals, the boards did adopt a strong unifying philosophy. This can best be described as the desire to achieve an equality of sacrifice, a concept that had two key elements. On the one hand, the members were convinced that military necessities had to be met in order to facilitate an Allied victory. The chairman of the Second Canterbury Board stated it was 'his clear duty to send as many men as possible', while his counterpart on the Second Wellington body stressed that each 'available man in the country will have to go to it'.[97] This outlook motivated a belief that every individual had to contribute as much as they possibly could to the war effort. One chairman considered a man's 'first duty' was to the forces, and another rhetorically asked an appellant 'does it matter nothing to you whether you are under German or British rule?'[98] The boards saw their role as being to investigate cases thoroughly in order to root out 'shirkers'. Relief would not be given lightly, with the appellant always having to satisfy the burden of proof.

On the other hand, the second element of the boards' mantra held that exemption should be granted if justified. Chairman Day of the Second Otago body maintained that he and his colleagues wanted 'to determine how best men can serve their country', and the members of the Second Auckland Board signalled their intention 'to deal with appellants with due regard to the military demands of the State, while inflicting no undue hardship on the individual or imperilling food production'.[99] Every man would be given a 'fair chance' to state his claim, with the

118 *Army first?*

members insisting that their extensive questioning was not motivated by a desire to fill reinforcement quotas, but to reach informed decisions.[100] When responding to criticism that they had acted too harshly, the boards rarely emphasised the need for men, but instead expressed disappointment that their earnest efforts to balance the needs of the country and the appellant had not been recognised. One chairman lamented that 'scarcely a day passes that we do not hear anathemas passed upon [our] decisions, still we have to keep on and carry out our functions to the best of our abilities'.[101]

This quest for an equality of sacrifice determined the boards' approach during appeal hearings. Men from families who had failed to send any sons to the front were routinely denounced. Charles Managh's father stated that his son did all the ploughing and cropping on their farm of 1,050 acres, which held 2,300 sheep and 80 cows. The land needed constant attention, as it was impossible to fatten the animals without cropping. Yet these arguments were insufficient to deflect the ire of the First Wellington Board when Managh admitted that he had three more sons who had not enlisted, with one member charging 'why should some families sacrifice all and some nothing?'[102] Henry and Joseph McNeill had equally a torrid time before the First Otago Board, they being the only sons in the family. Asked to explain their failure to join up, one brother's assertion that they had 'not been summoned' prompted the retort that they 'didn't need to be summoned. Sixty thousand of them weren't summoned. They went'.[103] Men who were perceived as placing an undue emphasis on having two or three brothers in the firing line were also criticised, it being pointed out that other families had managed to send five or six members. When Peter McLaren pleaded hardship to his mother on the grounds he had two brothers serving and another recently called up, he was told by the chairman of the First Otago Board that 'if we allow sentiment to rule us there might be a difficulty in getting a draft'.[104] So firm was the boards' initial stance in this regard that, in January 1917, the government had to instruct them to exempt automatically any appellant with two or more brothers killed in action.[105]

Other reservists were denied exemption after the boards refuted claims that their conscription would cause undue hardship to relatives. Thomas McCune of Whitianga had an ill wife and dependent father-in-law to support, and maintained that he contributed an essential proportion of his 9s. 6d. daily wage to their upkeep. This failed to satisfy a member of the First Auckland Board, who told McCune that with pay and allowances he would receive 47s. 3d. a week in the army.[106] Similar reasoning was used against Charles Connor, the sole provider for his aged father and invalid brother, to whom he sent a total of £30 each year.[107] Another of the boards' frequent ripostes was that family members or patriotic organisations would be able to fill the gap left by an appellant's absence. When George Grigg claimed that his wages were the only thing supporting his widowed mother, a member of the First Wellington Board informed him that 'I know of hundreds of cases where the War Relief Societies have assisted persons so situated'.[108] Likewise, the First Otago body turned down Charles Orr, a labourer who was the sole support of his widowed mother and partial support of his stepbrother, on the basis that 'there were the patriotic societies, whose duty it was to

Army first? 119

supplement the mother's income if necessary'.[109] The boards admitted that hardship would inevitably result in such cases, but asserted that other families were suffering just as much and that sacrifices had to be made in order to win the war.

Businessmen and tradesmen who cited economic hardship stood little chance of exemption if they were not engaged in essential work. When John Keen, a hairdresser and tobacconist, lamented he would be forced to give up his 'good business' if not given time to find a manager, he received little sympathy from the First Wellington Board. The members insisted that Keen would serve his country better by going to the front, and asked whether he was aware 'that thousands have actually given up their business and their good positions?'[110] Men in similar occupations who appealed for time to arrange their affairs were often accused of making an insufficient effort to do so previously. When a solicitor asked the Second Auckland Board for three months to find a manager, he was informed that 'other solicitors had arranged their affairs much more promptly'.[111]

Many employers also failed to satisfy the boards of their credentials. Where an enterprise was not considered vital to the war effort, the appeal bodies usually required it to work through the loss of an appellant, or to close down. Moreover, simply being engaged in a 'most essential' or 'essential' industry was not enough. The boards asserted that the man himself had to be indispensable, and frequently asked questions regarding precise roles and the steps that had been taken to secure a replacement. John Bell asserted that, as a foreman compositor, he was integral to the production of the *Ashburton Guardian*. Sensing that something was amiss, the First Canterbury Board delved into Bell's responsibilities and forced his employer to admit that a dismissal would in fact only cause an 'awful strain' to the publication. This prompted Chairman Evans to remark that 'the men at the front have also to endure an awful strain. We don't take into consideration the infliction of a strain'.[112] Other employers were probed over how their business would cope if the man they were appealing for suddenly took ill, died or 'was run over by a tramcar'.[113]

Some of the boards' strongest criticism was reserved for employers who had made no effort to replace their staff with men who were too old or unfit to fight, or, increasingly, women. John Linklater appeared on behalf of Thomas Linklater, a farm hand, and argued that he would not be able to carry on his team and agricultural work if his son were taken. Under questioning, John stated 'he had taken no steps to get another man, because it was no good', to which Chairman Poynton replied that it was 'no use his taking up that attitude; they knew that women were helping in agriculture in England'.[114] Members were also wont to seize on the failure of many industries to organise themselves. In criticising the apparently lackadaisical efforts of Taranaki farmers, a member of the First Wellington body remarked that 'this Board has been preaching co-operation for about eight months now. The people here seem only to wake up when they are hit'.[115]

Whatever the appellant's occupation, the boards adhered rigidly to three principles that made certain cases less likely to succeed. First was the conviction that 'every single man should be made to go before any married man is forced to go'.[116] The members believed that Second Division reservists had much greater

120 *Army first?*

responsibilities than those in the First Division and that their conscription would cause considerably more hardship. They often pointed out that exempting a single man would force a married man to serve in his stead, with a member of the First Otago Board asking an appellant whether 'your son should stay at home and let married men with families go?'[117] A second principle revolved around the situation at the front. If casualties were high or German attacks successful, the boards would prioritise getting men into camp. Fernando Fernandez had previously been granted *sine die* exemption owing to his being an engineer employed by the Public Works Department at the Addington sub-station. On reviewing his case in April 1918, the Second Canterbury Board argued that 'the position to-day is different to what it has been' and dismissed Fernandez's case with only a short period of leave.[118] Equally, the chairman of the Third Wellington body countered a bus proprietor's claim that 'the busy time is just coming on' by asserting 'yes, the busy time is on in Europe at the present time, too'.[119] The third principle that counted against appellants was a refusal to tolerate any attempt at exaggeration. When a sheep farmer appeared before the Second Wellington Board to claim that his properties would have to be sold in his absence, the rural member asked whether it was really 'likely that the farms would be shut up?'[120] Likewise, the First Otago body scornfully rejected the appeal of a farm hand, whose father claimed that his seventeen-year-old son was incapable of working with horses.[121] Evidence of outright duplicity could even prompt the appeal bodies to take punitive action. At a previous sitting of the First Canterbury Board, Ernest Ward, a Waipara farmer, had been granted *sine die* exemption on the grounds that his father owned a hotel in Dunedin, and was therefore unable to assist him on the property. However, police evidence then came to light showing the father had in fact sold his interest in the hotel and had been helping out on the farm for some time. Incensed by this blatant deception, Chairman Evans ordered that Ward be prosecuted for perjury.[122]

The boards do not seem to have unduly favoured appellants from the higher social classes. Despite the fact seven of the nine active appeal bodies contained a trade union official, there were numerous allegations that men of wealth and status were more likely to receive exemption. A correspondent to the *Hawke's Bay Tribune* lamented that 'when you achieve a certain amount of prosperity you become indispensable', while the *NZ Truth* kept up a series of sarcastic tilts at the appeal bodies' alleged inequities.[123] Perhaps the most controversial verdicts reached during conscription were the First Auckland Board's exemption of Robert Laidlaw, founder of the Laidlaw Leeds mail order business, and the Third Wellington body's refusal of an appeal for the working-class MP for Grey, Paddy Webb. One reason why Laidlaw's exemption prompted such a furore was that it coincided with the relief of several other wealthy and high-profile appellants, namely the Australasian head of the meat company Thomas Borthwick and Sons, the manager of the Bank of New Zealand and the prominent Auckland solicitor John Tole.[124]

However, there is little evidence to support claims of a wide-ranging class bias. Laidlaw's case was postponed several times to obtain additional information, and the board clearly acknowledged the import of its verdict by delivering

Army first? 121

it alongside a lengthy justification.[125] As for Webb, he failed even to attend his appeal hearing, which was something that all the appeal bodies regarded as *prima facie* grounds for dismissal.[126] There were also numerous instances of appellants being denied relief precisely because they possessed large amounts of money. The Second Otago chairman dismissed the appeal of Arthur King on the grounds his father could easily afford to employ a manager, before pointedly remarking that 'the well-to-do people seemed to be the first to ask for exemption'.[127] Likewise, a member of the First Auckland body stated that men of property were those who 'had the most at stake, and who should be prepared to defend it', and Chairman Evans asserted that his board always refused cases where men were in a 'sufficiently sound financial position to be able to carry on their properties while they went to the front'.[128] Ultimately, the individuals who were most likely to receive exemption from the boards were not wealthy industrialists, bankers or merchants, but rather slaughtermen, miners, merchant seamen and police constables.

The board members also resisted the temptation to prioritise men who shared their economic background, or who they knew in a personal capacity. As impartial overseers, the chairmen had numerous responsibilities. These included summing up the evidence, delivering the verdict and giving statements of their board's policies if the case had a wider significance. Yet the chairmen did not limit themselves to administrative functions, and often took a full part in assessing the validity of testimony through questioning. The other members usually divided their labour on the basis of expertise. If the appellant was engaged in a rural occupation, the farmer member would ask any technical questions and comment on the evidence from his own experience, with the trade unionist or businessman doing the same in urban cases. Members did endeavour to moderate their colleagues if they felt their questioning was overly harsh or uninformed.[129] However, there was no obvious favouritism, with expert knowledge also being used to identify dubious elements of an appellant's testimony. The trade unionist on the Third Wellington Board opposed his colleagues' decision to exempt several marine engineers, while the Farmers' Union petitioned Allen to increase the number of farmers on each appeal body, so as to include a specific representative for the main type of agricultural production in every district a board sat in.[130] As for individuals they knew outside of the appeals process, the boards typically observed strict standards of impartiality. Indeed, a member of the First Auckland body told an appellant 'I'm not supposed to know anybody. That's why I didn't nod to you'.[131]

Despite their wish to take every man who could reasonably be expected to serve, the boards clearly recognised that some exemptions had to be granted. This partly revolved around an attempt to mitigate the difficulties their decisions would cause. An insistence that 'we do not wish to inflict hardship on anyone' was not mere self-justification, as what were perceived as genuine cases provoked considerable sympathy.[132] Having studied George Adamson's written submission, the chairman of the Third Wellington Board proclaimed himself 'quite satisfied that, if his statements were true, appellant would have been a brute to enlist. It is clearly a case of "Les Miserables."'[133] Similarly, when Ralph Darling told the First Otago body he already had three brothers serving, the chairman agreed that taking the

122 *Army first?*

last boy from the family would be a hardship on the mother, and, therefore, 'the board did not feel justified in disturbing the existing arrangements'.[134]

Regardless of a man's situation, the appeal bodies always rewarded a tangible willingness to make sacrifices. While having two or three brothers at the front was usually insufficient to gain exemption on its own, it did lead the members to view a case more favourably. Hugh Russell asked for four months' exemption to dispose of his business, which the Third Wellington Board awarded after he outlined that three of his brothers were in the forces.[135] The appeal bodies' preparedness to grant exemption rose in proportion to the number of men a family had sent and they lauded the patriotism of parents who had five or six sons serving. Gordon Birnie testified that five of his brothers were at the front, while another had already been killed in action. Overjoyed with this example of sacrifice, a member of the First Auckland Board exclaimed 'I should like to congratulate you on this very fine showing. There are not many families with six sons away'.[136] Similarly appreciated were those appellants who had made an effort to ready themselves for conscription, either by making arrangements for their family or by trying to dispose of their assets. Edwin Kupli stressed that it would only take him two months to wind up his furniture business of twelve years' standing, and that he did not mind the sizeable financial loss this arrangement would cause. After the board had professed its admiration for the appellant's patriotism, and stated it 'thoroughly appreciated the big sacrifice he was prepared to make', Kupli was granted his two months.[137] For Percy Cramp, the issue was that he already had two brothers serving and would have to sell his dairy stock if he were taken as well. Nevertheless, Cramp stated that he considered it his duty to go and only wanted a period of relief for milking. This prompted a member to praise his 'good spirit' and for the appeal body as a whole to grant three months' leave.[138]

Recognition of the need to maintain essential businesses and industries was also apparent. John Greenslade, a merchant, only asked the First Canterbury Board for four months in which to sell his concern, but the chairman stated they were disinclined to compel people to wind up, and instead granted a *sine die* exemption.[139] Likewise, Patrick O'Gorman, the only bread baker left at a firm of grocers, was given an indefinite period of relief by the First Otago body because it had not 'adopted the policy of closing up necessary businesses'.[140] As for industries, the members constantly stressed that the needs of the army and the economy had to be balanced against each other, so as to minimise disruption to New Zealand's productive capacity. Indeed, a formal statement issued by the Second Auckland body maintained that 'they did not desire to damp the ardour of any young fellow anxious to go to the front, but they recognised that the affairs of the country had to be kept going'.[141] If the boards felt a particularly impressive effort had been made to release men, they asked the employer to read out the figures so they could be published in the press, both to highlight the achievement and to provide an example to others.

Another striking contrast is that there were scarcely any disagreements within individual boards. This is not to suggest the members were always of one mind. When the appeal of Thomas Green was referred to the NEB by the First Otago

Army first? 123

body, Alfred Bell expressed a desire to 'disassociate himself entirely from the views of his colleagues in this matter', as he believed such an indispensable blacksmith should have immediately been granted exemption.[142] In April 1917, another member of the same board issued a minority statement to the effect that his colleagues had been wrong to award *sine die* relief to Albert Wheeler, the superintendent of the Union Steamship Company. Yet such incidents were extremely rare. As part of his report on the Wheeler case, Edward Kellett stated that he 'regretted' having to stand against his colleagues, and noted this was the 'first time' he had done so.[143] When any board member cast an opposing vote, he always felt compelled to give a lengthy explanation for adopting such an irregular course. Moreover, the military representative attached to the First Canterbury body recorded that its members were 'harmonious in every respect', and there were no resignations caused by internal disputes during conscription.[144]

There were three reasons why the boards achieved a much greater consistency in attitudes, with the first being the more concise and better explained instructions that they received. The boards were told that the issuing of a ministerial certificate should result in exemption, provided with a classification of industries that clearly indicated their relative importance and informed that having two or more brothers killed in action, or at least three brothers serving, should always be considered sufficient grounds for relief. There was no equivalent of the VTC to which exempted men might be sent, and disaffected New Zealand appellants could only be medically re-examined if they had obvious physical ailments.[145] Furthermore, the boards' directives were issued by just two sources: cabinet members and the NEB. If a lack of clarity subsequently became evident, they were guaranteed a swift response to their enquiries from the Recruiting Board, Solicitor General Salmond or Attorney General Herdman. Any remaining doubts could then be cleared up at one of the frequent conferences called by Allen, with the board chairmen meeting him at least six times during conscription.

A second reason was the boards' smaller numbers and standardised memberships. Having only nine active appeal bodies made synchronisation far more achievable, and allowed the government to better monitor their activities and take steps to correct any inconsistencies. While differences did exist between the boards in terms of their members' politics, Allen's strictly applied appointment criteria meant all were united in supporting the war and conscription, in representing similar occupations and in being outside of the military age. In addition, each board only had three members, and these individuals usually held their positions for long periods of time. Only forty New Zealanders sat on an active appeal body during conscription.[146] In other words, there were fewer board *members* across the whole country than there were *tribunals* operating in the division.

The third explanation concerns the boards' wider conception of the exemption system. If the division's tribunals tended to approach their work from a local perspective, then the New Zealand appeal bodies sought to achieve an equality of sacrifice by adopting a national outlook. When discussing agricultural cases, the chairman of the Second Auckland Board stated an intention to 'give every possible consideration to the farming industry, not in the interests of the appellants simply,

124   *Army first?*

but of the country as a whole'.[147] Similarly, a member of the First Wellington Board affirmed his desire to avoid any decision that would 'injure the country', while the chairman of the Second Wellington body stressed the need to keep freezing works operating due to their importance for the dominion's productive capacity.[148]

This more national perspective led the boards to place a much greater emphasis on uniformity. In February 1917, the chairman of the First Otago body dismissed several appeals on the basis that Balclutha sharemilkers were proving less productive than those employed 'down south'.[149] Likewise, the First Wellington Board criticised Taranaki farmers for not organising themselves as effectively as their counterparts in the Manawatu, while Chairman Cooper frequently countered claims that elderly relatives were too infirm to work by referencing an unnamed 'lady, aged 63 years, who milks 25 cows night and morning'.[150] When discrepancies in their methods did come to light, the boards always sought a swift resolution. In June 1917, the three Wellington bodies held an impromptu discussion over how best to determine the claims of men employed in essential industries.[151] A year later, the two Canterbury boards met to consider the cases of farmers engaged in wheat production.[152] If such an immediate remedy were found to be insufficient, the chairmen would either correspond with each other, or adjourn the relevant cases until an official instruction had been received.

These three factors illuminate why the boards' attitudes were much more closely aligned than those of the division's appeal bodies. Ultimately, it is impossible to reach a strong conclusion on whether the tribunals prioritised getting soldiers or sought to balance the army's needs with those of others. They did concur on only exempting single, young and high category men in exceptional circumstances, and on showing little sympathy to families who were not represented at the front. Yet beyond these few similarities existed a plethora of different approaches. The members could not even agree on the fundamental purpose of their work and differed widely over whether to accept sentimental cases, whether to heed the claims of businesses and industries, whether to oppose the findings of the medical boards, whether to direct men to the VTC, and over how to deal with potential conflicts of interest. These discrepancies stemmed from confusing instructions, the large number of tribunals and the localism of many of their members. The situation regarding the boards was largely the opposite. They did not achieve complete uniformity, but came far closer to doing so than their British counterparts. All the New Zealand bodies sought to promote an equality of sacrifice, a conception of their role that led them to place a high emphasis on military requirements, but also to acknowledge that some cases were deserving of exemption. This relatively united effort was made possible by clearer and more concise instructions, by the existence of fewer appeal bodies and by the national perspective adopted by the members.

Claims based on hardship, occupation or medical unfitness constituted the vast bulk of the tribunals' and boards' workloads. However, they were also required to judge the validity of another ground of appeal, one that would provoke an immense amount of controversy, and that would cause difficulties out of all proportion to frequency with which it was raised.

Notes

1 *HE*, 16 Sep. 1916, 5.
2 *GT*, 4 Aug. 1916, 4.
3 *BC*, 30 Sep. 1916, 2.
4 *CSG*, 24 Nov. 1916, 6.
5 *PCE*, 4 May 1917, 5.
6 *CSG*, 9 Mar. 1917, 3.
7 *PCE*, 16 Jun. 1916, 3.
8 *HE*, 13 Jan. 1917, 6.
9 *BC*, 17 Jun. 1916, 1.
10 *CSG*, 3 Mar. 1916, 2.
11 *BN*, 28 Oct. 1916, 1.
12 *HEx*, 22 Mar. 1916, 2; *BC*, 4 Mar. 1916, 8.
13 *HEx*, 1 Mar. 1916, 2.
14 Ibid., 2 Mar. 1916, 2.
15 Ibid., 26 Jun. 1918, 2.
16 *BN*, 9 Dec. 1916, 5.
17 *CSG*, 14 Apr. 1916, 5.
18 *HE*, 11 Mar. 1916, 2; *BN*, 5 May 1917, 5.
19 *BC*, 8 Apr. 1916, 1.
20 *HE*, 18 Mar. 1916, 8; Gray to Richmond, 2 Aug. 1916, BLTF, RD 21/6/2, KA.
21 *BN*, 26 Feb. 1916, 5.
22 *BC*, 27 Jan. 1917, 8.
23 *BN*, 2 Feb. 1918, 2.
24 *HEx*, 1 Oct. 1917, 4.
25 *WE*, 1 Dec. 1917, 7.
26 *GT*, 30 Mar. 1917, 2.
27 *WE*, 30 Jun. 1917, 6.
28 *HE*, 13 Jan. 1917, 6.
29 *BN*, 28 Apr. 1917, 3.
30 *HE*, 25 Mar. 1916, 8.
31 *WE*, 17 Mar. 1917, 3.
32 *PCE*, 19 Apr. 1916, 3.
33 *GT*, 5 Jul. 1918, 5.
34 *HEx*, 27 Jun. 1917, 4; *WE*, 13 May 1916, 7.
35 Keith Grieves, "Total War? The Quest for a British Manpower Policy, 1917–18," *Journal of Strategic Studies* 9, no. 1 (1986): 79–95; McDermott, *British Military Service Tribunals*, 185.
36 *WE*, 16 Sep. 1916, 7.
37 *BN*, 14 Oct. 1916, 5, 7.
38 *HEx*, 20 Mar. 1916, 4.
39 Minutes, Huddersfield Local Tribunal, 27 Mar. 1916, KMT 18/12/2/52/1, KA.
40 *WE*, 2 Sep. 1916, 8; *CSG*, 6 Oct. 1916, 7; *BN*, 24 Mar. 1917, 3; *PCE*, 20 Apr. 1917, 1.
41 Circular, LGB R. 155, 3 Nov. 1917, MH 47/142, NA.
42 *WE*, 1 Jun. 1918, 2; *CSG*, 21 Jun. 1918, 2; *W*, 22 Jun. 1918, 3.
43 K. W. Mitchinson, *Defending Albion: Britain's Home Army, 1908–1919* (Basingstoke: Palgrave Macmillan, 2005).
44 *HEx*, 14 Jul. 1916, 2.
45 *PCE*, 14 Jul. 1916, 3.
46 Mitchinson, *Defending Albion*, 150–51.
47 *OO*, 21 Apr. 1917, 3; *WE*, 21 Jul. 1917, 5.
48 *HEx*, 8 Mar. 1917, 3.
49 *GT*, 23 Feb. 1917, 5; *OO*, 15 Sep. 1917, 5.

126   *Army first?*

50   *WE*, 27 Jan. 1917, 8; *BN*, 14 Jul. 1917, 1 and 18 Aug. 1917, 1.
51   *GT*, 2 Feb. 1917, 4; *OO*, 24 Nov. 1917, 3; *PCE*, 2 Nov. 1917, 1.
52   *GT*, 2 Mar. 1917, 6; Minutes, Huddersfield Local Tribunal, 17 Aug. 1916, KMT 18/12/2/52/1, KA; *OO*, 15 Sep. 1917, 5.
53   "The Military Service (Regulations) Order, 1916," 3 Feb. 1916, MH 47/142, NA.
54   *HE*, 26 Feb. 1916, 8.
55   *W*, 4 Mar. 1916, 6; *PCE*, 3 Mar. 1916, 6 and 31 Mar. 1916, 3.
56   *PCE*, 10 Mar. 1916, 6; *GT*, 25 Feb. 1916, 5; *BI*, 4 Mar. 1916, 8.
57   *W*, 11 Mar. 1916, 5.
58   *GT*, 25 Feb. 1916, 5, 17 Mar. 1916, 4 and 2 Jun. 1916, 2.
59   *W*, 25 Mar. 1916, 5; *HE*, 21 Oct. 1916, 6.
60   Boulton, *Objection Overruled*, 124; Mitchinson, *Saddleworth*, 61–62; Kenneth O. Morgan, "Peace Movements in Wales, 1899–1945," *Welsh History Review* 10, no. 3 (1981): 413; Pearce, *Comrades in Conscience*, 139.
61   *BN*, 23 Dec. 1916, 5.
62   *WE*, 5 Jan. 1918, 7.
63   *PCE*, 16 Jun. 1916, 1, 4 Aug. 1916, 3 and 2 Feb. 1917, 2.
64   *BN*, 8 Sep. 1917, 4.
65   "The Military Service (Regulations) Order, 1916," 3 Feb. 1916, MH 47/142, NA.
66   *GT*, 6 Oct. 1916, 6.
67   *OO*, 11 Nov. 1916, 3, 10 Nov. 1917, 8 and 15 Jun. 1918, 3.
68   *BN*, 23 Jun. 1917, 4.
69   *PCE*, 2 Nov. 1917, 2.
70   *CSG*, 17 Aug. 1917, 6.
71   *PCE*, 9 Aug. 1918, 3.
72   Ibid., 20 Jul. 1917, 3.
73   *WE*, 10 Aug. 1918, 3; underlining in original.
74   *BC*, 17 Jun. 1916, 1, 27 Jan. 1917, 8 and 29 Jun. 1918, 1.
75   *W*, 7 Oct. 1916, 3; Minutes, South Crosland Urban District Council, 2 Oct. 1916, KMT 38, KA.
76   *BN*, 24 Mar. 1917, 3; *PCE*, 2 Jun. 1916, 3; *HE*, 1 Jul. 1916, 6; *OO*, 11 Mar. 1916, 5.
77   *W*, 7 Jul. 1917, 3 and 3 Nov. 1917, 3; *HE*, 16 Feb. 1916, 6; *HEx*, 21 Jul. 1917, 4.
78   *BN*, 6 Jan. 1917, 6.
79   *CSG*, 18 Oct. 1918, 3.
80   *HEx*, 2 Mar. 1916, 2 and 16 Nov. 1916, 4.
81   *BC*, 8 Jul. 1916, 7.
82   J. H. Worrall, *The Tribunal Hand-Book* (London: W. H. Smith & Son, 1917), 59–60.
83   Circular, LGB R. 55, 23 Feb. 1916, MH 47/142, NA.
84   Circular, LGB R. 95, 6 Jul. 1916, Circular, LGB R. 113, 20 Jan. 1917 and Circular, LGB R. 107, 1 Dec. 1916, MH 47/142, NA.
85   *CSG*, 14 Apr. 1916, 5.
86   *PCE*, 15 Jun. 1917, 3; *BC*, 29 Jun. 1916, 1.
87   *PCE*, 15 Jun. 1917, 2.
88   *BN*, 21 Oct. 1916, 2; *CSG*, 8 Jun. 1917, 3.
89   *CSG*, 22 Jun. 1917, 3.
90   Gregory, *Last Great War*, 103.
91   *HEx*, 23 Nov. 1916, 3.
92   Ibid., 16 Nov. 1917, 4.
93   *PCE*, 23 Jun. 1916, 2 and 5 Aug. 1917, 2.
94   *EP*, 13 Jul. 1917, 6.
95   Gray to Allen, 31 Jan. 1917, AD 82 8 74, ANZ; *EP*, 26 Jun. 1918, 6.
96   Frostick to Gray, 12 Dec. 1917, AD 1 736 10/512, ANZ.
97   *Akaroa Mail and Banks Peninsula Advertiser*, 17 Apr. 1917, 2; *EP*, 1 Aug. 1917, 8.
98   *P*, 3 Feb. 1917, 13; *EP*, 13 Mar. 1917, 7.

99 *ST*, 14 Mar. 1917, 5; *NZH*, 21 May 1917, 7.
100 Evans to Gray, 9 Dec. 1918 and Widdowson to Allen, 13 Dec. 1918, AD 82 2 1/11/2, ANZ; *EP*, 14 Mar. 1917, 6.
101 Cooper to Ferguson, 27 Aug. 1917, NEB 1 16 703, ANZ.
102 *FS*, 8 Oct. 1917, 4.
103 Kelly, *Military Board Appeals: Dec 1916 to Feb 1917*, 22.
104 *ODT*, 8 Jun. 1917, 2.
105 Gray to Military Service Board Chairmen, 27 Jan. 1917, AD 1 1 1/3, ANZ.
106 *AS*, 14 Mar. 1917, 2.
107 *EP*, 29 Dec. 1916, 3.
108 *EP*, 7 Dec. 1916, 7.
109 Kelly, *Military Board Appeals: Dec 1916 to Feb 1917*, 17.
110 *EP*, 13 Dec. 1916, 3.
111 *WT*, 21 Jun. 1918, 2.
112 *P*, 4 Jan. 1917, 8.
113 *EP*, 1 Feb. 1917, 7.
114 *PBH*, 11 Oct. 1917, 4.
115 *TH*, 13 Jul. 1917, 3.
116 *EP*, 7 Feb. 1917, 8.
117 *ODT*, 27 Jul. 1917, 7.
118 *P*, 5 Apr. 1918, 6.
119 *EP*, 12 Oct. 1917, 6.
120 *HNS*, 13 Jun. 1917, 4.
121 *ODT*, 14 Jul. 1917, 11.
122 *P*, 13 Jul. 1918, 8.
123 *HBT*, 17 Jul. 1918, 3; *NZ Truth*, 27 Apr. 1918, 1, 11 May 1918, 1 and 28 Sep. 1918, 5.
124 Peter Clayworth, "'Lucky Laidlaw' and 'Worried Webb': The Robert Laidlaw Exemption Case and Public Attitudes to Conscription in 1918," *Journal of New Zealand Studies* 20 (2015): 75.
125 *NZH*, 19 Jan. 1918, 8, 8 Feb. 1918, 4, 19 Feb. 1918, 6 and 21 Feb. 1918, 4.
126 *EP*, 30 Oct. 1917, 10.
127 *ST*, 9 Feb. 1917, 2.
128 *WT*, 24 Jan. 1917, 4; *ME*, 20 Dec. 1918, 3.
129 *MES*, 13 Apr. 1917, 2.
130 Mack to Commandant Military Forces Wellington, 31 May 1917, AD 1 896 39/275, ANZ; Minutes, New Zealand Farmers' Union Dominion Executive, 17 Apr. 1917, MSY 0237, ATL.
131 *Northern Advocate*, 25 Jun. 1917, 2.
132 *WDT*, 24 Mar. 1917, 4.
133 *EP*, 1 Feb. 1917, 7.
134 *ODT*, 20 Dec. 1917, 6.
135 *EP*, 23 Jul. 1917, 8.
136 *AS*, 12 Apr. 1917, 6.
137 *EP*, 8 Feb. 1917, 8.
138 *ROT*, 21 Mar. 1917, 5.
139 *GRA*, 4 Apr. 1917, 3.
140 *ODT*, 2 Feb. 1917, 3.
141 *WT*, 14 Mar. 1917, 5.
142 *ODT*, 12 Jul. 1918, 2.
143 Kelly, *Military Board Appeals: March 1917 to June 1917*, 14–15.
144 Free to Tate, 24 Jan. 1917, AD 1 896 39/275, ANZ.
145 Minutes, Conference of Military Service Board Chairmen, 27 Apr. 1917, AD 1 765 20/43, ANZ.
146 Report, Members of the Military Service Boards, n.d., AD 82 2 1/11/1, ANZ.

128 *Army first?*

147 *WT*, 14 Mar. 1917, 4.
148 *TH*, 18 Oct. 1917, 4; *PBH*, 12 Oct. 1917, 5.
149 Kelly, *Military Board Appeals: Dec 1916 to Feb 1917*, 55–56.
150 *TH*, 19 Feb. 1917, 7 and 20 Feb. 1917, 4; *EP*, 6 Feb. 1918, 8.
151 Minutes, Conference of Wellington Military Service Boards, 26 Jun. 1917, AD 82 7 46/7, ANZ.
152 *ODT*, 25 Jun. 1918, 6.

6   Those troublesome few

From the moment Britain's and New Zealand's Military Service Bills were first made public, the treatment of conscientious objectors provoked a storm of debate. Both countries had officially entered the war to protect the rights and freedoms of small groups, but many of their people refused to accept that citizens could justifiably raise religious or political arguments against fighting for the national cause. Tasked with adjudicating between these perspectives, the appeal bodies were frequently accused of prejudice and unreasonableness by conscription's opponents, with the same charges being laid, and only occasionally countered, by historians ever since. Such allegations have tended to centre on how the tribunals and boards applied their official instructions, and on the way in which they questioned conscientious objectors during hearings.

There were substantial disagreements among the East Central Division's tribunals over what manner of conscientious scruples a man had to possess to be eligible for exemption. According to the Military Service Act of January 1916, relief could be granted to individuals who demonstrated a 'conscientious objection to the undertaking of combatant service'.[1] The only point on which the appeal bodies concurred was that this wording definitely encompassed members of the Society of Friends, whose historical opposition to performing military service was widely recognised. Indeed, one of the first questions put to objectors was often whether they were Quakers and, if not, how closely their beliefs aligned with those propagated by the society.[2] All other matters gave rise to a multitude of interpretations. For some tribunals, at least in the early months, a conscientious objection was only valid if it derived from the tenets of a Christian denomination. In March 1916, the Huddersfield Tribunal dismissed the appeal of a grocer's assistant on the grounds that 'if you had any very serious conscientious objection you would have joined your fellows in some religious body'.[3] Equally, the Linthwaite Tribunal turned down a Wesleyan because his denomination did not object to performing combatant service, with the same reasoning being used against James Walker, a member of the Church of Christ, at Birstall.[4] Other tribunals were prepared to look beyond pacifist groups, but still maintained that *bona fide* objections had to be grounded in some form of religious faith. When a prospective conscript informed the Cudworth Tribunal that he was a member of both the ILP and the Anti-Capitalist Movement, the chairman tersely remarked

130 *Those troublesome few*

that 'we cannot be influenced by either of these bodies'.[5] Similarly, the Mirfield members repeatedly asked a British Socialist Party (BSP) official if he held any religious objections, and refused him when he replied in the negative, while the Birkenshaw chairman turned down a man who proffered no Christian scruples by stating 'all the conscientious objectors I have come across have been shirkers'.[6] Nonetheless, a few tribunals were prepared to adopt a wider reading of the 'conscience clause'. The New Mill body granted relief to several socialist appellants during March and April 1916, and, of the five absolute exemptions awarded to conscientious objectors in the division, three went to men who based their claims solely on political arguments.[7]

The tribunals also failed to adopt a common approach over the types of relief that should be afforded. One point of contention was whether any conscientious objector deserved absolute exemption from military service. In March 1916, the Skelmanthorpe body granted this form of certificate to a weaver who had preached against war since 1910.[8] That same month, the Batley Tribunal awarded absolute relief to both Charles Hopkinson, a labour exchange clerk who cited a long-standing moral and ethical opposition to militarism, and Joseph Peel, a member of the ILP, who reminded the tribunal of his past protests against 'armaments, big navies, and all that tends to fasten the militarist yoke on the workers of the country'.[9] However, these were the only absolute exemptions awarded to conscientious objectors by the Skelmanthorpe and Batley tribunals. Indeed, the option then appears to have gone unused across the division until October 1916. It was at this juncture that the Holmfirth Tribunal granted a builder's labourer twenty-one days to find 'work of national importance', after he convinced them that his New Testament principles were opposed to joining the army. When the same individual was back before the appeal body several weeks later, he admitted to having made no effort to source an occupation that would contribute to the war effort. Remarkably, the Holmfirth members chose not to punish this defiance, but instead effectively rewarded it by upgrading the man's certificate to one of absolute exemption.[10] The granting of total relief then fell into another prolonged period of abeyance. Only in July 1918 did Martin Farrington, a socialist member of the West Riding County Council, manage to convince the Linthwaite Tribunal that he had dedicated his life to trying to 'destroy the rule of capitalism' and thereby secure absolute exemption.[11]

Further discrepancies took place over exemptions that were conditional on the appellant being engaged in 'work of national importance'. This form of certificate was granted very rarely until June 1916, when the Huddersfield Tribunal afforded provisional relief to four Christadelphians whose spokesman said they 'could not give any obligation to any other authority than Christ'.[12] The following month, the Wakefield Borough Tribunal conditionally exempted an appellant whose religious scruples would prevent him from opposing a German invasion, and the Spenborough body did likewise for a shaft manufacturer who had declined a war service badge on the grounds it would bring him under the control of the Ministry of Munitions.[13] Although most other appeal bodies started issuing provisional exemptions during the first year of conscription, the Barnsley Borough Tribunal

Those troublesome few   131

held out until March 1917, and some others never granted anything more than non-combatant certificates.[14] Even when the appeal bodies did begin to utilise the conditional form of relief, they often went about it in different ways. The Spenborough and Marsden tribunals allowed objectors to remain in their occupation if the work was of 'national importance', but the Huddersfield body regularly determined that compelling men to find new employment was the only way to ensure they were making the necessary degree of sacrifice.[15]

These variations were only partly remedied at a higher level. The ECAT did manage to nullify local inconsistencies over the granting of absolute exemptions, with all five of these certificates subsequently being overturned.[16] In all other matters, the appeal tribunal merely compounded the existing disparities. A crucial impediment was that local decisions could only be altered if the relevant military representative decided to refer the case. Some War Office appointees opposed the granting of anything more than a non-combatant certificate, but others were prepared to countenance the conditional exemption of deserving appellants. Therefore, while the ECAT could apply its own policies to certain claims, many were left solely in the hands of the local tribunals. This would have been less of an issue if the appeal tribunal had not demonstrated substantial irregularities itself. During a sitting in March 1916, the ECAT appeared to place the various types of conscientious objection on an equal footing by granting every appellant non-combatant service.[17] Yet at another hearing six months later, it first varied the non-combatant certificate afforded to Arthur Wilson, a religious objector, to conditional exemption, then altered the same award given to an ILP member by refusing his case entirely.[18] The ECAT also adopted a unique interpretation of the 'work of national importance' stipulation. It not only required men to give up their existing employment, but also insisted that they relocate at least twenty-five miles away from their home district.[19]

Significant differences were also apparent in how the tribunals questioned conscientious objectors during hearings. Although their initial guidance implored the members to 'interpret the Act in an impartial and tolerant spirit', many proved unable, or unwilling, to live up to these standards.[20] In March 1916, the No-Conscription Fellowship's *Tribunal* newssheet asserted that conscientious objectors were being 'rebuked, bullied and condemned' across the country, while Long wrote to the tribunals asking them to refrain from subjecting appellants 'to a somewhat harsh cross-examination'.[21] These admonishments were certainly applicable in parts of the division, where the clerk to the South Crosland Tribunal designated moral arguments against conscription as an 'ailment', Alderman Blamires derided 'conscientious objection fads' at Huddersfield, and the Birstall chairman beseeched a religious appellant to recognise that 'you are doing all you can to uphold the Devil and not Christ'.[22] Attacks on an individual's beliefs were often accompanied by accusations that he lacked the moral fibre to serve. A member of the Ossett body said the outlook of most objectors was enough to 'make any honest man sick', the Golcar chairman explicitly accused a Methodist of being 'too soft to fight' and Councillor Pearson bluntly described one Honley appellant as a 'coward'.[23]

132   *Those troublesome few*

Yet the notion that all conscientious objectors met with ridicule and hostility needs to be qualified. At a national level, even Labour MP Philip Snowden, who worked tirelessly to highlight the exemption system's various abuses, was prepared to acknowledge that 'many' appeal bodies 'tried to do their duty sincerely'.[24] In the division, one appellant gave the Holmfirth Tribunal 'credit for having listened attentively' to his claim, while another thanked the Spenborough body 'for the courteous hearing they had given him'.[25] Such praise was usually directed at those tribunals that adopted a list of ten questions, issued by the Central Tribunal in May 1916, as the basis for their examinations. These bodies thereby confined themselves to investigating the sincerity of an objector's beliefs and his willingness to perform alternative service, whereas other tribunals continued to rely on more rough-and-ready methods of interrogation.[26]

Discrepancies of procedure and attitude also occurred within individual appeal bodies. This most commonly involved a tribunal's trade unionist personnel advocating for one of the more comprehensive forms of exemption. At Huddersfield, Joseph Pickles often pleaded for the absolute or conditional relief of men to whom his Liberal and Conservative colleagues were only prepared to grant non-combatant service. This situation reached a tipping point in September 1917, by which time another labour representative, Councillor Law Taylor, had joined Pickles on the tribunal. Noting that the absence of several members had created an opportunity, these individuals tabled a motion to grant absolute exemption to an appellant who belonged to the BSP. However, the other two members present insisted that the case should be adjourned temporarily and, because Owen Balmforth was the acting chairman, it was his casting vote that proved decisive.[27] Trade unionist members were also the most likely to try and protect conscientious objectors from abuse. At the Barnsley Borough Tribunal, Councillor Bray remonstrated against the use of 'hypothetical questions' after his colleagues had repeatedly asked a man whether he would defend his mother from German rapists.[28]

Yet these instances of labour personnel acting as a moderating influence were not typical everywhere. William France adopted an extremely arbitrary approach at Ossett by opposing every claim where the objector was unable to quote from the work of Leo Tolstoy.[29] Equally striking is the attitude of Mrs. Walker at Holmfirth, who, as a Quaker, refused to accept that the Society of Friends was against military service and consistently voted against granting absolute exemption to her co-denominationalists.[30] On the other hand, Chairman Brook of the Meltham Tribunal, the owner of a cotton mill, first criticised his colleagues' predilection for asking hypothetical questions, and then described as 'ridiculous and nonsense' their refusal to award a well-known local objector anything more than non-combatant service.[31]

These differences in the tribunals' handling of conscientious objectors partly resulted from the ambiguous directions they received. Crucially, the Military Service Act of January 1916 provided no definition of what constituted a valid 'conscientious objection'. During the Parliamentary debates around the legislation, Conservative leader Andrew Bonar Law had insisted that the term must extend beyond pacifist religious groups.[32] Yet the only denominations that ever

Those troublesome few 133

received official recognition were the Quakers and the Christadelphians.[33] When it came to the vast number of other religious bodies, and to those men who relied on a personal interpretation of the scriptures, the tribunals were effectively left to make up their own minds. There was also very little guidance regarding the validity of politically based objections, which, given the prominence of socialist movements in towns like Huddersfield, were frequently voiced in the division. The only concrete prescription available to the appeal bodies was the Central Tribunal's ruling that political opposition to involvement in one particular war did not satisfy the Act's requirements.[34]

Even more confusing were the tribunals' instructions on what types of exemption could and should be granted. According to the Act,

> any certificate of exemption may be absolute, conditional, or temporary … and *also* in the case of an application on conscientious grounds, may take the form of an exemption from combatant service only, or may be conditional on the applicant being engaged in some work which in the opinion of the tribunal dealing with the case is of national importance.[35]

Uncertainty quickly emerged as to whether the key word 'also' in this section signified that every form of relief could be awarded to objectors, or whether they were only eligible for non-combatant service or conditional exemption. In his initial circular to the tribunals, Long affirmed that absolute relief could be given in 'exceptional cases'.[36] However, the government was not unanimous on this point, with the Home Secretary, Herbert Samuel, insisting that all exempted men 'must do something' for the war effort.[37]

Matters were further complicated by the fact the only ground of appeal available to conscientious objectors was an unwillingness to perform 'combatant service'. In the name of consistency, this seemed to indicate that the most an appellant could expect to receive was a non-combatant certificate. When one Huddersfield objector demanded that the local tribunal award him absolute exemption, the clerk replied they could not 'override the Act of Parliament'.[38] Aware of these difficulties, Long wrote to the tribunals on 23 and 27 March 1916 informing them that they could grant any of the mandated types of relief to conscientious objectors.[39] However, he contradicted himself in the Commons two weeks later, by stating that 'total' exemption was only available if an appellant was engaged in 'work of national importance'.[40] An even more restrictive interpretation was then applied at the High Court on 18 April, when it ruled that the maximum exemption a tribunal could award was non-combatant service.[41] In May, the Military Service Act, 1916 (Session 2) apparently removed the potential for differing interpretations by confirming that conscientious objectors could be granted absolute exemption.[42] Yet many applications had already been finally processed by this point, and both Long and the Central Tribunal still insisted that the circumstances of a case would have to be 'very exceptional' for an absolute certificate to be justified.[43] This issue was still causing concern as late as January 1918, when the new President of the LGB, W. Hayes Fisher, asked the appeal bodies if any conscientious objectors

134 *Those troublesome few*

had been refused absolute certificates 'not because the Tribunal considered that such exemption was not justified in the case in question, but because the Tribunal were under the impression that they had not power to grant absolute exemption'.[44]

Additional difficulties emerged over whether and how the tribunals should award exemptions that were conditional on the appellant undertaking 'work of national importance'. One major issue was that which bedevilled the question of absolute relief: did the Act's reference to 'combatant service' mean the most an appellant could receive was a non-combatant certificate? This was certainly the position indicated by the April 1916 verdict of the High Court. Indeed, the Linthwaite Tribunal refused to grant any conditional exemptions on the basis that applications were 'made on the ground of an objection to the undertaking of combatant service', with a similar interpretation being applied by the Middlesex Appeal Tribunal.[45] Another problem revolved around the concept of 'work of national importance'. Neither the Act nor Long's initial guidance attempted to define this term, and simply left the matter to 'the opinion' of the relevant tribunal.[46] Moreover, the government failed to develop any method for assigning conscientious objectors to essential occupations. A partial resolution was only achieved in late March 1916, when the government appointed a Committee on Work of National Importance, generally known as the Pelham Committee after its chairman, T. H. Pelham, who was an assistant secretary at the Board of Trade. On 14 April, this body circulated a list of occupations that the tribunals should regard as being of 'national importance'.[47] However, the Pelham Committee was only able to make recommendations, rather than decisions, and the tribunals were somewhat slow to make use of its services, with just 265 applicants having been referred by 11 May.[48] Only with the passage of the Military Service Act (Session 2) did it finally become clear that conscientious objectors could be granted a conditional exemption. It is surely no coincidence that this marked the point where many of the division's tribunals first began to award such certificates.

Another source of discrepancy was the presence of so many tribunals and members in the division. With several contentious issues to decide upon, it was hardly surprising that sixty-four appeal bodies adopted differing procedures. Indeed, even a much smaller number might have struggled to achieve uniformity, given the diversity that existed between their members in terms of politics, occupation and beliefs about the legitimacy of the war and compulsory military service. These variables worked together to generate a whole plethora of attitudes. On one side were men such as William Armitage of the Huddersfield Tribunal, who consistently pressed for the refusal of conscientious objectors and berated appellants for espousing pacifist principles. In November 1916, having lost patience with one particularly determined individual, Armitage earned himself the enmity of labour organisations throughout the division by exclaiming 'I am opposed to it, and I will never consent to it. I don't believe in the conscientious objector'.[49] At the other end of the spectrum were individuals like Councillor Thomas Brook, chairman of the Holmfirth Tribunal, who expressed the hope that no objector would leave their sittings 'and say that justice had not been done', and Councillor George Brook, who resigned from the New Mill body when it decided to impose

Those troublesome few   135

the VTC condition on a socialist.[50] Taking these more extreme positions could result in members becoming isolated, with the attempts made by the ECAT's two labour personnel to secure absolute or conditional exemptions invariably being overruled by their colleagues.[51] Yet there were times where the views of certain individuals profoundly influenced the decisions of an entire appeal body. Ben Turner sat as chairman of the Batley Tribunal for around ten weeks after conscription was introduced, during which two conscientious objectors were granted absolute certificates, and the overall exemption rate for this type of appellant was 75 percent. Following Turner's departure to sit on the ECAT, no more Batley objectors were awarded absolute certificates and their chances of gaining any form of exemption declined to only 46 percent.[52]

The final cause of inconsistency among the division's tribunals was the localism of their personnel. There can be no doubt that the appeal bodies considered their instructions when making decisions, with the Act and official correspondence often being quoted directly. Nonetheless, the fact members were beholden to the community in which they lived was particularly important during the claims of conscientious objectors, as these individuals tended to generate the strongest public reactions. There were districts in which men who espoused opposition to performing military service became pariahs, and some tribunals probably found justification for adopting an aggressive approach in this climate of opinion.[53] However, local sentiment could also mobilise in favour of certain appellants. One such incident occurred at Leeds in the Northern Division of the West Riding, where the City Tribunal's refusal to allow a socialist, Ernest Horner, to read a statement of his beliefs prompted a storm of protest from the gallery. Eventually, the chairman decided that the room would have to be cleared for a private discussion to take place. This proved easier said than done, with the spectators only being evicted after fifteen minutes and with the aid of several policemen. When more interruptions occurred during subsequent appeals, the tribunal decided to adjourn indefinitely all cases relating to conscientious objectors. This action prompted cries of 'shame' from the watching public, who also sang a rendition of 'the Red Flag' to signal their displeasure.[54]

Significant pro-appellant demonstrations also took place in the division. At the Barnsley Borough Tribunal, a conscientious objector received a lengthy chorus of support from the audience after refusing to answer a hypothetical question. Seemingly panicked by this interruption, the members first heard the rest of the case in private, and then decided to sidestep the issue by awarding relief on the grounds of occupation.[55] Deliberately avoiding the ethical or moral aspect of appeals was a commonly employed tactic, and one that points to a belief the matter was best avoided if possible. A second means of evasion was utilised at Huddersfield in March 1916. By that time the local tribunal had already indicated its reluctance to antagonise popular conscientious objectors. A number of claims had simply been adjourned, while several others had been dismissed with an accompanying entreaty for the appellant to take his case before the ECAT.[56] This approach reached a peak during the appeal of Arthur Gardiner, a founding member of the Huddersfield Socialist Party, whose presence drew between 300

136 *Those troublesome few*

and 400 people into the packed chamber.[57] What followed clearly made several tribunal members extremely nervous. Gardiner managed to parry any questioning of his principles, and the hearing was repeatedly interrupted by interjections and outbursts of laughter from the public. As soon as the case concluded, Chairman Blamires led his colleagues out of the room for a private discussion. When they returned fully twenty minutes later, the verdict laid bare the depth of their concerns:

> we have made a decision, a majority decision, we believe that the applicant ... has proved that he is entitled to call himself a conscientious objector ... in view of the fact that we believe in the sincerity of his convictions, we are disposed to grant temporary exemption for two months.[58]

At first glance, this verdict makes little sense. A man of Gardiner's convictions was scarcely likely to alter his views, meaning the tribunal would be faced with a second confrontation when the certificate came up for renewal. However, factoring in the members' local pre-occupations demonstrates that they had in fact made a calculated decision. They knew Gardiner would accept nothing short of absolute exemption and actively encouraged him to take his case before the ECAT. That is exactly what happened, meaning the local tribunal had managed to avoid refusing the claim, which would have infuriated the watching public, but had also avoided giving in to Gardiner, which would have incited the town's pro-conscriptionists. The Huddersfield body granted temporary exemptions to several more conscientious objectors over the following months, with the chairman remarking 'the sooner the better the other tribunal deals with these things'.[59]

Unlike the division's tribunals, the boards quickly developed a common understanding over what type of objector should be eligible for exemption. New Zealand's legislative provision recognised individuals who, since the outbreak of war, had continuously been 'a member of a religious body the tenets and doctrines of which ... declare the bearing of arms and the performance of any combatant service to be contrary to Divine revelation'.[60] The boards determined that only two denominations definitely qualified under this formula: the Society of Friends and the Christadelphians. These groups possessed long-standing traditions of refusing military service and had been officially recognised as genuine religious objectors in Britain.[61] Whenever a member of either denomination came up for hearing, he was automatically offered relief upon showing that his affiliation dated back to at least 4 August 1914. However, the Quakers and the Christadelphians were both relatively small groups, with only five of the former and eight of the latter making appeals before 24 April 1917.

The fact a reservist was deemed eligible for exemption was not the end of the matter. Under the Act, an appeal could only be allowed if the objector was prepared to sign an undertaking, addressed to the Commandant of the Defence Forces, stating his willingness to perform 'non-combatant work or services, including service in the Medical Corps and the Army Service Corps, whether in or beyond New Zealand'.[62] The Society of Friends held that taking up non-combatant roles

Those troublesome few   137

was incompatible with their principles, as it entailed 'supporting and becoming part of the vast military machine'.[63] This was the view articulated to the First Auckland Board by Percy Wright, who refused exemption because 'any service under the direction of the military authorities' would be 'helping on the war'.[64] Likewise, several Christadelphian congregations had written to Allen informing him that while they were prepared to 'do ANY CIVIL DUTY', their determination to avoid being yoked within an earthly body meant 'we cannot enter any Branch of Military Service'.[65] When Herbert Milverton was assured by the Third Wellington Board that 'all you would be asked to do' would be 'to succour the wounded', he replied 'no; it would be required that I should become part and parcel of an army'.[66] So despite the appeal bodies' willingness to exempt Quakers and Christadelphians, the theological scruples of these groups meant New Zealand's first religious exemption provision was virtually a dead letter. By April 1917, only two Quakers had agreed to sign the necessary undertaking.

It was the Defence Department that made the conditions of exemption more acceptable, thereby permitting the boards to develop a new orthodoxy. On 24 April 1917, modifications to the undertaking religious objectors were required to sign removed any mention of the Medical Corps or Army Service Corps, and stipulated that men would not be compelled to wear military uniform. Informally, the Defence Department went even further, with a promise of agricultural work on the state farm at Levin.[67] As well as making exemption more attractive to future appellants, many objectors who had previously refused to sign the undertaking had their cases reheard to give them the chance to accept the revised version.[68] These measures proved successful for the Christadelphians, with those individuals who had rejected the old undertaking being willing to sign the new one, and all but one member of this denomination who was subsequently deemed eligible for relief also choosing to accept it.[69] A slight difficulty did arise in September 1917, when the Third Wellington Board dismissed two Christadelphian claims on the basis that the Act required membership of a religious body prior to 1914, whereas the men concerned had been merely adherents. However, the appeals were swiftly re-assessed and granted after Allen instructed the boards to follow a section in the defeated Expeditionary Forces Amendment Bill that would have made adherents eligible for exemption.[70]

Another important rehearing involved David Jackson, a Seventh-day Adventist. Members of this denomination had previously been refused exemption on the grounds they did not possess a written constitution against bearing arms and 'as a body had not objected to being called up'.[71] This position changed in June 1917, when the Third Wellington Board received documentary evidence from the United States that proved the Seventh-day Adventist's creed was opposed to combatant service. Jackson was granted, and accepted, exemption at his rehearing, an outcome that was repeated whenever members of this denomination appealed to the boards subsequently.[72]

The situation regarding the Quakers was somewhat different. While they continued to be offered relief in every instance, members of this denomination proved less well disposed towards the amended undertaking. The society's officials were

138　*Those troublesome few*

suspicious that agricultural work had been suggested, but not guaranteed, and concerned that exempted men would still be placed under military authority.[73] These issues were raised at his hearing by John Rigg, who only accepted exemption after the military representative warned him that 'unless you sign that paper the board has no option but to dismiss your appeal'.[74] However, no amount of pressure was sufficient to sway Edward Dowsett, whose claim was rejected after he asserted that he wanted to continue on as a baker and would refuse to work under military control.[75]

Whereas these groups were given the chance to benefit from the religious exemption clause, the boards automatically dismissed the appeals of two other large categories of men. The first consisted of individuals who belonged to a religious denomination, but one whose principles were clearly not opposed to performing combatant duties. In terms of the major denominations, the First Wellington Board refused Robert Jones, who admitted there was nothing in the Church of England's tenets that prohibited military service, while the chairman of the Second Auckland Board described Robert Watson as a 'perfect humbug' for suggesting that bearing arms was contrary to the doctrines of the Catholic Church.[76] Baptists, Methodists and Presbyterians met with the same rebuttal, as did the members of a whole plethora of smaller sects, like the Auckland Central Mission, the Christian Scientists, the Church of Christ and the International Bible Students' Association.[77]

A second category of men who were quickly deemed ineligible were those who did not belong to a religious body. This included some individuals whose objections were based solely on their own literal or spiritual reading of the Bible. Hugh King was rejected by the Second Wellington Board as soon as he admitted to being guided 'purely by the teaching of the Holy Gospel', while several other appellants who simply referenced the commandment of 'thou shalt not kill' also received short shrift.[78] A much larger proportion of the second category consisted of men who advanced political arguments. David Williams was turned down by the Second Auckland Board after asserting that conscription was against the interests of the working classes, and Hugh Gray fared no better before the First Auckland body when stating that, as a Marxist, he objected to killing his German comrades at the behest of a capitalist elite.[79] A different kind of argument, but exactly the same result, occurred in the appeal of Thomas Spillane to the Second Wellington Board. After outlining his refusal to fight for Britain at the same time as its soldiers were oppressing his Irish homeland, Spillane was promptly informed by Chairman Poynton that he had 'no ground for appeal – nothing to sustain it at all'.[80]

The boards also adopted a uniform policy towards three denominations whose standing was slightly less straightforward. For the Brethren, this involved a collective decision that the group did not come within the scope of the Act. One reason why the boards reached this conclusion was the testimony given by the appellants themselves, which cast considerable doubt on whether the Brethren were opposed to performing combatant service. Whereas one reservist told the First Otago body it was contrary to the teachings of the denomination to join the infantry, another admitted to the First Wellington Board that although 'some

Those troublesome few 139

members' adhered to the principle of not bearing arms, 'others do not'.[81] Indeed, the president of the Auckland Brethren Bible Class Union renounced claims that it was against their doctrine to fight, while the New Zealand head of the denomination informed Allen that the question of enlisting had been left to each individual's conscience.[82] Another consideration was the apparent disconnect between the Brethren's alleged opposition to combatant service and the fact several of its members had volunteered. Questioning on this matter again produced varied and ambiguous replies. Gordon Rose maintained that all members believed it was wrong to enlist, but when asked 'how is it some of them have joined', he simply answered 'I don't know'. Rose further asserted that these men withdrew from the Brethren, but another appellant merely stated the issue had caused 'a lot of trouble', while Charles Doherty informed the Second Otago Board that membership did not cease upon engaging in combatant service.[83]

The boards used the same reasoning to dismiss appeals lodged by members of the Testimony of Jesus and the Richmond Mission. One preacher of the former denomination informed the First Canterbury Board that there was no definite doctrine regarding military service, while another wrote to Allen stating they had no leader and no headquarters, and had only adopted a name for administrative convenience, given that they were not a formal body at all.[84] Then, on 25 July 1917, sixteen men from this group whose appeals had previously been dismissed were granted a rehearing to determine finally their eligibility for exemption. The Third Wellington Board's questioning centred on whether the denomination was opposed to combatant service. In reply, one appellant claimed such a policy had only been agreed at a conference in 1915, prompting a furious response from their solicitor, who knew this was not enough to satisfy the legislation's requirements. Another reservist then further muddied the waters by stating that the conference had not achieved a resolution and that the Testimony of Jesus possessed no definite creed. When it was claimed that the denomination had preached against the bearing of arms before the war, the board wondered why it had then been necessary to raise the matter at their conference. The appellant's reply that 'there was some doubt in the minds of young members as to whether they should go or not' failed to satisfy the chairman, who inquired why there would be 'any doubt if it is a recognised tenet of your Church'.[85] A similar impasse occurred during cases involving the Richmond Mission, whose members were at least consistent in verbally opposing combatant service. However, they were unable to supply any proof that their sect was actually a 'religious body', or that they had any written 'constitution or tenets' against joining the army's frontline units.[86]

In addition to concurring over who was eligible for exemption, the boards adopted a uniform approach towards offering a lesser form of relief to other religious objectors. From January 1917, the appeal bodies began questioning men who were deemed to be outside the scope of the Act, but whose scruples they considered 'genuine', on their willingness to perform overseas non-combatant service. Although an amenable objector still had his appeal dismissed, this was accompanied by a recommendation that the army camp commandants should assign him to the Medical Corps. The main proponent of this initiative was again the Defence

140 *Those troublesome few*

Department, and particularly Adjutant General R. W. Tate who secured the participation of the military representatives and the support of the Recruiting Board.[87] In deciding whether to offer a recommendation to conscientious objectors, the boards applied a number of tests. The first was whether an individual troubled to attend his hearing, with the appeal bodies holding that anyone who could not, or would not, defend his principles in person lacked the necessary degree of sincerity. A second measure was whether an objector's beliefs could be traced back to before the outbreak of war. Under no circumstances would the boards allow a man to avoid fighting if he had only recently developed conscientious scruples, as they perceived such 'convenient' conversions as *prima facie* evidence of 'shirking'. The final test was whether a reservist's misgivings were based on religious faith. For the appeal bodies, beliefs that had their roots in the Bible were the only valid form of conscientious objection.

These means of assessment were utilised by all nine active boards. Almost certain to be offered recommendations were members of those sects that had narrowly missed out on exemption. The Second Auckland Board endorsed William Wallace of the Brethren 'on account of his genuine attitude', the First Auckland body offered non-combatant service to Wilfred Davey of the Testimony of Jesus, despite the fact he was a clerk at the Defence Department, and the First Canterbury Board reached the same decision in the case of Theodore Gibbs of the Richmond Mission.[88] Members of other Christian denominations, and even those individuals who held only personal religious beliefs, were also likely to be questioned on their willingness to tend to the wounded. Indeed, an increasing number of appellants came before the boards precisely to obtain such recommendations, rather than exemption.[89] On the other hand, socialist or Irish nationalist objectors were consistently deemed to be undeserving of endorsements for non-combatant service.

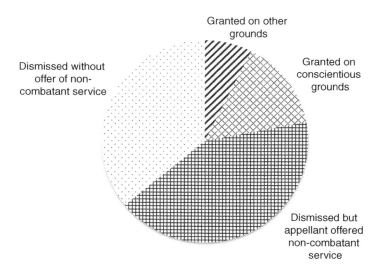

Figure 6.1 The boards' verdicts on appeals lodged by conscientious objectors

Those troublesome few 141

The boards' common approach towards these cases can also be illustrated statistically. Some of the 634 men who the newspapers reported as appealing on conscientious grounds were not considered. The majority of those who cited 'all grounds' did not allude to objections in their testimony, nor were they questioned on them by the boards or military representatives. Several other objectors either failed to attend their hearing or were classed as medically unfit, making it impossible to determine how the boards would have treated their claim. Discounting all the cases from these two categories leaves 501 for analysis. Figure 6.1 indicates that, of this number, seventy-three objectors (14.51 percent) were exempted on religious grounds, comprising of thirty-six Christadelphians, seven Quakers and thirty Seventh-day Adventists. Each of these men had their appeals allowed after they agreed to sign the relevant undertaking. A total of 391 objectors were deemed to fall outside the scope of the Act and had their claims rejected, while the remaining thirty-seven were granted exemption on the grounds of undue hardship or public interest. Significantly, of the 391 objectors who had their appeals dismissed, 149 accepted a recommendation for overseas non-combatant service, while another sixty-two refused the offer after being questioned on their attitude towards it. These individuals were all members of a Christian denomination, or had based their appeals on personal religious beliefs. Not one socialist or Irish nationalist objector was even considered for such an endorsement.

If the verdicts the boards delivered were striking in their uniformity, can the same be said for their attitudes during hearings? The appeal bodies did sometimes neglect the implementation of a common policy in favour of chastising an individual's beliefs. One objector was informed that 'unpatriotic people like you don't deserve to belong to the nation', and a second that his religious ideals were nothing short of 'madness'.[90] Likewise, John Olley, assistant school master of Hastings, was advised that 'it is a disgrace to the community that a man holding these views should be teaching our young'.[91] Other appellants were lambasted for a perceived willingness to enjoy New Zealand's freedom and prosperity while other men fought on their behalf. A member of the First Wellington Board told an objector that 'you get all the benefits and good of this earth, but will take no share in the work', while Jesse Morris was charged by the First Otago body with being 'prepared to take all the benefits and stand by and let others bear the brunt of the fighting'.[92] If the boards' tactics could be brutal, then some of their questions were simply unsavoury. Perhaps the worst was put to Eric Badger, who was asked 'if the Germans came here and attempted to violate your women, kill children and destroy the country, would you attempt to stop them?'[93] As Baker maintains, the knowledge they would suffer this kind of treatment is likely to have dissuaded some 'genuine' reservists from lodging a claim.[94] This was certainly the case for famous conscientious objector Archibald Baxter, who later recalled that the 'Appeal Boards were farcical as far as objectors were concerned, their members usually ridiculing the objectors who were rash enough to appeal'.[95]

Nevertheless, the overwhelming impression derived from the boards' operations is of a collective and measured approach. Their primary concern was always to determine a man's eligibility for relief, rather than to attack his convictions.

142   *Those troublesome few*

Each hearing began with an assessment of the objector's claim to come within the Act, during which he was allowed to state his beliefs, press his arguments and call numerous witnesses.[96] If this segment of the appeal was inevitably brief when the objector did not belong to a Christian denomination, or was the member of a church that obviously countenanced military service, then the extensive investigations into the Brethren, Testimony of Jesus and Richmond Mission demonstrate that the boards did endeavour to reach informed decisions.

When an appeal could not be allowed, the boards' second concern was establishing whether the objections were sufficiently 'genuine' to warrant a recommendation for non-combatant service. It was here that questions about the rape of womenfolk and the killing of infants were usually employed. However, any judgement of the boards must take into account the circumstances under which they operated. Sittings were busy, even hectic, occasions, with large numbers of cases up for hearing. Under these pressures, the boards simply did not have the time to conduct a detailed investigation of every objector's sincerity. Instead, all they could rely on were crude tests of his consistency. Asking what an appellant would do if his wife was attacked was a means of determining whether he was opposed to force in every circumstance. In a similar vein, farmer objectors were asked if they had 'not been helping the war by growing oats and wheat', with other men being challenged to explain parts of the Bible that seemed to encourage military service.[97] Those appellants who explained any apparent inconsistencies by reference to their religious faith were usually given a recommendation for the Medical Corps; those who floundered, or who relied on political precepts, were invariably denied one. Moreover, the frequency with which the boards criticised objectors' beliefs has been overstated. In many cases it is not reported to have taken place at all, with the sole focus being the appellant's eligibility for relief. When ridicule did occur, it constituted a small part of the proceedings, and usually only came after the objector had refused service in the Medical Corps. The boards could not comprehend the reluctance of Christian men to help those in distress, with one chairman remarking that he was at a loss to 'understand how succouring the wounded can be regarded as contrary to the teachings of the Bible'.[98]

The boards' attitudes towards conscientious objectors were also compatible with their overall efforts to promote an equality of sacrifice. What the appeal bodies always set out to discover was how much a man could reasonably be expected to do to help the war effort, and whether he was prepared to make the necessary sacrifices. If a conscientious objector demonstrated that he came within the scope of the Act then he was entitled to exemption, but must be prepared to work on the state farm. If he had personal religious scruples then he should be excused from combatant service, but must be amenable to treating the wounded. If he did not have any 'genuine' objections then the best place for him was serving on the front line. When viewed as a part of the boards' overall methodology, it becomes apparent that this means of assessing conscientious objectors was largely the same as that used for men who appealed on the other available grounds. Any individual who demonstrated a need to look after his family, or to continue in his occupation, was awarded the appropriate form of relief, whereas one who exaggerated his

Those troublesome few   143

circumstances or was unwilling to do his bit was dispatched to camp. Indeed, the attacks made on certain conscientious objectors were not fundamentally different from the comments levelled at other individuals whom the boards perceived as 'shirking'. Families who had sent no sons to the front were berated for letting others make all the sacrifices, miners were sharply criticised for going on strike and employers who argued their staff could not possibly be replaced were accused of a selfish dereliction of their duty. For the boards, any man who was reluctant to do his utmost for country and empire was open to criticism. While objectors were challenged on their beliefs rather than their actions, they were not being singled out especially.

There were three reasons why the boards adopted a more uniform approach than the division's tribunals. The first, and perhaps most important, is that the legislation and their subsequent instructions possessed a far greater degree of clarity. In its final form, the New Zealand Act outlined that a valid objection had to be religious rather than conscientious, had to be held by a body rather than an individual, had to be stated in official doctrine rather than just verbally agreed, and had to have been in existence before the outbreak of war. This constituted a vast amount of guidance and was far in excess of anything the tribunals ever had access to. It informed the boards that the Quakers and the Christadelphians, and later the Seventh-day Adventists, were eligible for exemption, while definitely excluding every appellant who was not the member of a religious body or whose denomination was not opposed to combatant service. The somewhat ambiguous positions of the Brethren, the Testimony of Jesus and the Richmond Mission might have caused considerable difficulty were it not for the carefully crafted provisions of the statute, which, according to the Solicitor General, justified the boards' insistence that an eligible denomination must possess a written constitution against bearing arms.[99] In determining whether an individual should receive a recommendation for non-combatant service, the boards were told to base their decision on whether his scruples were 'genuine'. Although this term was undoubtedly less specific, it did indicate what type of objector should, and should not, receive consideration. Allen and the Defence Department had always insisted that the only valid form of objection was one based on religious beliefs.[100] Moreover, the boards were specifically told that an appellant's scruples must have been evident prior to the outbreak of war.

This differing clarity of instructions not only had an impact when determining who was eligible for exemption, but also when deciding what type of relief ought to be granted. It was made readily apparent to the boards that men who were eligible for exemption had to sign the undertaking to perform non-combatant duties, altered by the April 1917 regulations to agricultural work, whereas those who had 'genuine' scruples outside of the legislation could be recommended for the Medical Corps.

The second factor behind the boards' consistency was their smaller numbers and similar memberships. Whereas achieving uniformity between sixty-four division tribunals, and hundreds of members, was always likely to prove impossible, the alignment of only nine active appeal bodies in New Zealand was a far

144   *Those troublesome few*

more realistic objective. Undoubtedly there were some differences in the board members' degree of tolerance for conscientious objectors. While Chairman Poynton of the Second Wellington body asserted that men who would do nothing to defend their 'home from destruction, or a child from murder or outrage' belonged in 'a mental hospital', Chairman Earl of the Second Auckland Board claimed to 'respect every man's religious principles, no matter how foolish and futile they may be'.[101] Yet, at the level that mattered most, their attitudes were largely the same. Due to Allen's rigorously applied selection criteria, there were no anti-conscriptionists or pacifists among the boards' personnel. All the members were firm supporters of compulsory service and ardent believers in the need to win the war. This background ensured they could be relied upon to apply the Act in the strict fashion that most MPs desired, by limiting exemption to the three 'lucky sects'.[102] Moreover, from their actions and statements, it is clear the members held a common belief that the most a 'genuine' conscientious objector deserved was a place in Medical Corps. While conflicting opinions were a common occurrence in division, not a single claim made by a conscientious objector is reported to have caused a split decision in New Zealand.

The final contributor to the boards' greater consistency was their national conception of the exemption system. If the division's tribunals were apt to be swayed, or even intimidated, by local feeling, then the New Zealand appeal bodies listened only to views that emanated from the government. Whenever objectors expressed disappointment or anger at failing to secure exemption, they were simply referred to the wording of the Act and to the obvious intentions of Parliament.[103] Likewise, the boards never wavered from an insistence that men must sign the officially mandated undertaking if they wished to secure relief. This national perspective meant the boards attached a tremendous degree of importance to uniformity. Whereas the division's tribunals rarely mentioned how conscientious objectors were being dealt with in other districts, the boards' sittings frequently turned on such considerations. When the initial appeal from a member of the Brethren came before the First Canterbury Board, Chairman Evans remarked that their verdict was 'rather an important question', as the appeal bodies had decided 'to adopt uniformity in those matters upon which the majority were agreed upon'.[104] Two months later, Chairman Widdowson of the First Otago body dismissed the claim of a Brethren member on the basis that 'he must hold with the finding of another board'.[105] A further example of this collective decision-making was in cases involving Seventh-day Adventists. Before June 1917, every man from this body was refused exemption. However, as soon as the Third Wellington Board determined that the denomination's creed was opposed to combatant service, all the other boards immediately fell into line and began offering relief under the revised undertaking.

These factors are crucial to explaining why the boards adopted a more consistent approach towards conscientious objectors than their British counterparts. The division's tribunals managed to agree on one point: that members of the Society of Friends deserved some form of relief. Yet this was a minor detail when compared to the myriad ways in which they defined 'conscientious objection', and to the

Those troublesome few 145

wide range of procedures they used to decide which forms of exemption should be granted to deserving appellants. Whereas some appeal bodies only entertained cases from men who belonged to a pacifist denomination, others were prepared to acknowledge those based on a personal interpretation of the Bible, or even on political principles. Similarly, a few tribunals offered conscientious objectors nothing more than non-combatant certificates, but many of their sister bodies granted *bona fide* applicants conditional, or occasionally absolute, exemption from military service. In terms of the way objectors were questioned, this ranged from a formulaic and measured analysis, to a concerted attack on all aspects of a man's principles. These discrepancies stemmed from ambiguous, and even contradictory, instructions, the large number of tribunals and the community sensitivities of their members. The situation regarding the boards could scarcely have been more different. They collectively determined that only three denominations were eligible for exemption, and excluded every appellant who did not belong to a group that opposed its members joining the frontline units of the army. Moreover, the boards concurred that men who possessed a genuine religious faith could be given a recommendation for non-combatant service, but always refused to grant such endorsements to politically motivated individuals. This uniform effort was facilitated by clear and concise instructions, by the existence of fewer appeal bodies, and by the national perspective adopted by their members.

As controversial and time-consuming as they undoubtedly were, the claims of overt conscientious objectors were always too few to have any major impact on Britain's and New Zealand's war efforts. A much greater concern for the respective governments and militaries was how the appeal bodies determined the vast number of cases that came before them in their entirety.

Notes

1 Military Service Act, 1916, 5 & 6 Geo. 5, c. 104, sec. 2(1)(d).
2 *WE*, 15 Apr. 1916, 2; Mitchinson, *Saddleworth*, 65; *HE*, 18 Mar. 1916, 2.
3 *HEx*, 9 Mar. 1916, 4.
4 Ibid., 16 Mar. 1916, 2; *BN*, 25 Aug. 1916, 1.
5 *WE*, 6 May 1916, 7.
6 *DR*, 11 Mar. 1916, 6; *CSG*, 2 Aug. 1918, 1.
7 *HE*, 25 Mar. 1916, 6 and 1 Apr. 1916, 3.
8 *W*, 22 Apr. 1916, 3.
9 *BN*, 4 Mar. 1916, 2 and 18 Mar. 1916, 12.
10 *HE*, 12 Aug. 1916, 4 and 7 Oct. 1916, 6.
11 *W*, 27 Jul. 1918, 3.
12 Ibid., 25 Mar. 1916, 5 and 3 Jun. 1916, 6.
13 *WE*, 15 Jul. 1916, 3; *CSG*, 21 Jul. 1916, 2.
14 *WE*, 15 Jul. 1916, 3 and 12 Aug. 1916, 7; *BC*, 17 Mar. 1917, 6.
15 *CSG*, 21 Jul. 1916, 2; *HEx*, 12 Sep. 1916, 4; *W*, 22 Jul. 1916, 5 and 19 Aug. 1916, 5.
16 *W*, 22 Jul. 1916, 4.
17 *BN*, 1 Apr. 1916, 3.
18 Ibid., 2 Sep. 1916, 3.
19 *W*, 1 Jul. 1916, 4 and 26 Aug. 1916, 3.
20 Circular, LGB R. 36, 3 Feb. 1916, MH 47/142, NA.

146 *Those troublesome few*

21 *Tribunal*, 8 Mar. 1916, 1; Circular, LGB R. 70, 23 Mar. 1916, MH 47/142, NA.
22 *W*, 11 Mar. 1916, 5 and 18 Mar. 1916, 3; *BN*, 18 Mar. 1916, 12.
23 *OO*, 5 Aug. 1916, 7; *W*, 11 Mar. 1916, 3 and 25 Mar. 1916, 6.
24 Snowden, 82 Parl. Deb., H.C. (5th ser.) (1916), 1044.
25 *HE*, 7 Oct. 1916, 6; *CSG*, 21 Jul. 1916, 2.
26 Circular, LGB R. 87, May 1916, MH 47/142, NA; *WE*, 8 Jul. 1916, 1 and 18 Nov. 1916, 6.
27 *W*, 15 Sep. 1917, 3.
28 *BC*, 25 Mar. 1916, 1.
29 *OO*, 25 Mar. 1916, 5 and 15 Jul. 1916, 7.
30 *HE*, 11 Mar. 1916, 8.
31 *W*, 1 Apr. 1916, 5.
32 Bonar Law, 78 Parl. Deb., H.C. (5th ser.) (1916), 428.
33 Circular, LGB R. 76, 27 Mar. 1916 and Circular, LGB R. 77, 27 Apr. 1916, MH 47/142, NA.
34 Minutes, Central Tribunal, 2 May 1916, MH 47/1, NA.
35 Military Service Act, 1916, 5 & 6 Geo. 5, c. 104, sec. 2(3) (italics added).
36 Circular, LGB R. 36, 3 Feb. 1916, MH 47/142, NA.
37 Samuel, 78 Parl. Deb., H.C. (5th ser.) (1916), 452.
38 *HEx*, 23 Mar. 1916, 4.
39 Circular, LGB R. 70, 23 Mar. 1916 and Circular, LGB R. 76, 27 Mar. 1916, MH 47/142, NA.
40 Long, 81 Parl. Deb., H.C. (5th ser.) (1916), 1460.
41 R v. the Central Tribunal, *ex parte* Parton, 18 Apr. 1916, *The Times Law Reports* 32, 476–77.
42 Military Service Act, 1916 (Session 2), 6 & 7 Geo. 5, c. 15, sec. 4(3).
43 Circular, LGB R. 84, 1 Jun. 1916, MH 47/142, NA; Minutes, Central Tribunal, 6 Jul. 1916, MH 47/1, NA.
44 Circular, LGB R. 168, 2 Jan. 1918, MH 10/82, NA.
45 *W*, 18 Mar. 1916, 5; Minutes, Middlesex Appeal Tribunal, 29 Mar. 1916, MH 47/5, NA.
46 Military Service Act, 1916, 5 & 6 Geo. 5, c. 104, sec. 2(3); Circular, LGB R. 36, 3 Feb. 1916, MH 47/142, NA.
47 Rae, *Conscience and Politics*, 125.
48 Minutes, Central Tribunal, 11 May 1916, MH 47/1, NA.
49 *W*, 4 Nov. 1916, 5.
50 *HE*, 1 Apr. 1916, 8; *HEx*, 21 Jul. 1916, 4.
51 *HE*, 1 Apr. 1916, 3; *W*, 20 May 1916, 3.
52 Register of Cases, Batley Local Tribunal, KMT 1, KA.
53 Thomas C. Kennedy, "Public Opinion and the Conscientious Objector, 1915–1919," *Journal of British Studies* 12, no. 2 (1973): 107–17; McDermott, *British Military Service Tribunals*, 38–39.
54 *BC*, 1 Apr. 1916, 5.
55 Ibid., 8 Jul. 1916, 1.
56 *W*, 11 Mar. 1916, 3.
57 Pearce, *Comrades in Conscience*, 140.
58 *W*, 25 Mar. 1916, 3.
59 Ibid., 6.
60 New Zealand Military Service Act, 1916, 7 Geo. 5, no. 8, sec. 18(1)(e).
61 O'Connor, "Awkward Ones," 124.
62 New Zealand Military Service Act, 1916, 7 Geo. 5, no. 8, sec. 18(4); *NZG*, 1916, 3211.
63 Statement to Auckland Military Service Board, Jan. 1917, AD 1 733 10/407/1, ANZ.
64 *NZH*, 27 Jan. 1917, 11.
65 Such to Allen, 10 Sep. 1916, AD 1 733 10/407/1, ANZ (emphasis in original).
66 *EP*, 13 Mar. 1917, 7.

Those troublesome few 147

67 *NZG*, 1917, 1399; Gray to Military Service Board Chairmen, 24 May 1917, AD 1 733 10/407/1, ANZ.
68 Tate to Gray, 5 May 1917 and Tate to Director of Recruiting, 11 Jun. 1917, AD 1 733 10/407/1, ANZ.
69 *ODT*, 16 May 1917, 6; *WC*, 19 Jul. 1917, 6; *EP*, 23 Aug. 1917, 3.
70 *EP*, 27 Sep. 1917, 8; Robin to Allen, 12 Jan. 1918, AD 1 734 10/407/2, ANZ; O'Connor, "Awkward Ones," 124–25.
71 *P*, 20 Feb. 1917, 3; *MES*, 28 Feb. 1917, 5.
72 *AS*, 9 Jul. 1917, 2; *MES*, 7 Jun. 1917, 7 and 10 Aug. 1917, 3; *WT*, 4 May 1918, 4.
73 Gill to Tate, 11 Jul. 1917 and Gill to Allen, 20 Aug. 1917, AD 1 734 10/407/2, ANZ.
74 *EP*, 23 May 1917, 8.
75 *NZH*, 3 Oct. 1917, 6.
76 *EP*, 13 Dec. 1916, 3; *NZH*, 22 Apr. 1918, 6.
77 Baughan to Allen, 17 Jan. 1917, AD 1 733 10/407/1, ANZ; *EP*, 13 Dec. 1916, 3 and 28 Jan. 1917, 8; *WDT*, 11 Jan. 1917, 3; *NZH*, 22 Feb. 1917, 8 and 14 Aug. 1917, 6; *MES*, 7 Nov. 1917, 3.
78 *EP*, 20 Apr. 1917, 8; *AS*, 4 May 1917, 6.
79 *NZH*, 21 Feb. 1917, 8 and 22 Sep. 1917, 6.
80 *HBT*, 11 May 1917, 6.
81 Kelly, *Military Board Appeals: Dec 1916 to Feb 1917*, 13; *TH*, 30 Jan. 1917, 7.
82 *AS*, 1 Dec. 1916, 6; Compton to Allen, 9 Feb. 1917, AD 1 733 10/407/1, ANZ.
83 *EP*, 14 Dec. 1916, 3; *ODT*, 7 Aug. 1917, 3.
84 *P*, 4 Jan. 1917, 8; Holtham to Allen, 23 May 1917, AD 1 733 10/407/1, ANZ.
85 *EP*, 25 Jul. 1917, 8 and 26 Jul. 1917, 7; *FS*, 4 Aug. 1917, 2.
86 *P*, 6 Feb. 1917, 4.
87 *EP*, 10 Feb. 1917, 5; Tate to Gray, 5 May 1917 and Gray to Tate, 3 Jun. 1917, AD 1 733 10/407/1, ANZ.
88 *NZH*, 23 Feb. 1917, 8 and 21 Aug. 1917, 4; *P*, 6 Feb. 1917, 4.
89 *MES*, 21 Jul. 1917, 2 and 3 Oct. 1917, 5.
90 *EP*, 23 Aug. 1917, 3; *P*, 6 Feb. 1917, 4.
91 *HBT*, 20 Jun. 1917, 2.
92 *WC*, 19 Jul. 1917, 6; *ODT*, 29 Sep. 1917, 5.
93 *MES*, 13 Jan. 1917, 7.
94 Baker, *King and Country Call*, 176.
95 Archibald Baxter, *We Will Not Cease* (Whatamongo Bay: Cape Catley, 1983), 11.
96 *EP*, 25 Jul. 1917, 8 and 26 Jul. 1917, 7.
97 *WDT*, 9 Jan. 1917, 2 and 11 Jan. 1917, 3.
98 *EP*, 31 Jan. 1917, 8.
99 Salmond to Tate, 22 May 1917, AD 1 733 10/407/1, ANZ.
100 Gray to Adjutant General, 21 Nov. 1916 and Allen to Baughan, 23 Jan. 1917, AD 1 733 10/407/1, ANZ.
101 Poynton to Gray, 2 Dec. 1918, AD 1 1046 66/57, ANZ; *WT*, 24 Aug. 1917, 4.
102 O'Connor, "Awkward Ones," 124.
103 *MES*, 28 Mar. 1917, 5; *EP*, 20 Apr. 1917, 8.
104 *P*, 29 Nov. 1916, 3.
105 Kelly, *Military Board Appeals: Dec 1916 to Feb 1917*, 30.

7 Work or fight?

Reflecting on his experiences as a civil servant in the British Ministry of Munitions, Humbert Wolfe wrote that 'there is no single factor in modern war which contributes so much to defeat or victory as the failure or success in handling the man-power problem'.[1] The tribunals and boards played an integral role in deciding which of these eventualities came to pass. Through the verdicts they reached on all types of exemption claims, the appeal bodies determined how many men would be available to the army, and how many men would be available to the home front, at a time when Britain's and New Zealand's reserves of manpower were approaching critical levels.

The records produced by some of the East Central Division's tribunals have been used to assess the likelihood of them granting exemption. For two reasons, this appraisal is restricted to only those appeal bodies for which minute books, annotated sitting agendas or registers of case are available. First, several tribunals automatically confirmed the recommendations made by their military representatives and advisory committees, meaning that the relevant appeals never underwent a formal hearing and were, therefore, not mentioned in the newspapers. Second, press coverage in the division tended to focus on only the more 'interesting' or 'informative' cases from each sitting, with many others going unreported. As a result, relying on newspaper evidence alone would provide a very partial and unbalanced account, whereas the surviving tribunal records detail most, or sometimes all, of the verdicts reached in the County Borough of Huddersfield, the Borough of Batley and the urban districts of Birstall, Marsden and Spenborough.

Several filters have been applied to these verdicts to remove potential distortions. The first concerns instances where cases were simply adjourned to a later date. By following this course, the tribunals were displaying uncertainty over how a claim should be treated, and indicating that more evidence was required before they could reach a fully informed decision. As the *Batley News* explained, 'in cases of doubt [the] Tribunal defers a decision for independent enquiries. At the adjourned hearing the result sometimes establishes the claimant's case, sometimes not'.[2] Given this inherent flexibility, it would be misleading to count temporary adjournments either for or against an appeal body's record of granting relief. Instead, only the positive 'concrete verdicts' of absolute, conditional and temporary exemptions, and the negative 'concrete verdicts' of refusals, are included. A different rationale underlies the discounting of cases that were dismissed because the appellant had already been classified as medically unfit. Here the tribunal's verdict was effectively redundant, as the man's physical condition meant he was excused from joining the army anyway. Dismissing the claim was simply an administrative means of ensuring he would not be called up again unless his health improved. The final excluded category is those cases that were withdrawn before an official hearing took place. This occurred when an appellant had a change of heart over his willingness to join the army, or where proceeding with a claim was found to be unnecessary because the man already possessed another form of exemption, such as a war service badge or a protection certificate. Either way the outcome was taken out of the tribunal's hands, with the members never having an opportunity to judge the appeal before dismissing it.

With these filters applied, Figure 7.1 demonstrates that the five division tribunals conducted their operations with a striking degree of leniency. All of them granted absolute, conditional or temporary exemptions far more often than they dismissed cases. The most liberal was the Marsden Tribunal, which returned a positive 'concrete verdict' fully 85.56 percent of the time. Both the Batley and Huddersfield bodies granted exemptions in over three-quarters of the cases they determined, while the Birstall Tribunal was only slightly less favourable to appellants, recording a total of 74.14 percent positive decisions. Even the Spenborough members, the strictest in the sample, and described by one solicitor as 'the smallest sieve people had to go through', only refused around one-third of all the claims

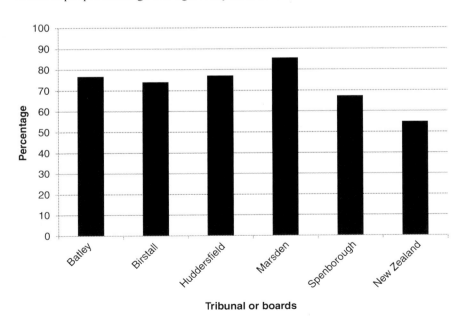

Figure 7.1 Positive 'concrete verdicts' as a proportion of all verdicts delivered

150 *Work or fight?*

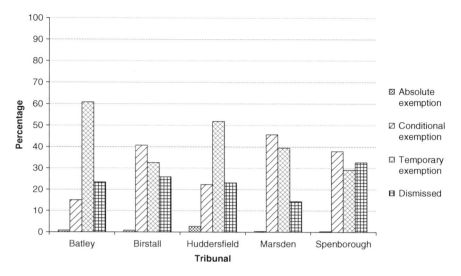

Figure 7.2 Types of 'concrete verdict' delivered by the division's tribunals

that came before them.[3] Across these five appeal bodies, 74.77 percent of the 'concrete verdicts' gave the appellant some form of exemption from military service.

Figure 7.2 provides a detailed breakdown of these 'concrete verdicts'. It illustrates that absolute exemptions were extremely rare, with the highest proportion being the 2.73 percent of decisions reached at Huddersfield. Although some appeal bodies were prepared to issue this form of certificate in the early months of their operations, its use quickly became restricted to claims where the appellant was palpably unfit to serve in any military capacity.[4] Conditional exemptions were far more common, and constituted the most frequently awarded type of relief at Birstall, Marsden and Spenborough. These certificates often went to men who were engaged in essential wartime occupations, usually requiring the bearer to remain in his present employment, or to individuals who already had several family members serving in the forces.[5] Despite the relative ubiquity of conditional certificates, temporary exemptions were the most prevalent verdict delivered at Batley and Huddersfield, and, indeed, across the five tribunals. The stipulated period of relief could be anywhere from one week to six months, but typically excused a man from reporting to camp for around eight weeks. Unless the award had been designated as 'final', it was always open to the appellant to apply for a renewal, at which point the relevant tribunal would rehear the case to determine whether the circumstances had changed in the interim. Some men never received anything more than a temporary exemption, but still managed to avoid performing military service by having their certificate renewed up to seven or eight times over conscription.

Even these findings do not divulge the full extent of the tribunals' leniency. From mid-1916, most of the division's appeal bodies began to deliver a new type

Work or fight? 151

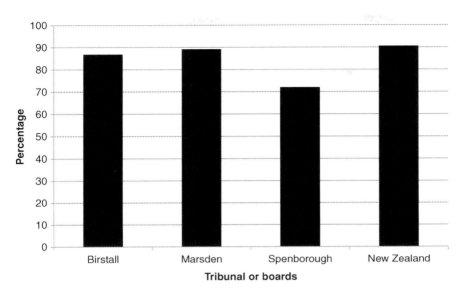

Figure 7.3 Positive 'concrete verdicts' and dismissals with time as a proportion of all verdicts delivered

of verdict, whereby a man's claim would be refused, but with the proviso that he not be summoned by the military authorities until after a specified period of 'grace' had elapsed.[6] Although undoubtedly less favourable than a temporary exemption, as there was no possibility of applying for a renewal, this verdict did afford individuals a valuable opportunity to arrange their domestic or business affairs, while giving employers the chance to hire or train replacements. Indeed, a few weeks or months to attend to such matters were all that many appellants requested from the tribunals. Therefore, any comprehensive analysis of an appeal body's verdicts requires a distinction to be draw between dismissals with and without 'grace'. While the surviving records for Batley and Huddersfield do not disclose the necessary information, the relevant figures are obtainable for the other three tribunals. On the one hand, the Marsden Tribunal afforded 'grace' to only 42 out of 165 refused men, perhaps due to the fact its members awarded so many exemptions anyway, while only 148 out of 1,076 individuals were granted extra time at Spenborough.[7] On the other hand, the Birstall Tribunal utilised the option of 'grace' far more readily, attaching it to 105 dismissals from a total of 216.[8]

Figure 7.3 demonstrates that taking these decisions into account can have a significant impact on an appeal body's record. The Marsden Tribunal is revealed to have been even more lenient than was previously suggested, granting a form of relief to 89.24 percent of the men who came before it, while the figure for Spenborough shows that only around a quarter of the appellants to that body left their hearing with nothing. Most illustrative of all is the situation regarding the

152 *Work or fight?*

Birstall Tribunal, which granted exemption in 74.14 percent of cases, but awarded at least a period of 'grace' 86.89 percent of the time.

It is impossible to say for sure whether the decisions reached by these division tribunals are representative of a wider pattern. There are no surviving records that provide a breakdown of the 'concrete verdicts' delivered throughout Britain, while those appeal bodies that have been the subject of detailed studies constitute only a small proportion of the total. Nevertheless, analysing the available sources does offer strong *prima facie* grounds for contending that the lenient approach evident in the division was the norm rather than the exception. Official statistics supplied to the cabinet indicate that 1,120,656 tribunal-issued exemptions were in force on 1 October 1916.[9] Although this figure had declined to 926,400 by 1 November, examining the period from 9 September 1916 to 6 December 1916 in its entirety reveals an overall increase in tribunal certificates of 94,432.[10] This is particularly significant, as the latter months of 1916 saw the appeal bodies come under sustained pressure from both the government and the military to refuse more cases. Even after further 'comb-outs', and the review of all certificates held by men under thirty-one years of age, there were still 779,936 tribunal exemptions in force on 30 April 1917.[11]

A similar picture emerges from the verdicts delivered by appeal bodies operating outside the division. Among the most generous must surely have been the Calne and Stratford-upon-Avon Borough tribunals, which, in cases that were pressed to a conclusion, returned a negative 'concrete verdict' only 9.15 percent and 14.81 percent of the time, respectively, and the Stratford Rural Tribunal, which 'refused an exemption certificate' to only seven out of fifty men from the village of Kineton.[12] A study of eight appeal bodies in the Welsh county of Carmarthenshire has found that 'approximately one man was enlisted for every nine exempted', while the Scottish Haddington Burgh Tribunal granted relief in 82.76 percent of its verdicts.[13] If the approach of the East Lothian County Tribunal in Scotland, the bodies covering Stourbridge and Dudley in the Black Country, and the Audenshaw Tribunal in Lancashire were slightly less liberal, they still afforded exemption in 75 percent, 78.18 percent and 74.77 percent of their verdicts, respectively.[14]

Further evidence of the tribunals' leniency can be found in the actions and communications of official agencies. The fact the government felt it necessary to direct the appeal bodies so frequently to refuse more cases is a compelling indication that substantial numbers of exemptions were being granted. Indeed, it took only twelve months of conscription before the cabinet began considering proposals to remove the claims of young single men from the tribunals' jurisdiction.[15] This measure was eventually implemented by using the 'clean cut' to terminate automatically the certificates of men below a certain age. By March 1918, Auckland Geddes had become so frustrated by the appeal bodies' perceived tardiness that he drafted legislation which would have completely overhauled the exemption system, and replaced the local tribunals with more pliable county advisory committees.[16] There would have been no need to formulate such schemes, or to impress continually on the tribunals the 'urgent' requirements and

Work or fight? 153

'immediate demands' of the army, if a high proportion of appellants were already being refused.[17]

Of even greater importance are the views advanced by the military. Far from regarding the tribunals as partners in a collaborative effort to meet the army's demands, the War Office saw their members as overly sentimental obstructionists who were doing more to hinder the national cause than to advance it. Why would the military hierarchy have felt compelled to hold several meetings with the tribunal chairmen to stiffen their resolve if the appeal bodies were already dismissing most of the claims that came before them? As early as March 1916, the Director General of Recruiting lamented the 'disquieting attitude of certain Tribunals' in refusing to send married men to the front, while a correspondent for *The Times* noted that 'exemptions are being freely granted, despite the protests of the representatives at the tribunals of the Military Authorities'.[18] These complaints became increasingly bitter as the war dragged on. The Army Council lambasted the appeal bodies for being 'only too anxious' to exempt men for personal and family reasons, and the Adjutant General greeted the overall increase of tribunal certificates during late-1916 with undisguised fury.[19] An even greater sense of betrayal is apparent among the army's generals, who portrayed the appeal bodies as working in conjunction with government departments such as the Ministry of Munitions to 'nullify to a great extent the object of the Military Service Acts'.[20]

There are two significant explanations for the tribunals' willingness to grant relief. The first is the considerable amount of protection that the British exemption system afforded to many industries. Despite a series of revisions, the list of certified occupations remained a substantial document throughout conscription, and the tribunals attached a great deal of importance to its content. One reason why the government waited so long before implementing the 'clean cut' mechanism was a belief that the only young men who had been afforded exemption were those who were absolutely vital to the wartime economy.[21] Moreover, during both November 1916 and April 1917, official statistics indicate that the number of men holding tribunal certificates on the basis of being engaged in a protected occupation was greater than the total exempted on all the other appeal grounds combined.[22] The division's tribunals certainly shared this wider appreciation of the need to safeguard essential industries. While accepting their military representative's claim that employment in a certified occupation did not guarantee an appellant's exemption, the chairman of the Spenborough body contended that it nevertheless put him 'in a strong position, and makes your case more difficult to prove'.[23] Likewise, the Dewsbury members signalled their intention to always have 'regard to the importance of the work' men were doing when reaching their decisions, and the chairman of the Marsden Tribunal stated that the overarching purpose of his body was to keep vital industries functioning.[24] The tribunals also held regular meetings with the representatives of major firms, partly to establish how many men they could afford to release, but also to ensure that an indispensable core were kept back.[25]

These practices further demonstrate a conviction that supplying men for the army was not the be all and end all of Britain's war effort. Even the most

154 *Work or fight?*

bellicose tribunal members only ever asserted that the military's needs were their *primary* concern, or that each man who could *possibly be spared* should serve. The Wakefield Borough Tribunal excused several employees of the District Light Railway Company on basis that 'they could not run the risk of workmen not being able to get to their work, especially when they were doing important war work'.[26] Likewise, a member of the Goole Urban body asserted 'it is no use getting an army if it is going to cripple industry'; the Featherstone chairman opined that a coke-oven bricklayer was '100 times more valuable to the country where he is' than he would be at the front; and Mr. Radley of the Whitwood Tribunal supported the exemption of a farm hand because 'if we don't get food they will have to stop fighting altogether'.[27]

A second contributor to the tribunals' leniency was the localism of their members. If adhering to the list of certified occupations accounts for a sizeable proportion of the certificates awarded, it does not explain why men engaged outside of protected industries were given exemption on employment grounds, or why individuals were relieved because of domestic or business hardship. The most persuasive rationalisation for the high volume of these other awards is that the primary criterion for appointment to a tribunal was prominence in the local economy and the local community. As businessmen, manufacturers or trade union leaders, it would have been irrational for the members to reduce trade by forcing the widespread closure of local enterprises. Likewise, involvement in charitable and patriotic organisations would have given most of them a fulsome appreciation of the difficulties that the war had already caused to many families in their area. Self-interest would have also exercised a degree of influence. Being mostly elected councillors, the members needed to retain the goodwill of their district's population. Refusing to send any men to the front would undoubtedly have seen them charged with a lack of patriotism, but depriving families of their breadwinners, or local industries of their essential workers, must surely have struck the members as being equally damaging to their political ambitions.

The most compelling evidence that localism was behind the members' approach is the fact their fiercest critics clearly believed this to be the case. One War Office memorandum cited the 'inherent objection to a body appointed ... by a small local authority, having committed to it the decision whether men shall be sent to the Army'.[28] Similarly, an exasperated member of the military hierarchy in South-East England wrote that

> the organisation of the Tribunals is such that they are composed of local men who owe their position to local popularity and local influences and who have had neither training in judicial or imperial matters nor that experience in official administration which developed the judicial faculty and the instinct of placing the affairs of the Nation first.[29]

The verdicts reached by the boards have been used to discern the relative likelihood of gaining exemption in New Zealand. While the available sources necessarily restrict the scope of investigation to a few of the division's tribunals, the surviving evidence makes it possible to analyse the boards' work as a collective. New Zealand's exemption system contained no advisory committees to carry out preliminary screenings, while the press coverage was far more comprehensive and detailed than that in Britain. Therefore, studying the reports carried by a large quantity of New Zealand newspapers divulges a sample of verdicts (33,133) that constitutes a sizeable proportion of the total number delivered.

Nonetheless, several categories of verdict have still been discounted. The first is where claims were adjourned temporarily. Such a postponement certainly indicated a belief that the case had not been substantiated, but it also pointed to a desire to consider the matter further, and the board might well have granted exemption at a subsequent hearing. Counting temporary adjournments against the percentage of appeals granted would ignore this latter scenario and effectively label these decisions as refusals. A second category of excluded verdicts were instances where an appeal came up for hearing after the reservist had been classed as medically unfit. Here the board's decision was redundant, as the state of the individual's health had already afforded him a *de facto* exemption. To allow the appeal would have been counter-productive as, unless the man was found to be outside the parameters of the Military Service Act, he would have been returned to the reserve and become eligible for reballoting while still unfit. The remaining options of a dismissal or a *sine die* adjournment both held the same implications; the individual would remain at home as long as he was unfit and, if he was later reclassified, his right of appeal would be re-instated.[30] The third point of omission was where the appellant failed to attend his hearing without prior notice. The boards understandably felt compelled to dismiss these cases, as the man's absence made it impossible to assess his circumstances through questioning. A non-appearance was seen as an indication that the appellant had either withdrawn his claim, was not committed to it, or had chosen to default.[31] A final exclusion encompassed those appeals that were withdrawn prior to a hearing taking place. Here the boards played no part in the outcome and were never given a chance to grant exemption.

Analysing the remaining 25,347 verdicts produces the striking findings displayed in Figure 7.1. Whereas the proportion of exemptions awarded in the division ranged from 85.56 percent to 67.34 percent, the boards were stricter than all five of these tribunals, with only 54.83 percent of cases being allowed or adjourned *sine die*. Nevertheless, the most important conclusion to be drawn from Figure 7.1 is that, despite extensive public pressure and the constant need for soldiers to fill reinforcement quotas, the boards were more likely to grant a man's appeal than to order him into camp.

Figure 7.4 provides further details on the sample 'concrete verdicts' delivered by the boards. It shows that relatively few claims, 10.66 percent, were allowed outright, which, at first glance, appears to validate the claim that their decisions afforded appellants 'little certainty'.[32] However, this situation largely resulted from technicalities within the Military Service Act, rather than from intransigence on the boards' part. The legislation only permitted the granting of complete relief to men who were deemed not to be 'a member of the Reserve': those outside the

156 *Work or fight?*

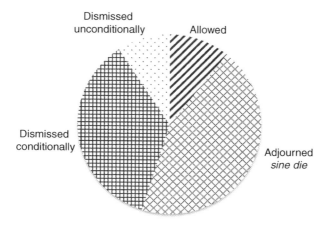

Figure 7.4 Sample 'concrete verdicts' delivered by the boards

military age or who were not British subjects. In every other instance, allowing an appeal would mean the individual became eligible for subsequent ballots, whereas a *sine die* adjournment remained in force until the relevant board made a conscious decision to review the case. Given that some claims never came up for re-assessment, a *sine die* adjournment often afforded the appellant a longer period of exemption.[33] Indeed, the decision to permit the boards to postpone cases indefinitely arose from the government's desire to secure the exemption of men employed in essential industries. Concerned that allowing such appeals would result in the men being balloted time after time, Allen created the provision for *sine die* adjournments so the government could 'hang these fellows up like Mahomet's coffin, and not let them go into the ballot until we may find it necessary'.[34] This calculated use of indefinite postponements is crucial to bear in mind, as, at 44.17 percent of the total, they were the most commonly reached 'concrete verdict' in New Zealand.

Even many of the negative 'concrete verdicts' delivered by the boards still gave appellants a period of relief from military service. Like their British counterparts, the New Zealand appeal bodies possessed the ability to refuse a claim while simultaneously stipulating that the reservist should not be expected to enter camp before a certain date.[35] Known as conditional dismissals, these decisions typically afforded men between one and six months of unpaid leave to put their affairs in order. It is vital to separate these partial refusals from claims that were dismissed outright for two reasons. First, many appellants only wanted a temporary respite from military service and, if this was all they requested, the boards could hardly have been expected to give them more when the army's need for men was so pressing.[36] Second, granting leave was clearly a more lenient act than dismissing a case unconditionally, so not distinguishing between the two would obscure some of the boards' willingness to afford relief. The appeal bodies certainly recognised that some extra time could go a long way towards reducing the impact of an

Work or fight? 157

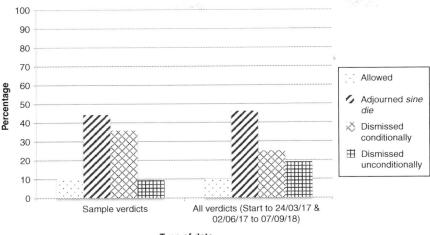

Figure 7.5 Sample 'concrete verdicts' compared to all 'concrete verdicts' delivered by the boards

appellant's conscription. One member asserted 'the Military Boards should give all appellants a reasonable opportunity to wind up their affairs', while another assured the press that 'reasonable time will be given appellants to get others to take their places'.[37] Figure 7.4 illustrates that, in the sample, some 79.27 percent of dismissals were conditional rather than unconditional, which is a much greater ratio than for any of the division's tribunals. Furthermore, when the positive 'concrete verdicts' and conditional dismissals are combined, it becomes apparent that 90.64 percent of the boards' decisions granted at least a temporary reprieve from joining the army. This is a higher figure than even that for the Marsden Tribunal in the division, and is only exceeded by the Calne Rural body among all the British tribunals whose verdicts have been analysed in detail.

To what extent are these sample verdicts representative of all those delivered in New Zealand? Although it is impossible to provide a comprehensive answer, an analysis of two returns produced by the Defence Department does allow conclusions to be drawn for twenty out of the twenty-five months that the appeal bodies held sittings. Figure 7.5 illustrates some differences, but also a crucial similarity. The sample verdicts contain a higher percentage of allowed appeals, but marginally fewer *sine die* adjournments. A much greater divergence is evident over the two types of dismissal, with the sample including 35.81 percent conditional refusals and only 9.36 percent unconditional, against 24.93 percent conditional and 18.97 percent unconditional overall. Yet when it comes to positive and negative 'concrete verdicts' the two data sets are remarkably similar. In the sample, 54.83 percent of the decisions were allowed or adjourned *sine die,* compared to 56.1 percent overall. The effect of these similarities and differences becomes apparent when the New Zealand decisions are compared to those

158 *Work or fight?*

reached by the tribunals. While the sample verdicts suggest the boards awarded at least temporary relief with greater regularity than any of the division's bodies, the overall figures indicate that both the Birstall and Marsden tribunals were more lenient. Nonetheless, whichever of the New Zealand figures is used, it is evident that the boards granted exemption in over half their verdicts, and afforded at least some form of relief to the clear majority of men who came before them.

Two major factors underlay this approach. The first was the boards' official instructions, which often encouraged them to afford a virtually blanket exemption to certain occupational groups. Alongside the 'strategic unions' of slaughtermen, merchant mariners and coal miners, other callings singled out for preferential treatment included farmers, railway workers, clerics, shearers and ship builders, while the Minister of Justice himself appeared before the appeal bodies to request the exemption of all police constables.[38] The boards attached considerable weight to these directions, with many sittings in Wellington City witnessing whole swathes of essential men being granted exemptions. Moreover, the chairman of the First Otago body stated that 'as long as a man was carrying on an essential industry he would not be disturbed', while Chairman Evans insisted that his First Canterbury Board 'quite recognised that the industries of the country had to be carried on'.[39]

The fact many other individuals were afforded relief despite being employed outside of these industries suggests the members' desire to achieve an equality of sacrifice also played a significant role. At the heart of this philosophy was a belief that married men carried far greater domestic and business responsibilities than their single counterparts and were, therefore, less likely to be able to serve immediately. During 1916 and 1917, when unmarried individuals lodged most claims, the proportion of positive 'concrete verdicts' in the sample was 50.74 percent, while some form of relief was granted 89.18 percent of the time. Once the appeal bodies started hearing cases from large numbers of Second Division reservists in 1918, these statistics rose to 59.55 percent and 92.32 percent, respectively.

Attempts to equalise the degree of sacrifice went beyond an appellant's marital status. In March 1917, one board member remarked that his appeal body had always examined 'each case in the light of the consideration whether a man could be more useful as a fighter or a producer'.[40] Likewise, the chairman of the Third Wellington Board asserted that although they 'did not want to keep a man back who should be [at the front]', equally important was that they 'did not want to send any man who should not go'.[41] The high rate of favourable decisions delivered throughout conscription demonstrates that these statements were not mere self-justification. That nearly half the overall verdicts ordered a man to camp means the boards cannot be said to have granted exemptions lightly. However, they also held true to the other side of their mantra: that relief would be awarded if the circumstances demanded it and that many appellants had too many responsibilities, or were too important to the country's economy, to be sent into the army straight away.

The surviving records provide compelling evidence that both the division's tribunals and the New Zealand boards were highly likely to afford at least temporary relief to the men who came before them. All five of the featured bodies in the division granted exemption more than two-thirds of the time, while even many dismissals were accompanied by a period of 'grace' before the appellant was required to mobilise. Furthermore, there are *prima facie* grounds for believing that such a charitable outlook was the norm across the rest of Britain, with the tribunals coming in for constant criticism from the military authorities for their perceived reluctance to release men to the army. These lenient practices derived from the substantial protection that the British exemption system afforded to many occupations and the localist sentiments of the tribunals' members. The situation regarding the boards contained more similarities than differences. While they were less likely to grant exemption than their British counterparts, the Zealand appeal bodies also delivered a positive 'concrete verdict' on over half the occasions where it was both possible and relevant for them to do so. Given that most dismissals were accompanied by a period of leave, the vast majority of appellants obtained at least a temporary relaxation of their obligations under conscription. This lenient approach can be explained by the official instructions that the board members received and by their earnest desire to promote an equality of sacrifice.

Notes

1   Wolfe, *Labour Supply*, 1.
2   *BN*, 22 Jul. 1916, 1.
3   *CSG*, 30 Mar. 1917, 7.
4   Minutes, Huddersfield Local Tribunal, KMT 18/12/2/52/1, KA; *BN*, 26 Feb. 1916, 4 and 4 Mar. 1916, 2; *HEx*, 20 Mar. 1916, 4.
5   Register of Cases, Batley Local Tribunal, KMT 1, KA; Minutes, Spenborough Local Tribunal, KMT 39/1/2/1/1, KA; *HEx*, 8 Mar. 1916, 2 and 28 Jun. 1916, 2.
6   *BN*, 3 Jun. 1916, 8 and 24 Feb. 1917, 8.
7   Sitting Agendas, HHP, S/NUDBTW/34, KA; Minutes, Spenborough Local Tribunal, KMT 39/1/2/1/1, KA.
8   Sitting Agendas, BLTF, RD 21/6/2, KA.
9   Report, "Numbers of Men due to the Army and the Number of those Remaining in Civil Life," 24 Oct. 1916, CAB 17/158, NA.
10 Report, "Man-Power Distribution Board to the War Committee," 9 Nov. 1916, CAB 17/156, NA; Memorandum, "Recruiting Prospects So Far as they Can Be Foreseen," 10 Jan. 1917, CAB 17/158, NA.
11 *Statistics of the Military Effort*, 367.
12 Slocombe, "Recruitment," 110; Spinks, "War Courts," 214; Gillian Ashley-Smith, *Kineton in the Great War, 1914–1921* (Studley: Brewin Books, 1998), 22.
13 Barlow, "Military Tribunals in Carmarthenshire," 18; Cranstoun, "Impact of the Great War," 115–17.
14 Cranstoun, "Impact of the Great War," 115–17; Levine-Clark, *Unemployment*, 128; Grieves, "Mobilising Manpower," 28.
15 Report, "Director-General of National Service to the War Cabinet," 3 Feb. 1917, CAB 1/23/14, NA; Memorandum, "Exemptions by Tribunals," 9 Feb. 1917, CAB 1/23/27, NA.
16 Memorandum, Minister of National Service, 26 Mar. 1918, CAB 24/46/4036, NA.
17 Circular, R. 122, 1 Mar. 1917 and Circular, LGB R. 167, 17 Dec. 1917, MH 47/142, NA.
18 Derby to Long, 27 Mar. 1916, Walter Long Papers, GB 947/497, WSHC; MacDonagh, *In London*, 99.

19 Mitchinson, *Defending Albion*, 152; Memorandum, Adjutant General, 10 Jan. 1917, CAB 17/158, NA.
20 Military Members of the Army Council to the Secretary of State for War, 28 Nov. 1916, CAB 37/160/25, NA.
21 Memorandum, "Exemptions by Tribunals," 9 Feb. 1917, CAB 1/23/27, NA.
22 Report, "Man-Power Distribution Board to the War Committee," 9 Nov. 1916, CAB 17/156, NA; *Statistics of the Military Effort*, 367.
23 *CSG*, 5 Oct. 1917, 3.
24 *BN*, 19 May 1917, 6; *HEx*, 23 Nov. 1916, 3.
25 *BN*, 3 Jun. 1916, 8.
26 *WE*, 14 Oct. 1916, 2.
27 *GT*, 28 Sep. 1917, 4; *PCE*, 21 Jul. 1916, 5 and 15 Jun. 1917, 3.
28 Report, "Amendments Desirable in the Present Military Service Acts," n.d., WO 32/5614, NA.
29 General Officer Commanding-in-Chief Eastern Command to Secretary of State for War, 27 Oct. 1917, NATS 1/876, NA.
30 Report, "Recruiting 1916–1918," 31 Mar. 1919, AD 1 712 9/169/2, ANZ.
31 *EP*, 28 Feb. 1917, 7.
32 Parsons, "Many Derelicts," 49.
33 New Zealand Military Service Act, 1916, 7 Geo. 5, no. 8, sec. 28; Report, "Recruiting 1916–1918," 31 Mar. 1919, AD 1 712 9/169/2, ANZ.
34 Allen to Massey, 1 Sep. 1916, AP, ALLEN 1 9, ANZ.
35 Report, "Recruiting 1916–1918," 31 Mar. 1919, AD 1 712 9/169/2, ANZ.
36 Baker, *King and Country Call*, 119.
37 *FS*, 14 Mar. 1917, 2; *EP*, 2 Feb. 1917, 6.
38 *NZH*, 24 Nov. 1916, 8; Gray to Military Service Board Chairmen, 31 Mar. 1917 and 5 May 1917 AD 82 2 1/11/1, ANZ; Gray to Military Service Board Chairmen, 12 Oct. 1917, AD 82 2 1 1/5, ANZ.
39 Kelly, *Military Board Appeals: Dec 1916 to Feb 1917*, 57; *P*, 20 Dec. 1916, 9.
40 *ME*, 27 Mar. 1917, 3.
41 *EP*, 31 Jan. 1917, 7.

Conclusions

In July 1917, Auckland Geddes, then British Director of Recruiting, advised the War Cabinet that the current method for issuing exemptions was preventing an efficient allocation of manpower. His rationale concerned the tribunal members' propensity for basing their verdicts 'almost entirely on individual or local considerations'. Not only was this causing inconsistency of procedure and decision from one district to the next, it was also fomenting a dangerous 'sense of injustice' among the public.[1] Four months later, the Rodney Chamber of Commerce passed a resolution criticising New Zealand's exemption system. Its delegates asserted that the national interest would be better served by prioritising the opinions of local people, who, unlike the travelling board members, possessed 'the requisite knowledge of the facts' and were highly attuned to community sentiment.[2] These two remonstrations encapsulate the main findings of this book.

The current historiography implies too great a similarity between the tribunals' and boards' operations. This has largely come about due to a focus on only those appellants who cited conscientious objections, who, it has been correctly argued, were often denied exemption and subjected to hostile questioning in both countries. Yet such a narrow scope ignores the overwhelming volume of the appeal bodies' work, as overt conscientious objectors were a tiny minority when compared to individuals whose claims rested on hardship or occupational grounds. By adopting a wider perspective, it becomes apparent that localism and decentralisation were the defining characteristics of the British exemption system. Although government departments issued numerous policy statements, most of the division's tribunals continued to insist that local circumstances must be their overriding concern when judging appeals. Given that New Zealand introduced conscription several months later, one might anticipate that its exemption system would have simply followed the British example. However, this was not the case. The dominion's government chose to retain the ability to exert a substantial influence over the course of appeal hearings. Moreover, the frequent use of this prerogative occurred with the general compliance of the boards' members, who believed that official directions were of vital assistance in their efforts to achieve uniformity.

This book identifies only two parallels between the tribunals' and boards' operations, although both are immensely significant. First, most British and New

162   *Conclusions*

Zealand appellants expressed their desire to join the army were it not for existing commitments; a stance that the available evidence suggests was predominately genuine. Second, while it has often been asserted that a large proportion of claims were rejected in both countries, many appeal bodies did not set out simply to get men for the army. Instead, they performed a careful balancing act between the needs of the military, the needs of the appellants and the social and economic fabric of a locality or a country at war. This approach meant that men were far more likely to be granted some form of relief from military service than not.

Significant disparities between the two exemption systems were created at the beginning. The voluntary period saw decentralisation and an emphasis on local participation emerge as the primary facets of British recruitment policy. To forestall potential opposition, these principles were further embedded in the legislation and regulations that introduced conscription. Over two thousand local tribunals were established to determine claims, each staffed by local people chosen by the local authorities. The task of administering the appeal bodies was entrusted to the LGB, whose president, Long, was a firm believer in their capacity to reach sound judgments. Not every member of the government shared Long's faith, as several checks were placed on the tribunals' discretion. Yet by involving a whole range of agencies, these measures increased the amount of delegation in the appeals process. The War Office had no authority to control the tribunals and even its military representatives and advisory committees were prone to putting the interests of their locality before those of the army. The situation in New Zealand could scarcely have been more different. Only ten boards were established, meaning that each of them had a vast area of jurisdiction. When combined with the fact it was the government who appointed their members, this automatically made the boards less local and easier to monitor. The government demonstrated a willingness to circumscribe the boards' discretion by issuing directions regarding the relief of men employed in essential industries. Moreover, while the military possessed only a limited degree of influence in Britain, it was the Minister of Defence, Allen, who became the *de facto* head of New Zealand's exemption system.

Contrasting approaches were also evident when it came to appointing personnel. In Britain, both the legislation and Long's ambiguous guidance effectively left the local authorities to make up their own minds. As a result, the council's internal dynamics, the nature of local politics and the structure of an area's economy all played a major role in determining who was chosen to sit on any tribunal. With each of these factors varying across the division's sixty-three districts, it was inevitable that the selection process would produce substantial inconsistencies. Most members were male, middle-class and locally prominent dignitaries who fully supported the war effort, but there were also women, trade unionists, anti-conscriptionists and individuals who had never taken on a prominent community role. Similarly, the men chosen as military representatives and advisory committees personnel differed from district to district by their occupation, background and level of involvement with the army. On the other hand, the New Zealand appointments were made in a highly centralised manner. Although the government received many applications from prominent individuals, Allen decided that

Conclusions 163

local imperatives should not be allocated any importance. Instead, he imposed a rigid selection criterion that was designed to filter out undesirables and give each appeal body a uniform constitution. The resulting boards were largely identical in terms of their occupational profiles, and in terms of their members' attitudes towards the war. Likewise, the selection of military representatives deliberately fell on men who shared a common background, but who were not residents of the area in which they operated.

Further discrepancies are apparent between the rates of appealing, although here the underlying reasons are more troublesome to discern. Most eligible British men became the subjects of exemption claims. In contrast, less than a third of balloted New Zealanders appealed or had appeals lodged on their behalf. Degrees of confidence in the national exemption system, the varying scales of conscription, the omission of Maori from appellant statistics, the more rural structure of New Zealand society, Britain's relative proximity to the frontline, and the differing financial hardships associated with military service are all inadequate for explaining the degree of this variance. Of much greater import were the wide-ranging protection that the British system afforded to essential industries and the stigma attached to appeals by the New Zealand public. The fact both British and New Zealand historians have focused on conscientious objectors has obscured their relatively small numbers. A much greater proportion of claims were based on domestic, business or occupational grounds, with most men insisting they were quite willing to fulfil their patriotic duty. Although the possibility that some opted to conceal a reluctance to serve cannot be discounted, the evidence suggests most of them were genuinely prepared to go.

The operations of the two sets of appeal bodies took divergent paths as soon as sittings began. The tribunals received a huge volume of official instructions, most of which implored them to send more men to the front. While the division's appeal bodies were usually prepared to dismiss the claims of young, single and medically fit individuals, directives that made stronger demands often met with resistance. Members protested the frequency with which their decisions were overturned and the injustice of being asked to refuse men with dependents at a time when government departments were protecting thousands of single men. This unrest was partly motivated by a sense of undermined authority, but also had more fundamental origins. As men who lived within, and who had been appointed by, their community, the tribunal members believed that only they had the local knowledge and moral sanction to reach verdicts. They resented the inequities caused by interference from ill-informed 'outsiders' and feared their own reputations would suffer by association. For the same reasons, the tribunals' relationship with the military representatives and advisory committees could easily be damaged by a perception that these War Office-appointees were too quick to place the army's needs above those of the district. This state of affairs did not exist in New Zealand. Its military commitment declined during conscription, meaning the boards came under less pressure to refuse appeals. Most directives were designed to ensure that men from essential industries would be guaranteed exemption. Having been appointed by the government, and lacking an immediate connection to the areas in which

164 *Conclusions*

they operated, the boards adopted a different outlook to their British counterparts. Rather than highlighting the unique requirements of a locality, their members instead looked to the government for guidance. This approach also facilitated amicable relationships with the NEB and the military representatives. Indeed, the only time the boards baulked at outside involvement was over the farmers' trustees, who they perceived as being tainted by local sentiment.

The format of the respective exemption systems also led to differences in how the tribunals and boards approached appeal hearings. Most division members shared a belief that young, single and high category men were the best able to serve, and that families who were unrepresented in the forces deserved scant consideration. However, this marked the limits of a common approach. The tribunals could not even agree on the purpose of their work, with some arguing that obtaining soldiers should be the overriding concern, while others advocated balancing the military's needs against the merits of each claim. Such inconsistency resulted from the chaotic state of national manpower policy and the sheer number of agencies responsible for implementing it, which meant that the tribunals received a mass of ambiguous directions. Furthermore, it was never realistic to expect so many appeal bodies to work in tandem, particularly when they had diverse memberships and tended to prioritise the unique circumstances of their districts. These issues did not affect the boards, whose members were united in trying to achieve an equality of sacrifice. They believed every man should join the army unless he had clear grounds for exemption, but simultaneously acknowledged that many could not be expected to serve. This mutual understanding was partly enabled by clear and definitive guidance. In addition, bringing only nine active appeal bodies into line was a relatively straightforward task, particularly when the board members believed that following official policy was the best way to spread the war's burdens equally.

The tribunals were far more inconsistent than the boards in their dealings with conscientious objectors. Those operating in the division agreed that Quakers deserved some form of relief, but otherwise developed a range of interpretations over what constituted a 'valid' objection. Many only allowed cases lodged by the members of pacifist denominations, whereas others accepted personal interpretations of the scriptures, and others still recognised socialist precepts. Even where uniformity was achieved on this issue, the tribunals frequently differed over what types of relief should be available. Some refused to award anything more than non-combatant certificates, but their counterparts elsewhere in the division were willing to grant conditional, or even absolute, exemption. Likewise, the way in which conscientious objectors were questioned ranged from detailed and methodical investigations, to relentless and vitriolic personal attacks. These inconsistencies arose from the same factors that divided the tribunals' attitudes towards other appellants: ambiguous instructions, the large number of appeal bodies and the local sensitivities of their members. The situation in New Zealand was virtually the opposite. Here the boards unanimously determined that only the Society of Friends, Christadelphians and Seventh-day Adventists were eligible for exemption. They also concurred that other men who possessed 'genuine' religious scruples could be given a recommendation for non-combatant service, but always refused to grant these endorsements to politically motivated individuals. This cohesive approach came about from a handful of straightforward official directions, the existence of fewer appeal bodies and the national perspective adopted by the boards' members.

The only substantive similarity between the tribunals and boards was that both adopted a lenient approach towards awarding exemptions. All five tribunals at Batley, Birstall, Huddersfield, Marsden and Spenborough afforded at least some form of exemption over two-thirds of the time, while even their rejection of claims was regularly mitigated by permitting men to spend several additional weeks at home. The available statistics further indicate that a broadminded outlook was the norm across Britain, especially given that the tribunals were constantly criticised by the War Office and the army's generals. These liberal practices derived from the protection that the British exemption system afforded to many occupations and the local sentiments of the tribunal members. The situation regarding the boards was very similar. Certainly, they were less likely to grant exemption than their British counterparts. However, the New Zealand appeal bodies also delivered a positive 'concrete verdict' on over half the occasions where it was possible and relevant for them to do so. The fact even that most dismissals were accompanied by a period of leave meant the majority of appellants obtained at least a temporary relaxation of their obligations. This lenient approach can be explained by the official instructions that the board members received and by their belief that many individuals were already doing enough for the war effort.

While this book has compared the tribunals' and boards' operations over a range of areas, it has deliberately steered clear of attempting some highly subjective assessments. In maintaining that 'few meaningful *comparative* deductions can be drawn' from the surviving statistics relating to the tribunals, McDermott surely overstates the case.[3] By contrasting the ratio of positive to negative 'concrete verdicts', it is possible to draw illuminating conclusions on the appeal bodies' relative willingness to grant exemptions, and thereby inform an analysis of how closely they followed official policies. Adopting a transnational perspective makes the use of comparative statistics even more vital, as it helps identify the degree to which differing circumstances affected the operation of the two exemption systems.

Where McDermott's cautionary note does carry merit is in critiquing those historians who have treated the fact an appeal body allowed more claims than it refused as an indicator of 'fairness'.[4] Such an extrapolation is deeply flawed, not least because it is anachronistic. Many observers, particularly in New Zealand, maintained that the appeal bodies were granting far too many exemptions. They believed relief should be limited to certain occupational groups and would have ardently rejected the notion that delivering a high volume of positive verdicts was 'fair'. In addition, affording plentiful exemptions does not necessarily mean the 'correct' decisions were being reached. The relief of certain individuals generated extensive protests, or even accusations of bribery and corruption, and there

166   *Conclusions*

were frequent arguments that pitted town against country, district against district and working class against middle class over which sections of society were more deserving of exemption.[5] Given this lack of consensus, it would overly simplistic to suggest the tribunals were more 'fair' than the boards just because they granted a higher proportion of appeals.

These considerations should also be applied on a wider scale. New Zealand's appeal mechanism was undoubtedly more streamlined and transparent than Britain's, with fewer agencies involved and with clearer policy guidelines. Yet while a man who received *sine die* exemption would have appreciated this simplicity, it would have given scant consolation to a compatriot who blamed the refusal of his case on the boards' lack of local knowledge, and who had no recourse to a higher tribunal or to a government department. It is striking that, as the war moved into its final year, several local bodies and organisations within New Zealand began to insist that a greater degree of community sentiment and understanding should be accommodated.[6] This was precisely the opposite conclusion that Geddes and the military hierarchy drew in Britain, and would have been challenged by a man from the division who attributed the rejection of his case to the fact a personal or professional rival was sitting on the local tribunal. Ultimately, any contemporary view on the 'fairness' or merits of the exemption systems would have depended on who was asked.

Notwithstanding these provisos, the historiographies of Britain and New Zealand during the Great War must take the tribunals' and boards' operations into account. As one New Zealand MP prophesied, their verdicts became 'the pivot' on which the success or failure of conscription revolved.[7] Without their co-operation, any manpower policy was always destined to fail, regardless of what the government, War Office or Defence Department may have desired. However, it would be a mistake to perceive the exemption systems merely as bureaucratic sorting machines. They provided the setting for some of the most striking human dramas of the war, with individuals from all classes and backgrounds being brought together to decide how young men could best serve their country. There were scenes of joy and despair, of relief and disappointment and of rancour and hilarity, mostly played out in full public view. Some men were sent to fight and die while others were allowed to remain at home, and it is no surprise that everyone had an opinion on whether these decisions were 'right' or 'wrong'. Therefore, accounts of exemption hearings provide an almost unparalleled view of British and New Zealand society at war. By comparing what took place in these two countries, it is possible to gain a much fuller understanding of the policies, attitudes and prejudices that had such significant impacts on their respective home fronts.

Notes

1 Memorandum, "The Theory and Practice of Recruiting," 23 Jul. 1917, CAB 24/20, NA.
2 *ROT*, 7 Nov. 1917, 5.
3 McDermott, *British Military Service Tribunals*, 220.

Conclusions   167

4 Rusiecki, *Impact of Catastrophe*, 103; Ivor Slocombe, *First World War Tribunals in Swindon* (Devizes: Wiltshire Family History Society, 1997), 5; Spinks, "War Courts," 214.
5 Baker, *King and Country Call*, 119–32.
6 *ME*, 5 Jun. 1918, 2 and 11 Jul. 1918, 8.
7 Wilford, 178 NZ Parl. Deb., H.R. (1916), 717.

Bibliography

Primary sources (Britain)

Bodleian Library, Oxford

Asquith, Herbert Henry. Papers.

British Library, London

Forty-Fifth Annual Report of the Local Government Board, 1915–1916, Cd. 8331.
Forty-Seventh Annual Report of the Local Government Board, 1917–1918, Cd. 9157.
Forty-Sixth Annual Report of the Local Government Board, 1916–1917, Cd. 8697.
Report on Recruiting by the Earl of Derby, K.G., Director General of Recruiting, 1916, Cd. 8149.
The War Cabinet: Report for the Year 1917, Cd. 9005.

Imperial War Museum, London

Lockwood, Frank. Papers.
Slack, Arthur. Papers.

National Archives, Kew

CAB: Records of the Cabinet Office.
MH: Records created or inherited by the Ministry of Health and successors, local government boards and related bodies.
NATS: Records created or inherited by the Ministry of National Service.
WO: Records created or inherited by the War Office, Armed Forces, Judge Advocate General and related bodies.

West Yorkshire Archive Service: Calderdale, Halifax

Halifax Local Tribunal. Minutes.
Hipperholme Local Tribunal. Files.

Bibliography 169

West Yorkshire Archive Service: Kirklees, Huddersfield

Batley Borough Council. Minutes.
Batley Local Tribunal. Register of Cases.
Birstall Local Tribunal. Files.
Birstall Urban District Council. Minutes.
Dewsbury County Borough Council. Minutes.
Golcar Urban District Council. Minutes.
Heckmondwike Urban District Council. Minutes.
Holmfirth Urban District Council. Minutes.
Hoyle, Harris. Papers.
Huddersfield Branch of the General Union of Textile Workers. Minutes.
Huddersfield County Borough Council. Minutes.
Huddersfield and District Trades and Labour Council. Minutes.
Huddersfield Local Tribunal. Minutes.
Lepton Urban District Council. Minutes.
Linthwaite Urban District Council. Minutes.
Mirfield Urban District Council. Minutes.
New Mill Urban District Council. Minutes.
South Crosland Urban District Council. Minutes.
Spenborough Local Tribunal. Minutes.
Spenborough Urban District Council. Minutes.

West Yorkshire Archive Service, Leeds

Leeds City Council. Minutes.
Leeds City Tribunal. Minutes.

West Yorkshire Archive Service, Wakefield

Ossett Borough Council. Minutes.

Wiltshire & Swindon History Centre, Chippenham

Calne Local Tribunal. Files.
Long, Walter Hume. Papers.

Official Publications

Census of Great Britain.
Central Tribunal. *Report of the Central Tribunal Appointed Under the Military Service Act, 1916* (London: HMSO, 1919).
Statistics of the Military Effort of the British Empire during the Great War, 1914–1920 (London: HMSO, 1922).
Official Report, House of Commons (Fifth Series).
The Times Law Reports.

170 *Bibliography*

Newspapers and Newssheets

Barnsley Chronicle.
Barnsley Independent.
Batley News.
Cleckheaton & Spenborough Guardian.
Colne Valley Guardian.
Dewsbury District News.
Dewsbury Reporter.
Goole Times.
Holmfirth Express.
Huddersfield Chronicle.
Huddersfield Examiner.
Ossett Observer.
Pontefract & Castleford Express.
The Times.
Tribunal.
Wakefield Express.
Worker.

Primary sources (New Zealand)

Archives New Zealand, Wellington

AD: Army [Defence] Department. Files.
Allen, Sir James. Papers.
NEB: National Efficiency Board. Files.
Numerical List of Reservists.

Alexander Turnbull Library, Wellington

McCaw, John. "Biography of My Life for the Benefit of My Children." Unpublished
manuscript, 1929.
New Zealand Farmers' Union Dominion Executive. Minutes.
Roth, Herbert Otto. Papers.
Wellington Branch of the Farmers' Union. Minutes.

Official Publications

Appendix to the Journal of the House of Representatives.
Census of New Zealand.
New Zealand Gazette.
New Zealand Official Yearbook.
New Zealand Parliamentary Debates.

Newspapers and Newssheets

Akaroa Mail and Banks Peninsula Advertiser.
Ashburton Guardian.

Auckland Star.
Bay of Plenty Times.
Colonist.
Dannevirke Evening News.
Dominion.
Evening Post.
Evening Star.
Farmers' Union Advocate.
Feilding Star.
Grey River Argus.
Hawera & Normanby Star.
Hawke's Bay Tribune.
Manawatu Evening Standard.
Maoriland Worker.
Marlborough Express.
New Zealand Herald.
New Zealand Times.
Northern Advocate.
NZ Truth.
Ohinemuri Gazette.
Otago Daily Times.
Poverty Bay Herald.
Press.
Rodney and Otamatea Times, Waitemata and Kaipara Gazette.
Round Table.
Southland Times.
Taranaki Herald.
Thames Star.
Timaru Herald.
Waikato Times.
Wairarapa Daily Times.
Wanganui Chronicle.

Secondary sources

Unpublished

Baker, Paul. "New Zealanders, the Great War, and Conscription." PhD thesis, University of Auckland, 1986.

Cranstoun, James G. M. "The Impact of the Great War on a Local Community: The Case of East Lothian." PhD thesis, Open University, 1992.

Hucker, Graham. "The Rural Home Front: A New Zealand Region and the Great War, 1914–1926." PhD thesis, Massey University, 2006.

Inder, Sonia. "Middlemarch, 1914–1918." Research essay, University of Otago, 1992.

James, Lisa. "Doing Their Duty: The Impact of Conscription on Farming Families in New Zealand during the Great War." Research essay, Victoria University of Wellington, 2006.

Parsons, Gwen A. "The Christchurch Community at War, 1914–1918: Society, Discourse and Power." Master's thesis, University of Canterbury, 2003.

172 *Bibliography*

Parsons, Gwen A. "'The Many Derelicts of the War'? Repatriation and Great War Veterans in Dunedin and Ashburton, 1918 to 1928." PhD thesis, University of Otago, 2008.

Stratton, Kerry. "'Doing Their Bit': The Impact of the First World War on the Inhabitants of Tuapeka County." Research essay, University of Otago, 1992.

Published

Adams, R. J. Q., and Philip P. Poirier. *The Conscription Controversy in Great Britain, 1900–18*. Columbus: Ohio State University Press, 1987.

Addison, The Rt. Hon. Christopher. *Four and a Half Years: A Personal Diary from June 1914 to January 1919*. London: Hutchinson, 1934.

Andrews, E. M. *The ANZAC Illusion: Anglo-Australian Relations during World War I*. Cambridge: Cambridge University Press, 1993.

Armitage, F. P. *Leicester, 1914–1918: The War-Time Story of a Midland Town*. Leicester: Edgar Backus, 1933.

Ashley-Smith, Gillian. *Kineton in the Great War, 1914–1921*. Studley: Brewin Books, 1998.

Auerbach, Sascha. "Negotiating Nationalism: Jewish Conscription and Russian Repatriation in London's East End, 1916–1918." *Journal of British Studies* 46, no. 3 (2007): 594–620.

Baker, Paul. *King and Country Call: New Zealanders, Conscription and the Great War*. Auckland: Auckland University Press, 1988.

Bannister, Andrew. *One Valley's War: Voices from a Yorkshire Community in the Great War and Its Aftermath, 1914–1919*. Pudsey: Outremer, 1994.

Barker, Rachel. *Conscience, Government and War: Conscientious Objection in Great Britain, 1939–45*. London: Routledge and Kegan Paul, 1982.

Barlow, Robin. "Military Tribunals in Carmarthenshire, 1916–1917." In *The Great War: Localities and Regional Identities*, edited by Nick Mansfield and Craig Horner, 7–26. Newcastle: Cambridge Scholars, 2014.

Barnes, Felicity. *New Zealand's London: A Colony and Its Metropolis*. Auckland: Auckland University Press, 2012.

Baxter, Archibald. *We Will Not Cease*. Whatamongo Bay: Cape Catley, 1983.

Beaven, Brad. *Visions of Empire: Patriotism, Popular Culture and the City, 1870–1939*. Manchester: Manchester University Press, 2012.

Beckett, Ian F. W. *The Amateur Military Tradition, 1558–1945*. Manchester: Manchester University Press, 1991.

Beckett, Ian F. W. "The Nation in Arms, 1914–18." In *A Nation in Arms: A Social Study of the British Army in the First World War*, edited by Ian F. W. Beckett and Keith Simpson, 1–35. Manchester: Manchester University Press, 1985.

Belich, James. *Paradise Reforged: A History of the New Zealanders from the 1880s to the Year 2000*. Auckland: Penguin, 2001.

Belich, James. *Replenishing the Earth: The Settler Revolution and the Rise of the Anglo-World, 1783–1919*. Oxford: Oxford University Press, 2009.

Bet-El, Ilana R. *Conscripts: Lost Legions of the Great War*. Phoenix Mill: Sutton, 1999.

Bibbings, Lois S. *Telling Tales about Men: Conceptions of Conscientious Objectors to Military Service during the First World War*. Manchester: Manchester University Press, 2009.

Boulton, D. *Objection Overruled*. London: MacGibbon and Kee, 1967.

Bibliography 173

Bourke, Joanna. *Dismembering the Male: Men's Bodies, Britain and the Great War.* London: Reaktion Books, 1996.

Brazier, Reginald H., and Ernest Sandford. *Birmingham and the Great War, 1914–1919.* Birmingham: Cornish Brothers, 1921.

Buckner, Phillip, and R. Douglas Francis. "Introduction." In *Canada and the British World: Culture, Migration, and Identity*, edited by Phillip Buckner and R. Douglas Francis, 1–9. Vancouver: University of British Columbia Press, 2006.

Byrnes, Giselle. "Introduction: Reframing New Zealand History." In *The New Oxford History of New Zealand*, edited by Giselle Byrnes, 1–18. Melbourne: Oxford University Press, 2009.

Cartmell, H. *For Remembrance: An Account of Some Fateful Years.* Preston: George Toulmin and Sons, 1919.

Ceadel, Martin. *Pacifism in Britain, 1914–1945: The Defining of a Faith.* Oxford: Clarendon Press, 1980.

Ceadel, Martin. *Semi-Detached Idealists: The British Peace Movement and International Relations, 1854–1945.* Oxford: Oxford University Press, 2000.

Chamberlain, W. J. *Fighting For Peace: The Story of the War Resistance Movement.* London: No More War Movement, 1928.

Childs, Major-General Sir Wyndham. *Episodes and Reflections: Being some Records from the Life of Major-General Sir Wyndham Childs.* London: Cassell, 1930.

Clayworth, Peter. "'Lucky Laidlaw' and 'Worried Webb': The Robert Laidlaw Exemption Case and Public Attitudes to Conscription in 1918." *Journal of New Zealand Studies* 20 (2015): 72–86.

Clegg, Malcolm. *A History of Birstall: The Last 200 Years.* Batley: Malcolm Clegg, 1994.

Cooke, Peter, and John Crawford. *The Territorials: The History of the Territorial and Volunteer Forces of New Zealand.* Auckland: Random House, 2011.

Cowan, James. *The Maoris in the Great War: A History of the New Zealand Native Contingent and Pioneer Battalion.* Auckland: Whitcombe and Tombs, 1926.

Crawford, John. "'I Get Blamed for Everything': Enduring the Burdens of Office, James Allen as Minister of Defence in 1915." In *Endurance and the First World War: Experiences and Legacies in New Zealand and Australia*, edited by David Monger, Sarah Murray and Katie Pickles, 14–30. Newcastle: Cambridge Scholars, 2014.

Dearle, N. B. *An Economic Chronicle of the Great War for Great Britain & Ireland, 1914–1919.* London: Humphrey Milford, 1929.

DeGroot, Gerard J. *Blighty: British Society in the Era of the Great War.* London: Longman, 1996.

Dewey, Peter. *British Agriculture in the First World War.* London: Routledge, 1989.

Douglas, Roy. "Voluntary Enlistment in the First World War and the Work of the Parliamentary Recruiting Committee." *Journal of Modern History* 42, no. 4 (1970): 564–85.

Edmonds, Brigadier-General Sir James E. *Military Operations: France and Belgium, 1916: Sir Douglas Haig's Command to the 1st July: Battle of the Somme.* London: Macmillan, 1932.

Eldred-Grigg, Stevan. *The Great Wrong War: New Zealand Society in WWI.* Auckland: Random House, 2010.

Ellsworth-Jones, Will. *We Will Not Fight: The Untold Story of the First World War's Conscientious Objectors.* London: Aurum, 2007.

Englander, David. "Soldiering and Identity: Reflections on the Great War." *War in History* 1, no. 3 (1994): 300–18.

174 *Bibliography*

Fenton, Damien. *New Zealand and the First World War, 1914–1919.* Auckland: Penguin, 2013.

Ferguson, Niall. *The Pity of War.* London: Penguin, 1998.

Flynn, George Q. *Conscription and Democracy: The Draft in France, Great Britain, and the United States.* Westport: Greenwood Press, 2002.

Franks, Peter and Jim McAloon. *Labour: The New Zealand Labour Party, 1916–2016.* Wellington: Victoria University Press, 2016.

Fraser, Mike. *"Does My Country Really Need Me?": The Work of the Berwick-upon-Tweed Military Service Tribunal, 1916–1918.* Berwick-upon-Tweed: Blue Button, 2015.

Gibbons, Peter. "The Far Side of the Search for Identity: Reconsidering New Zealand History." *New Zealand Journal of History* 37, no. 1 (2003): 38–49.

Graham, John W. *Conscription and Conscience: A History, 1916–1919.* London: George Allen and Unwin, 1922.

Granatstein, J. L., and J. M. Hitsman. *Broken Promises: A History of Conscription in Canada.* Toronto: Oxford University Press, 1977.

Grant, David. *Field Punishment No. 1: Archibald Baxter, Mark Briggs & New Zealand's Anti-Militarist Tradition.* Wellington: Steele Roberts, 2008.

Gregory, Adrian. "British 'War Enthusiasm' in 1914 A Reassessment." In *Evidence, History and the Great War: Historians and the Impact of 1914–18,* edited by Gail Braybon, 67–85. New York: Berghahn Books, 2003.

Gregory, Adrian. *The Last Great War: British Society and the First World War.* Cambridge: Cambridge University Press, 2008.

Gregory, Adrian. "Military Service Tribunals: Civil Society in Action, 1916–1918." In *Civil Society in British History: Ideas, Identities, Institutions,* edited by Jose Harris, 177–90. Oxford: Oxford University Press, 2003.

Grieves, Keith. "Military Tribunal Papers: The Case of Leek Local Tribunal in the First World War." *Archives: The Journal of the British Record Association* 16, no. 70 (1983): 145–50.

Grieves, Keith. "Mobilising Manpower: The Audenshaw Tribunal in the First World War." *Manchester Region History Review* 3, no. 2 (1989): 21–29.

Grieves, Keith. "Total War? The Quest for a British Manpower Policy, 1917–18." *Journal of Strategic Studies* 9, no. 1 (1986): 79–95.

Gullace, Nicoletta F. *"The Blood of our Sons": Men, Women, and the Renegotiation of British Citizenship during the Great War.* New York: Palgrave Macmillan, 2002.

Gustafson, Barry. *Labour's Path to Political Independence: The Origins and Establishment of the New Zealand Labour Party, 1900–19.* Auckland: University of Auckland Press, 1980.

Haigh, E. A. Hilary, ed. *Huddersfield, A Most Handsome Town: Aspects of the History and Culture of a West Yorkshire Town.* Huddersfield: Kirklees Cultural Services, 1992.

Halifax, Stuart. "'Over by Christmas': British Popular Opinion and the Short War in 1914." *First World War Studies* 1, no. 2 (2010): 103–22.

Hamer, David. *The New Zealand Liberals: The Years of Power, 1891–1912.* Auckland: Auckland University Press, 1988.

Harper, Glyn. *Johnny Enzed: The New Zealand Soldier in the First World War, 1914–1918.* Auckland: Exisle, 2016.

Holmes, Richard. *Tommy: The British Soldier on the Western Front, 1914–1918.* London: Harper Perennial, 2005.

Housden, Christine. "Researching Kingston's Military Tribunal, 1916–1918." *Occasional Papers in Local History* 2 (2004): 5–6.

Bibliography   175

Kelly, M. J. *Military Board Appeals: Otago Witness, Dec 1916 to Feb 1917*. Auckland: Old News Publications, 1993.

Kelly, M. J. *Military Board Appeals: Otago Witness, March 1917 to July 1917*. Auckland: Old News Publications, 1994.

Kelly's. *Kelly's Directory of the West Riding of Yorkshire, 1917*. Kelly's Directories, 1917.

Kennedy, Thomas C. *The Hound of Conscience: A History of the No-Conscription Fellowship, 1914–1919*. Fayetteville: University of Arkansas Press, 1981.

Kennedy, Thomas C. "Public Opinion and the Conscientious Objector, 1915–1919." *Journal of British Studies* 12, no. 2 (1973): 105–19.

King, Michael. *The Penguin History of New Zealand*. Auckland: Penguin, 2003.

King, Michael. *Te Puea: A Life*. new ed. Auckland: Reed, 2004.

Levine-Clark, Marjorie. *Unemployment, Welfare, and Masculine Citizenship: "So Much Honest Poverty" in Britain, 1870–1930*. Houndmills: Palgrave Macmillan, 2015.

Littlewood, David. "The Dutifully Reluctant: New Zealanders' Appeals for Exemption from Conscription, 1916–1918." *New Zealand Journal of History* 50, no. 2 (2016): 26–43.

Littlewood, David. "Personal, Local & Enduring: Masculine Citizenship in First World War Britain." In *The Citizen: Past and Present*, edited by Andrew Brown and John Griffiths, 171–95. Auckland: Massey University Press, 2017.

Littlewood, David. "'Willing and Eager to go in Their Turn'?: Appeals for Exemption from Military Service in New Zealand and Great Britain, 1916–18." *War in History* 21, no. 3 (2014): 338–54.

Lloyd George, David. *War Memoirs of David Lloyd George*. rev. ed. London: Odhams Press, 1938.

Lockwood, Ernest. *Colne Valley Folk*. London: Heath Cranton, 1936.

Long, Walter. *Memories*. London: Hutchinson, 1923.

Loveridge, Steven. *Calls to Arms: New Zealand Society and Commitment to the Great War*. Wellington: Victoria University Press, 2014.

McDermott, James. *British Military Service Tribunals, 1916–1918: "A Very Much Abused Body of Men"*. Manchester: Manchester University Press, 2011.

MacDonagh, Michael. *In London during the Great War*. London: Eyre and Spottiswoode, 1935.

Macdonald, Charlotte. *Strong, Beautiful and Modern: National Fitness in Britain, New Zealand, Australia and Canada, 1935–1960*. Wellington: Bridget Williams Books, 2011.

McGibbon, Ian. "The Price of Empire, 1897–1918." In *Frontier of Dreams: The Story of New Zealand*, edited by Bronwyn Dalley and Gavin McLean, 216–45. Auckland: Hachette Livre NZ, 2005.

McKernan, Michael. *The Australian People and the Great War*. Melbourne: Nelson, 1980.

McQuilton, John. "Doing the 'Back Block Boys Some Good': The Exemption Court Hearings in North-Eastern Victoria, 1916." *Australian Historical Studies* 31, no. 115 (2000): 237–51.

Mallalieu, J. P. W. *On Larkhill*. London: Allison and Busby, 1983.

Martin, John E. "Blueprint for the Future? 'National Efficiency' and the First World War." In *New Zealand's Great War: New Zealand, the Allies and the First World War*, edited by John Crawford and Ian McGibbon, 516–33. Auckland: Exisle, 2007.

Mein, Jonathan, Anne Wares and Sue Mann, eds. *St Albans: Life on the Home Front, 1914–1918*. Hatfield: University of Hertfordshire Press, 2016.

Messenger, Charles. *Call-To-Arms: The British Army, 1914–18*. London: Cassell, 2005.

176   *Bibliography*

Mitchinson, K. W. *Defending Albion: Britain's Home Army, 1908–1919.* Basingstoke: Palgrave Macmillan, 2005.

Mitchinson, K. W. *Saddleworth, 1914–1919: The Experience of a Pennine Community during the Great War.* Saddleworth: Saddleworth Historical Society, 1995.

Monger, David. *Patriotism and Propaganda in First World War Britain: The National War Aims Committee and Civilian Morale.* Liverpool: Liverpool University Press, 2012.

Montgomery, J. K. *The Maintenance of the Agricultural Labour Supply in England and Wales during the War.* Rome: International Institute of Agriculture, 1922.

Moon, Paul. *New Zealand in the Twentieth Century: The Nation, the People.* Auckland: HarperCollins, 2011.

Moorehead, Caroline. *Troublesome People: Enemies of War, 1916–1986.* London: Hamish Hamilton, 1987.

Morgan, Kenneth O. "Peace Movements in Wales, 1899–1945." *Welsh History Review* 10, no. 3 (1981): 398–430.

Nolan, Melanie. *Breadwinning: New Zealand Women and the State.* Christchurch: Canterbury University Press, 2000.

O'Connor, P. S. "The Awkward Ones – Dealing with Conscience, 1916–1918." *New Zealand Journal of History* 8, no. 2 (1974): 118–37.

O'Connor, P. S. "The Recruitment of Maori Soldiers, 1914–1918." *Political Science* 19, no. 2 (1967): 48–83.

Osborne, John Morton. *The Voluntary Recruiting Movement in Britain, 1914–1916.* New York: Garland, 1982.

Peacock, A. J. *York in the Great War: 1914 to 1918.* York: York Settlement Trust, 1993.

Pearce, Cyril. *Comrades in Conscience: The Story of an English Community's Opposition to the Great War.* rev. ed. London: Francis Boutle, 2014.

Pearce, Cyril and Helen Durham. "Patterns of Dissent in Britain during the First World War." *War & Society* 34, no. 2 (2015): 140–59.

Pennell, Catriona. *A Kingdom United: Popular Responses to the Outbreak of the First World War in Britain and Ireland.* Oxford: Oxford University Press, 2012.

Phillips, Jock. *A Man's Country?: The Image of the Pakeha Male – A History.* rev. ed. Auckland: Penguin, 1996.

Pickles, Katie. "The Obvious and the Awkward: Postcolonialism and the British World." *New Zealand Journal of History* 45, no. 1 (2011): 85–101.

Pugsley, Christopher. *On the Fringe of Hell: New Zealanders and Military Discipline in the First World War.* Auckland: Hodder and Stoughton, 1991.

Rae, John. *Conscience and Politics: The British Government and the Conscientious Objector to Military Service, 1916–1919.* London: Oxford University Press, 1970.

Repington, Lieut.-Col. C. À Court. *The First World War, 1914–1918: Personal Experiences of Lieut.-Col. C. À Court Repington.* London: Constable, 1921.

Robbins, Keith. *The Abolition of War: The "Peace Movement" in Britain, 1914–1919.* Cardiff: University of Wales Press, 1976.

Rusiecki, Paul. *The Impact of Catastrophe: The People of Essex and the First World War (1914–1920).* Chelmsford: Essex Record Office, 2008.

Scholefield, Guy H. *Who's Who in New Zealand and the Western Pacific, 1925.* Napier: G. W. Venables, 1924.

Scott, Keith Douglas. *Before ANZAC, Beyond Armistice: The Central Otago Soldiers of World War One and the Home They Left Behind.* Auckland: Activity Press, 2009.

Scott, William Herbert. *Leeds in the Great War, 1914–1918: A Book of Remembrance.* Leeds: Leeds Libraries and Arts Committee, 1923.

Bibliography 177

Seccombe, Wally. "Patriarchy Stabilized: The Construction of the Male Breadwinner Norm in Nineteenth-Century Britain." *Social History* 11, no. 1 (1986): 53–76.

Self, Robert, ed. *The Neville Chamberlain Diary Letters, Volume One: The Making of a Politician, 1915–20.* Aldershot: Ashgate, 2000.

Sheftall, Mark David. *Altered Memories of the Great War: Divergent Narratives of Britain, Australia, New Zealand and Canada.* London: I. B. Tauris, 2009.

Silbey, David. *The British Working Class and Enthusiasm for War, 1914–1916.* London: Frank Cass, 2005.

Simmonds, Alan G. V. *Britain and World War One.* Abingdon: Routledge, 2012.

Simpkins, Peter. *Kitchener's Army: The Raising of the New Armies, 1914–16.* Manchester: Manchester University Press, 1988.

Sinclair, Keith. *A Destiny Apart: New Zealand's Search for National Identity.* Wellington: Allen and Unwin, 1986.

Slocombe, Ivor. *First World War Tribunals in Swindon.* Devizes: Wiltshire Family History Society, 1997.

Slocombe, Ivor. "Recruitment into the Armed Forces during the First World War: The Work of the Military Tribunals in Wiltshire, 1915–1918." *Local Historian* 30, no. 2 (2000): 105–24.

Snowden, Philip (Viscount). *An Autobiography: Volume One, 1864–1919.* London: Ivor Nicholson and Watson, 1934.

Spinks, Philip. "First World War Conscientious Objection in South Warwickshire." *Local Historian* 42, no. 4 (2012), 280–91.

Spinks, Philip. "'The War Courts': The Stratford-upon-Avon Borough Tribunal, 1916–1918." *Local Historian* 32, no. 4 (2000): 210–17.

Stephen, Adrian. "The Tribunals." In *We Did Not Fight: 1914–18 Experiences of War Resisters*, edited by Julian Bell, 377–92. London: Cobden-Sanderson, 1935.

Stone, George F., and Charles Wells, eds. *Bristol and the Great War, 1914–1919.* Bristol: J. W. Arrowsmith, 1920.

Strachan, Hew. *The First World War: Volume I: To Arms.* Oxford: Oxford University Press, 2001.

Studholme, E. C. *Te Waimate: Early Station Life in New Zealand.* Wellington: A. H. and A. W. Reed, 1940.

Studholme, Lt.-Colonel John. *New Zealand Expeditionary Force: Record of Personal Services during the War of Officers, Nurses, and First-Class Warrant Officers; and other Facts Relating to the N.Z.E.F.: Unofficial, but based on Official Records.* Wellington: Government Printer, 1928.

Summers, Anne. "Militarism in Britain before the Great War." *History Workshop Journal* 2, no. 1 (1976): 104–23.

Taylor, A. J. P. *English History, 1914–1945.* Oxford: Clarendon Press, 1965.

Tosh, John. *A Man's Place: Masculinity and the Middle-Class Home in Victorian England.* New Haven: Yale University Press, 1999.

Turner, Ben. *About Myself, 1863–1930.* London: Humphrey Toulmin, 1930.

Turner, Ben. *Short History of the General Union of Textile Workers.* Heckmondwike: Labour Pioneer and Factory Times, 1920.

Watson, James. "Patriotism, Profits and Problems: New Zealand Farming during the Great War." In *New Zealand's Great War: New Zealand, the Allies and the First World War*, edited by John Crawford and Ian McGibbon, 534–49. Auckland: Exisle, 2007.

Weitzel, R. L. "Pacifists and Anti-Militarists in New Zealand, 1909–1914." *New Zealand Journal of History* 7, no. 2 (1973): 128–47.

178 *Bibliography*

White, Bonnie. "Volunteerism and Early Recruitment Efforts in Devonshire, August 1914 – December 1915." *Historical Journal* 52, no. 3 (2009): 641–66.

Wilson, Kathleen, ed. *A New Imperial History: Culture, Identity and Modernity in Britain and the Empire, 1660–1840.* Cambridge: Cambridge University Press, 2004.

Winegard, Timothy C. *Indigenous Peoples of the British Dominions and the First World War.* Cambridge: Cambridge University Press, 2012.

Winter, J. M. *The Great War and the British People.* Cambridge: Harvard University Press, 1986.

Wolfe, Humbert. *Labour Supply and Regulation.* Oxford: Humphrey Milford, 1923.

Woollacott, Angela. *Gender and Empire.* Basingstoke: Palgrave Macmillan, 2006.

Worrall, J. H. *The Tribunal Hand-Book.* London: W. H. Smith and Son, 1917.

Wright, Matthew. *Reed Illustrated History of New Zealand.* Auckland: Reed, 2004.

Wright, Matthew. *Shattered Glory: The New Zealand Experience at Gallipoli and the Western Front.* Auckland: Penguin, 2010.

Index

Admiralty 11–13
advisory committees 13–14, 19, 23, 47, 96–9; *see also* War Office
Allen, James: and board membership 38–9, 43–7, 123; and defence of boards 92, 94; and instructions to boards 26–7, 83–6, 91, 137, 143, 156; and military representatives 25, 27; role in exemption system 20–2, 26–7; and voluntary recruitment 16–17
Amery, Leo 17
appeals: grounds cited for 62–3, 65–72; permissible grounds for 13, 17–24, 80–2; rate of 53–7
appellants to military service boards, named: Adamson, George 121; Badger, Eric 141; Bell, John 119; Bennett, James 72; Birnie, Gordon 122; Blackie, Harry 71; Campbell, Peter 69; Casey, John 68; Coffey, Edward 62; Condon, John 99; Connor, Charles 118; Cook, George 68; Cramp, Percy 68, 122; Darling, Ralph 121–2; Davey, Wilfred 140; Denham, Albert 70; Doherty, Charles 139; Dowsett, Edward 138; Duckworth, Robert 69–70; Fernandez, Fernando 120; Fiddis, George 68; Gibbs, Theodore 140; Gray, Hugh 138; Greenslade, John 122; Green, Thomas 122–3; Green, William 71; Grigg, George 118; Hardwick, William 68; Hitchcock, Alfred 62; Howe, Charles 68; Hudner, William 68; Hunt, Vernon 71; Jackson, David 137; Johnston, Andrew 71; Jones, Robert 138; Keen, John 119; King, Arthur 121; King, Hugh 138; King, Jeremiah 71; Kupli, Edwin 122; Laidlaw, Robert 120–1; Laurie, Charles 64; Linklater, John 119; Linklater, Thomas 119; Longhurst, Arthur 66; McCune, Thomas 118; McLaren, Peter 118; McNeill, Henry 118; McNeill, Joseph 118; Managh, Charles 118; Milverton, Herbert 137; Mitchell, Thomas 69; Mohring, Leslie 69; Morris, Jesse 141; O'Gorman, Patrick 69–70, 122; Olley, John 141; Orr, Charles 118–19; Rigg, John 138; Robson, D. W. 72; Rose, Gordon 139; Russell, Hugh 122; Sneddon, Charles 1, 71; Sparrow, Arthur 93; Spillane, Thomas 138; Taylor, Reginald 68; Tole, John 120; Walker, John 70; Wallace, William 140; Ward, Ernest 120; Watson, Robert 138; Webb, Paddy 120–1; Wheeler, Albert 123; Wild, Colin 68; Williams, David 138; Wright, Percy 137
appellants to military service tribunals, named: Arrand, Mr. 108; Broadhead, Fred 67; Bruce, William 113; Byram, Alfred 109; Cooper, Eric 110; Coult, Andrew 67; Cowling, Mrs. 110; Farrington, Martin 130; Fox, Charles Edward 113; Gardiner, Arthur 135–6; Hartley, Leonard 67; Hepworth, John 111; Hopkinson, Charles 130; Horner, Ernest 135; Lockwood, Frank 58; Munns, Edgar 108; Murgatroyd, Herbert 71; Peel, Joseph 130; Percy, Frank 67; Pontefract, Norman 66; Porter, F. W. 113; Ramsden, Thomas 109; Rooke, John 99; Rosse, Casandra Countess of 113; Slack, Arthur 3; Smeaton, Joseph 109; Thompson, G. H. 110; Thurman, Benjamin 70; Walker, Albert 1; Walker, James 129; Wilson, Arthur 131
Army Council 80–1, 115, 153

180 *Index*

Asquith, Herbert 11–12, 14, 18
Auckland City Recruiting Committee 45
Auckland Labour Representation
  Committee 39, 45, 47
Australia 6, 56

'badging' 11–13
Baker, Paul 2–3, 55–6, 71–2, 141
Barlow, Robin 2
Batley News 70, 148
Baxter, Archibald 141
Belich, James 2, 59
Bet-El, Ilana 53
Board of Agriculture 13, 54, 115
Board of Education 115
Board of Trade 13, 54, 134
Boer War 10, 15
Bonar Law, Andrew 132
British Army, reinforcement of 11–12, 14,
  79–82
British Socialist Party (BSP) 130, 132
'British World' scholarship 4
'business as usual' 11–12
Byrnes, Giselle 4

Canada 6, 56–7
Canterbury Labour Representation
  Committee 39, 45
Canterbury Trades and Labour Council 47
Catholic exemption crisis 83–4, 91, 94; *see
  also* Allen, James
certified occupations 25–6, 63, 71, 79, 115,
  153; cuts to list of 80–2, 87; *see also*
  essential industries
Chamberlain, Austen 12
Churchill, Winston 12
citizenship, notions of 4, 15; among
  appellants 65–73; among boards 117–
  24; among public 57–8, 64–5; among
  tribunals 107–10, 114–17
'clean cut' 81–2, 152–3
coal miners 27, 63, 69, 85, 93–5; *see also*
  'strategic unions'
colliery courts 13
Colne Valley Guardian 34, 65
compulsory military training 5–6, 10–11,
  15, 56
conscientious objection: boards' attitude
  re 141–4; exemption available for 22,
  133–4, 136–40; provision for 19, 24–5,
  129, 132, 136; tribunals' attitude re
  131–2; *see also* appeals; citizenship,
  notions of

conscientious objectors: Brethren 138–40,
  144; Christadelphians 130, 132–3,
  136–7, 141; Irish 138, 140–1; Maori
  66; other religious 129, 133, 138–40;
  political 129–31; Quakers 24, 129,
  132–3, 136–8, 141; Richmond Mission
  139–40; Seventh-day Adventists 137,
  141, 144; Testimony of Jesus 139–40;
  see also appeals
country agricultural executive committees
  81–2
Cranstoun, James 65
Crewe, Lord 18
Curzon, Lord 12, 17

Dannevirke Evening News 58
Defence Department 48, 56; and
  conscientious objectors 137, 139–40,
  143; role in exemption system 20–2,
  25, 100–1; and voluntary recruitment
  15–16; *see also* Allen, James
Derby Scheme 12–14, 18–19
Derby tribunals 13–14, 33–5
Dewsbury Reporter 58

essential industries: boards' attitude re
  91–5, 117, 119, 122, 158; definition
  of 13, 17, 19, 23, 25–7, 54–5 63–4,
  79–82, 84–6; loss of men from 11–12;
  tribunals' attitude re 153–4
equality of sacrifice, notions of 117–18,
  123–4, 142–3, 158
Expeditionary Forces Amendment Bill 84,
  137

farmers: appeals by 60–1, 67–71;
  instructions re 27, 63–4, 80–2, 85–6;
  protests re 58, 91–2; *see also* essential
  industries
Farmers' Union 58, 85, 91, 121
Final Appeal Board 23–4, 84
Financial Assistance Scheme 62
First Division 20, 59, 83, 119–20; *see also*
  Second Division
Fisher, W. Hayes 133–4
'Fourteen', the 71
Fraser, Mike 65
Frostick, William 117

Gallipoli Campaign 16, 61
Geddes, Auckland 81–2, 152, 161, 166
German Spring Offensive (1918) 55, 82–3,
  86, 93

Godley, Lieutenant General Alexander 92
Goole Times 112
Goole Trades and Labour Council 45
Gregory, Adrian 2, 62
Grieves, Keith 2, 65
Gullace, Nicoletta 64–5

Halifax, Stuart 62
Hawke's Bay Tribune 64
Henderson, Arthur 12
Herangi, Princess Te Puea 59
Herdman, Alexander 26–7, 123
Home Office 13
Housden, Christine 65
Hucker, Graham 2–3
Huddersfield and District Trades and Labour Council 34–5, 38, 42, 44, 112
Huddersfield Friendly and Trade Societies' Club 58

imperial defence 5–6, 15
Independent Labour Party (ILP) 37–8, 42, 115, 129–31
Inder, Sonia 2
'industrial compulsion' 22
Industrial Conciliation and Arbitration Act, 1894 39

James, Lisa 2

Kitchener, Lord 12, 18

labour representatives: appointment of 34–5, 37–9, 41–7; attitudes of 114–15, 121, 132, 134–5; provision for 22–3, 35; *see also* Allen, James; Long, Walter
Lawson, General 116
Legislative Council 23–4, 84
Levine-Clark, Marjorie 63, 65
Liberal Party, Britain 11–12, 19
Liberal Party, New Zealand 20, 23
local councils, Britain, named: Ardsley 33–4; Ardsley East and West 37; Barnsley Borough 36; Batley 36–7; Birstall 34; Castleford 36; Cudworth 37; Darfield 36; Dewsbury 35–6, 44; Dodworth 36–7, 41; Featherstone 36–7; Golcar 36; Goole Urban 44–5; Holmfirth 36–7; Horbury 34, 36; Hoyland Nether 114; Huddersfield 34–8, 44; Knottingley 36; Leeds 37; Lepton 36; Linthwaite 33–4; Methley 36; New Mill 37–8; Ossett 34, 36–7;

Pontefract Borough 35–6; Saddleworth 44; St Albans 37; Wakefield Borough 36; Worsborough 34, 114; York 37
Local Government Board (LGB) 13, 19–20, 25, 80, 115–16; *see also* Long, Walter
Long, Walter: and advisory committees 19, 23; and defence of tribunals 58; and instructions to tribunals 13, 22, 25–6, 80, 115, 131, 133–4; and military representatives 19–20, 23; role in exemption system 13, 20, 25; and tribunal membership 13, 22–3, 34–7, 42, 45

Man-Power Distribution Board 80
Maori, appeals by 59–60, 66
Massey, William 17, 38, 92
Martin, John 2
Maxwell, General 116
McDermott, James 2, 165–6
McGibbon, Ian 2
McKernan, Michael 56
McQuilton, John 56
medical examinations 81, 110–11, 123
members of military service boards, named: Bell, Alfred Dillon 43, 122–3; Bishop, Chairman 58; Breen, Robert 46–7; Burgess, Frederick 43, 73, 100; Cooper, Daniel 43, 101, 124; Curtice, Frederick 46; Day, Chairman 101, 117; Earl, Chairman 144; Eldridge, Frederick 46; Elliott, George 43; Evans, James 43, 73, 93, 95, 119–21, 144, 158; Hockly, Frank 73; Kellett, Edward 43–4, 123; Mack, Matthew 46; McCaw, John 43; McLaren, David 43–4; Milton, James 43, 93; Moorhouse, Chairman 92; Perry, William 43, 100; Poynton, Chairman 64, 119, 138, 144; Robbins, Henry 46; Rosser, Arthur 46–7; Studholme, Edgar 43, 93–4; Widdowson, Howell 43, 73, 144
members of military service tribunals, named: Armitage, William 115, 134; Atkin, Mr. 115; Baines, Hannah 40; Balmforth, Owen 40–1, 132; Banks, Councillor 114; Barker, William 41; Beach, Councillor 108; Blackburn, Alderman 114; Blamires, Chairman 131, 136; Bray, Councillor 132; Brook, Chairman 132; Brook, George 115, 134–5; Brook, Thomas 134; Bruce, Edward

182 Index

42; Burns, Councillor 108; Cartmell, Harry 53, 71; Chamberlain, Neville 53; Clarke, Councillor 115; Colbridge, Percy 45; Cone, John 45; Crowther, John 40; Dennison, Mr. 110; Edwards, John 44; Firth, Cooper 40; Flynn, Alfred 34, 40, 90; France, William 34, 41, 132; Freer, Councillor 33–4; Furniss, John 40; Gartside, John 41, 44; Gill, Councillor 108; Haigh, Councillor 89; Haley, Joe 42; Halstead, Councillor 44; Hill, Councillor 89; Holden, Henry 40; Holton, William 34, 114; Hoyle, Harris 5, 41; Jagger, Councillor 115; Jagger, Mr. 108; Jenkins, Mr. 44; Kingswell, William 40; Lancaster, Edward 42; Littlewood, Ben 42; Livesey, Councillor 34; Lockwood, Arthur 40; Mallalieu, Frederick 42; Maxwell, Councillor 37; McCann, Chairman 115; Naylor, Albert 34, 98; Norton, Thomas 42; Pearson, Councillor 131; Pickles, Joseph 38, 42, 114–15, 132; Platt, Councillor 44; Porter, Councillor 98; Proctor, William 41; Radley, Mr. 154; Raley, William 40; Raynor, William 89; Rideal, Edmund 40; Roebuck, Councillor 107; Saxton, Councillor 109; Simmonds, Councillor 109; Sowden, Ernest 34, 42; Stonehouse, Edmund 42; Stott, Andrew 41; Taylor, Law 114–15, 132; Tinker, C. 40, 109; Turner, Ben 42, 135; Turner, Benjamin 44; Walker, E. 40, 132; Wilson, Alderman 113–14; Wood, Frank 33

militarism, pre-war 10–11, 15

military representatives, Britain, named: Baines, Mr. 99; Bradbury, Captain 96–7; Crosland, Arthur 47, 98; Featherston, Captain 98; Greenwood, Captain George 47, 96, 99; Hewitt, Lieutenant Colonel James 47, 98; Leather, H. D. 47, 98; Mallalieu, Captain 97; Mellor, Colonel 72; Neal, Lieutenant 98; Oddy, Mr. 72, 96; Quarmby, Mr. 97; Renny, Major 97; Repington, Charles 53; Richmond, Mr. 96; Strachan, Lieutenant 98–9, 113; Tanner, Major 97

military representatives, New Zealand, named: Barrett, Captain 101; Conlan, Major John 48, 73, 100; Free, Captain Cuthbert 48, 99; Gresson, Major 73, 100; Walker, Captain 100–1

Military Service Act, 1916, Britain 23, 35, 54, 79, 129, 132–4

Military Service Act, 1916, New Zealand 25–6, 83, 136–7, 143–4, 155–6

Military Service Act, 1918 81–2

Military Service Act (Session 2), 1916 80, 133–4

Military Service Bill, Britain 14, 17–20, 22–3

Military Service Bill, New Zealand 17, 20–5

military service boards, named: First Auckland 94, 99, 118, 120–2, 138, 140; First Canterbury 85, 91, 93, 95, 119, 122–3, 140, 158; First Otago 84, 92–3, 95, 99, 118–24, 141, 144, 158; First Wellington 72, 84, 91–2, 94–5, 100, 118–19, 124, 138, 141; Native 60; Second Auckland 58, 94, 117, 119, 122–4, 138, 140; Second Canterbury 91, 100, 117, 120; Second Otago 55, 91, 95, 117, 121; Second Wellington 58, 84–5, 117, 120, 124, 138; Third Canterbury 55; Third Wellington 55, 84, 91–2, 120–2, 137, 139, 158

Military Service (Convention with Allied States) Act, 1917 81

Military Service (No. 2) Act, 1918 82

Military Service (Review of Exceptions) Act, 1917 81

military service tribunals, named: Ardsley 33–4, 40, 98; Audenshaw 5, 152; Barnsley Borough 40, 97–8, 107–9, 114, 116, 130–2, 135; Barnsley Rural 87, 98, 109; Batley 5, 37, 42, 66, 86, 108–11, 113–14, 130, 135, 149–51; Berwick-upon-Tweed 65; Birkenshaw 88, 130; Birmingham 5, 53; Birstall 5, 34, 61–2, 66, 86, 90, 96, 98, 109, 112, 114, 129, 131, 149–52; Bristol 5; Calne 5, 152, 157; Carmarthen Rural 53; Castleford 58, 89, 96, 99, 112, 114, 117; Central 5, 13–14, 19, 114–15, 132–3; Cudworth 96, 99, 129–30; Dewsbury 1, 35, 44, 96, 98–9, 112–13, 115, 117, 153; Dodworth 37, 41; East Central Division Appeal (ECAT) 42, 86–90, 96–9, 131, 135–6; East Lothian County 65, 152; Golcar 58, 97, 108, 131; Goole Rural 67, 87, 110, 112; Goole Urban 44–5, 87, 89, 96–8, 107, 110, 112–13, 154; Haddington Burgh 152; Hampstead 53; Heckmondwike

41, 44, 86, 89–90, 96, 115; Hemsworth Rural 89, 97, 108, 115; Honley 108, 112, 115, 131; Horbury 88, 112; Huddersfield 5, 34–5, 37–8, 44, 54, 66, 89, 96, 98, 109, 111, 114–15, 129–36, 149–51; Kirkburton 35; Knottingley 90, 111, 114; Leeds 5, 37, 54, 135; Leek 5, 65; Leicester 53; Linthwaite 33–4, 58, 97, 108, 111, 129–30, 134; Lothian and Peebles Appeal 5; Marsden 5, 40–1, 87–90, 96–7, 116, 131, 149–51, 153; Meltham 112, 132; Middlesex Appeal 5, 65, 134; Mirfield 44, 109, 111, 130; Morley 54; Normanton, 110, 114; Northamptonshire Appeal 5, 65; Ossett 34, 36–7, 41–2, 72, 96, 99, 112–14, 131–2; Pontefract Rural 112–13; Pontefract Borough 35–6, 71, 97, 107–8, 111–12; Preston 5, 53, 71; Royston 41; Saddleworth 41, 44, 66; St Albans 37, 65–6; Shepley 110; Skelmanthorpe 130; Slaithwaite 96, 108, 112, 114, 116; South Crosland 112, 114, 131; Spenborough 5, 44, 70, 86, 90, 96–7, 107–9, 114–15, 130–2, 149–51, 153; Stanley 110; Stratford Rural 65, 152; Stratford-upon-Avon Borough 5, 65, 152; Wakefield Borough 86, 89, 109–13, 130, 154; Whitwood 89, 99, 114–16, 154; Wombwell 112

ministerial certificates 26–7, 83–4, 91–2, 94, 117; *see also* Catholic exemption crisis; essential industries

Ministry of Munitions 12–13, 19, 54, 115, 153

Ministry (department) of National Service 63, 80–2, 111, 115; *see also* Geddes, Auckland

Mitchinson, K. W. 66

Munitions Area Recruiting Officers (MAROs) 81, 88

Myers, Arthur 17, 20–2

National Defence League 15

National Efficiency Board (NEB) 84–5, 91, 94–5, 123; *see also* essential industries

National Register, Britain 12

National Register, New Zealand 16–17

National Service League 10–11

Newfoundland 6

New Zealand Expeditionary Force, reinforcement of 15–17, 82–3

New Zealand Herald 38, 61, 64

numerical list of reservists 56, 59

NZ Truth 47, 120

O'Connor, P. S. 2

Otago Trades and Labour Council 39, 45–7

Parliamentary Recruiting Committee 11

Parsons, Gwen 2–3, 69

Paul, J. T. 47

Pearce, Cyril 66

Pelham Committee 134

Pennell, Catriona 60, 62

Pickles, Katie 4

Pontefract Trades and Labour Council 35

Press 61

Rae, John 66

Recruiting Board 17, 26, 38–9, 84–5, 91, 123

Recruiting Scheme 17

'reductionist' movement 82–3

Reform Party 20, 23

Reserved Occupations Committee 13, 87; *see also* essential industries

Robin, Major General Alfred 45, 55

Rodney Chamber of Commerce 161

Round Table 58

Rusiecki, Paul 65

Salmond, John 26–7, 123, 143

Samuel, Herbert 133

schedule of protected occupations 81–2, 115; *see also* essential industries

Scott, Keith 2

Seamen 27, 69, 92; *see also* 'strategic unions'

Second Division 20, 57, 82–4; appeals from 59, 68, 72; boards' attitude re 119–20, 158; *see also* citizenship, notions of; equality of sacrifice, notions of

Selborne, Lord 12

'shirking', notions of 16–17, 24–5, 64–5, 71–3, 140, 143; *see also* citizenship, notions of

Silbey, David 60

Simon, John 18–19

Sinclair, Keith 43

slaughtermen 27, 85, 92, 117; *see also* 'strategic unions'

Slocombe, Ivor 2, 65

Smith, Frederick 17

184 *Index*

Snowden, Philip 22, 132
sources: Defence Department files 6, 154–5; newspapers 5–6, 63–5, 148; tribunal records 5, 148
South Africa 6
Southland War Funds Committee 45
Spen Valley Trades and Labour Council 44
Spinks, Philip 2, 65
'starred' and reserved occupations 12–14, 25–6, 79; *see also* essential industries
'strategic unions' 27, 85, 158
Stratton, Kerry 2

Tate, R. W. 100, 140
textile industry 41–2, 70, 87, 110, 116
Times, The 53, 153
Trade Card Scheme 80
Tribunal 131
trustee boards 85–6, 91, 94–5; *see also* farmers

verdicts: by boards 154–8; re conscientious objection 140–1; by tribunals 148–52

voluntary recruitment 11–17, 20, 53, 60, 62; *see also* Defence Department; War Office
Volunteer Training Corps (VTC) 111–12, 115–17

War Cabinet 81, 161
Ward, Joseph 17, 38
War Office 11–12, 18, 63, 115–16; role in exemption system 13–14, 19–20, 96–9; opinion of tribunals 53, 57, 153–4
War Policy Committee 12
Wellington Trades and Labour Council 39, 45–7
White, Bonnie 60
Wolfe, Humbert 148
women: appellants' opinions re 67–8, 71, 108; boards' opinions re 119, 124; tribunal members 22–3, 35, 37, 40, 132; tribunals' opinions re 87
Worker 58
Wright, Matthew 64

youth organisations 10–11